Love and Other Letters

Nancy Oestreich Lurie

Copyright

Milwaukee County Historical Society
910 North Old World Third Street
Milwaukee, Wisconsin 53203

© 2010

ISBN Number 978-0-615-37969

Published by
Milwaukee County Historical Society
910 North Old World Third Street
Milwaukee, Wisconsin 53203

All rights reserved. This book may not be reproduced
in part or in total, in any form or manner, without the
express written consent of the publisher.

Printed in the United States of America
Burton & Mayer, Inc.
Brookfield, WI

Love and Other Letters
Nancy Oestreich Lurie

Contents

Milwaukee, Wisconsin
2010

1

Rayline

You know how it is when you move. All the big stuff you worry about is quickly installed in nearly accustomed places—chairs, tables, beds, rugs. It's the little stuff that's the problem, the stuff you hadn't paid attention to in years and didn't have time to decide whether to keep or ditch when you moved but just dragged along to the new place to deal with once you were settled. Well, the time had come or I had finally made time to deal with a big paper shopping bag filled with packets of letters and other papers that had belonged to my mother, Rayline Danielson Oestreich.

The bag was among her things when she sold her house on Layton Boulevard on Milwaukee's south side in 1970 and came to live with me in a house I had bought on the city's northeast side, close to where I was then teaching at the University of Wisconsin-Milwaukee (UWM). UWM had been established in 1956, evolving from a merger of the Milwaukee Center of the University of Wisconsin Extension Division and a State Teachers College. Originally, the latter was called the Milwaukee Normal School that, coincidently, my mother had attended for nearly two years. She had gone to high school at the adjacent Milwaukee Downer Seminary, a private girls school. UWM had acquired the Seminary campus in 1961 and the associated Downer College campus in 1964, the year after I had joined the UWM faculty, following a stint of teaching at the University of Michigan and a divorce. I had no idea that the Normal School and Downer would figure in the bag of letters along with my mother's south side house on Layton Boulevard that had been built by her father in 1902 when she was four years old. At that time it was 22nd Avenue. It became 27th Street in 1909 and the stretch of over a mile with a center plot, between Lincoln Avenue on the south and National Avenue on the north, achieved Boulevard status. As it finally turned out, that bag of letters dealt with nearly everything except what I assumed it was about, Norway in 1906.

While the letters in the bag and related papers derive almost entirely from members of my family and, for the most part, are closely associated with Milwaukee, they transcend these parochial boundaries in recording the effect of national and world wide events on the everyday life of Americans during the first quarter of the 20th century. It will help if I begin to introduce the people those letters really concern. My mother had lived on Layton Boulevard virtually her entire life except for a period of a little less than a year when as newly weds in 1921 she and my father lived in Dallas, Texas. They returned to her family home where they remained and where I was born in 1924 and grew up. For any readers who might not be familiar with Milwaukee, the city is bisected by the deep and broad valley of the Menomonee River that flows east into Lake Michigan where it is joined from the north and south by the Milwaukee and Kinnickinnic Rivers, respectively. Long a corridor for railroad lines and industry, the valley is spanned by a number of viaducts that connect but also clearly define the city's north and south sides geographically and, to some extent, socially. My mother grew up on the south side, my father on the north side.

During my early childhood, there were six of us in the house on Layton Boulevard: my maternal grandparents, my grandmother's father, my parents and me. We don't know how it came about, but I called them by their given names. My parents were Rayline and Carl (though I usually called him Carly) and my grandparents were Lalla and Daniel. A few of my great grandfather's contemporaries called him Bill or Billy, but as the oldest male in the family he was the patriarch and just about everyone, family and friends, called him Pa. In the beginning I thought that was his name, just as I didn't learn until much later that my grandmother's first name was Florence because she was always called Lalla, a shortening of her middle name, Lalla Rookh, the heroine of a long romantic poem about a beautiful Hindu princess by the Irish poet Thomas Moore that had caught her mother's fancy.

Eventually only my parents survived in the house on Layton Boulevard; I had gone off to school, married, and lived far from Milwaukee. They remodeled the house a few years before Carl died in 1955, reserving the second floor as a flat for themselves and partitioning the first floor into two smaller rental apartments. When Rayline sold the house in 1970, she disposed of a lot of furniture and other household items, bringing only the better pieces from Layton Boulevard that included items from the family summer home on Phantom Lake, about 25 miles from Milwaukee, that she had sold in 1961. It too figures importantly in the letters. Many of her things had achieved the status of antiques or nearly so. While we could use practically everything she had in her flat, she still had to reckon with the contents of her attic.

Rayline always claimed that while the rest of the human race might have descended from apes, we came from squirrels. Although she accused her mother of being incapable of throwing anything away, she did not touch my grandmother's attic accumulation, even after the remodeling, and it was augmented by stuff my mother had squirreled away up there, too. After some initial culling, she simply moved the old trunks, including her huge cedar hope chest made by her paternal grandfather, and an assortment of boxes, baskets, and bags, including the one full of letters, from her attic to my attic "to go through later." Of course, we never did.

Rayline died on August 13, 1996—she would have been 98 on September 20—and I began making plans to sell my house and move into an apartment, which I did in 1999. I inventoried all the inherited furniture and other items according to family

lines—Danielson, Martin, Schuette (pronounced SHOOTee)—
and sent copies of the list to my Milwaukee kindred to come and
get what they wanted. My only caveat was that anyone interested
in the trunks and chests in the attic had to take what was in them.
Having lived this long in ignorance of the contents, I figured I had
no need for them. The recipients were delighted with their discov-
eries—a black plumed hat dating to the 1890s, embroidery floss
and directions for many pieces of "fancy work" my grandmother had
started but folded away and never finished, my mother's wedding
veil, books, linens and other useful things, and a lot of disposable
junk that my relatives, not I, were left to cope with.

They also were free to claim things with no particular family
pedigree that I would not need in smaller quarters or was happy
to replace, such as all my house plants. They came with vans and
pick-ups so when it came time for me to move from my eight room
house plus attic and basement to my new four room apartment I
didn't even have to hire a mover. Two strong second cousins with
large vehicles moved everything for me over the course of a week. I
made the final run in my car with the cat and her litter box.

Predictably, in the process of settling into my apartment I
still had items I didn't know what to do with and simply stashed
them away in the garage and the backs of closets "to go through
later." Well, we've heard that line before. I was saved the trouble of
having to make decisions about a large portion of the cache when I
was away in 2003 on a lovely lecture gig on the American Queen
plying the Mississippi between Davenport and the Twin Cities. The
garage was struck by lightning and everything in it burned up.

When I finally got around to reorganizing my closets in the
spring of 2005, there was that bag full of letters that I thought
had gone up in smoke two years earlier. It never occurred to me
that this trove Rayline had kept through the years could have
been anything but letters Lalla wrote to Daniel, from Norway in
1906. Lalla, a second to fourth generation American with roots
in England, Germany and Switzerland, became Norwegian by
marriage. From embracing the cuisine to learning Hardanger style

Rayline Danielson in Hardanger style Norwegian costume, a souvenir
of her visit to Norway with her mother and paternal grandmother in the
summer of 1906.

embroidery, she even incorporated a smattering of the language into
the household lexicon along with the German words and phrases
that were ubiquitous in the speech of many otherwise English
speaking Milwaukeeans, even of my generation. The Land of the
Midnight Sun exerted such a powerful influence that although
my ancestry also includes Sudeten and Prussian German on my
father's side, my really active ethnic identification is with Norway.
I am a member in good standing of the Milwaukee chapter of Sons
of Norway that Daniel's father helped to found.

It all goes back to my mother's paternal grandparents,
Bernhard Julius Danielson and a young widow, Caroline Pederson

Caroline and Bernhard Julius Danielson and their children,
left to right: Charles, Benjamin, Inga, Daniel, and Lou, ca.1893.

Matthiesson, both 26 years of age when they emigrated as newly-weds from Bergen on Easter Sunday, 1872. A ship's carpenter and cabinet maker, my great grandfather was well traveled with a fair command of English and was drawn to Chicago by the high wages that were being paid to rebuild the city after the great fire of the previous year. My mother's father, Daniel, their oldest child, was born in Chicago but soon after his birth the family moved to Milwaukee where my great grandfather became a general contractor and for a while owned a sash and door company. He did very well between what were called "panics" and claimed to have gone broke and recovered from seven such economic depressions in his lifetime. I don't know why they left Chicago except that there was a fairly large settlement of Norwegians and other Scandinavians on the south side of Milwaukee.

Daniel became a general contractor like his father, as did the youngest son, Charles. There were three other siblings between them—Inga, Lou, and Benjamin, besides a set of twins and another boy who died as infants. Inga and Lou both married and their families eventually left Milwaukee. Ben, a bachelor, was the family black sheep—a drifter and drinker but handsome and charming, a beloved uncle who, according to Rayline, knew magic tricks and sent enchanting post cards and gifts from exotic places. My great Uncle Charlie and his wife, Elisabeth Storr, "the C.B.s" for Charles Bernhard, had Jule and Richard, and daughters Dorothea, Betty (Elisabeth) and Anita. The last two and their families remained in the Milwaukee area; I think of them as the Danielson cousins although their names through marriage are O'Sullivan and Schroepfer, respectively.

My great grandparents occasionally returned to the homeland to see their relatives. In the spring of 1906, my great grandmother, her daughter-in-law—my grandmother Lalla—and my mother, not quite eight years old, went to Norway, timing their visit to take advantage of the national festivities marking the coronation of the new king and queen after Norway had gained its independence from Sweden the previous year. They had rooms in the apartment building where "Tante Dina," Bernard's sister Geraldine, lived in Bergen.

Daniel and his father were to join them during the summer and then they would all go home together in the fall, but the Danielson men had landed such a big building contract that they could not get away. Lalla, barely 28 years old at the time and determined to make the most of her European journey, happily made all the arrangements for the return trip, departing from the original plans to include extended sight seeing in London and its environs. Their return ship docked in Boston where Daniel met them and they spent the night at a hotel, leaving for Milwaukee the next day. In the excitement of the reunion, he shipped the baggage ahead that contained most of their clothes. After two days on the train, Rayline said she must have looked like "a grubby little immigrant" as the Norwegian costume she had worn to greet her father was wrinkled and dirty by the time they reached Milwaukee. When they finally got home, tired and disheveled, Daniel dashed in the house ahead of Lalla and Rayline and cranked up the Edison cylinder record player.

Although she laughed about it later, Lalla was not amused at the time as a tinny voice sang a welcoming song about separated lovers that ended: "Your letters all start, 'How I love you, Honey!' But why don't you write when you don't want money?"

I really didn't expect to learn anything new from the letters in

Florence Lalla Rookh Martin Danielson and Daniel B. Danielson at about the time of their marriage in 1897.

the shopping bag because I had heard about the Norway summer over and over, as evidenced by the detailed remembrance of the above incident. Still, I looked forward to reading them and passing them on to Betty and Anita who, as the two youngest of Charles's children, and tag-alongs at that, are only a few years my senior although of my mother's generation. They both have big families so there would be a lot of descendants to cherish the letters as they did the hope chest and other Danielson mementos. It was Betty's sons, Jerry and Bill, who had helped me move.

When I finally began taking the letters out of the bag I was assailed by mixed feelings. Except for a single letter, they were not about Norway at all but mainly love letters, more than *500* of them, that my father had written to my mother on a nearly daily basis between June 1, 1919 until shortly before their marriage on June 11, 1921, most of them from Canton, Ohio where he was working. There are a few later letters he wrote from Dallas when he transferred there from his job in Canton shortly before my parents were married and after their marriage when my mother was in Rochester, Minnesota where her father underwent surgery at the Mayo Clinic. I was glad the letters had not been destroyed in the garage fire when I still thought they concerned Norway, but now I had no idea what to do with them. As the childless only child of two only children, I not only have no direct descendants, I have no nieces or nephews, or even first cousins. What was I to do with this correspondence from someone only I was related to directly? I was already anguished over the disposition of my mother's diaries for the years 1918 through half of 1921 that also had escaped the fire and I had put aside unread. As a scholar accustomed to working with documentary materials I instinctively recoil at the thought of destroying original records of any kind. Furthermore, with the rise of ephemeral electronic communication historians bewail the future absence of practically any personal paper records. Yet, love letters and diaries are so personal, it almost seemed improper for me to open them. I finally decided to read everything and then have a bonfire.

My mother had kept the letters in consecutive order and when they stacked up to about 30 or 40 letters, including the occasional postcard or telegram, she made a packet tied with odd bits of ribbon or twine. The letters were in their original envelopes with a red two-cent stamp or two green one-cent stamps, bearing the same sculptured likeness of George Washington. Now and then Carl used higher denomination stamps for lack of the red or green ones and in 1920 often used two-cent stamps commemorating the 300th anniversary of the landing of the Pilgrims at

Plymouth Rock. Considering Carl had been an avid philatelist, I was amused that most of the envelopes had been torn open through the postage end so there weren't even many old stamps worth salvaging. Sandwiched in among the letters are the address sections of wrapping paper from some of the gifts from my father. Although some envelopes are addressed in cursive script, many of them are addressed in neat draftsman's lettering.

None of my mother's letters to my father survive because he was living in a rooming house and didn't want to risk anyone else seeing them. As he explained in one of his letters, "You know after I finish reading a letter I tear it up," reporting with amusement that he was warned when his landlady's little boy, Ralph, said, "Don't tear your letters, Carl, 'cause mother wants to read them." Carl's letters were frequent but brief, usually only both sides of a page or two, whereas my mother wrote less often but, according to her diary, her letters sometimes ran from four to eight pages or more.

As I took out the 16 packets of my father's letters, I discovered that there were some miscellaneous papers at the bottom of the bag along with two packets of letters from young men, Tuve ("2V" as he sometimes signed his name) Floden, 1916-1919, and George P. Gustafson, 1918, and two packets from girls with whom my mother had attended the Milwaukee Downer Seminary, Frances Roberts and Mary Ball, written between 1915-1917 and 1919-1920, respectively, and two letters my grandmother had written to my mother in Dallas in 1922. A number of miscellaneous items were jumbled together at the bottom of the bag—a valentine she had received as a child, a picture of my father in his cap and gown, graded papers she had written for French, English, and science classes at Downer, picture post-cards, and the single letter from Norway from my mother's best friend during the 1906 visit, Ragna Vikøren. Ragna was a few years older than Rayline and had assumed the role of big sister and teacher, insisting Rayline learn Norwegian although she herself was learning English in school. Her beautiful penmanship more than compensates for any shortcomings in her English.

Bergen 23/11-1915

Dear Rayline!

It is a long time since you have heard anything from me now, but I am sure that you still remember you old friend i Bergen—I often think of the funny days we had together. Therefor I send you my photography with my best wishes for a good Christmas and a happy New Year.

Your sincerely
Ragna Vikøren

The envelope and photograph were not with the letter.

Ragna and Rayline lost track of each other about the time the United States entered World War I when Rayline's diary record begins, but through the kind of plot twist we might question in a novel they were reunited exactly sixty years after their childhood summer together. In 1966, at the end of my year as a Fulbright lecturer at the University of Aarhus, Denmark, Rayline joined me for a summer of sightseeing in Europe. When we got to Bergen we looked up Vikøren in the phone book and found a florist shop owner who was Ragna's nephew. He immediately presented each of us with a rose and was quite perturbed that we were leaving the next day for Trondheim and couldn't spend the weekend with his family at their summer home. He was touched that Rayline still had the list Ragna had written when they were children of all her siblings' names, and he brought us up to date on what had become of them. Giving us Ragna's married name and address near Oslo, he sensitively filled us in on the hard life and less than happy marriage she had endured, including her husband's support of the Nazi collaborator, Vidkun Quisling, during World War II, so we would not blunder into painful topics to mar the reunion. Since we would be in Oslo in a few days Rayline wrote to Ragna and she met us at our hotel, bringing photographs from their childhood in Bergen that they reminisced over with laughter and tears. Ragna also brought a gold chain to hold a watch or locket that she had received at the time of her confirmation and insisted my mother keep as a remembrance. Ragna's little used English was still surprisingly good and with my Berlitz Danish adapted to Norwegian we had a wonderful time together. When my mother returned home they resumed their correspondence until Ragna's death some ten years later.

As I began going through the bag of letters, little mysteries would arise that usually were solved in the course of reading the diaries. I was puzzled, for example, that the stamps had been clipped off the envelopes of all the letters from Frances Roberts and Tuve Floden through 1917. The diary entry of January 19, 1918 reads, "Cut stamps off of envelopes this evening for Mother. I had 334 stamps." Evidently, then as now, philanthropic organizations raised money from the sale of cancelled stamps to collectors. While I have no idea what worthy cause this stamp clipping supported, the entry attests to the fact that Rayline's correspondence greatly exceeded the number of letters she had kept from Frances and Tuve. The diaries also mention many more letters than those I fell heir to. There seems to be no reason why she kept the particular selection of letters from Frances and Mary. She had, however, kept letters from a number of boy friends until March 19, 1920 when she wrote in her diary: "Cleaned out my cedar chest and thru [sic] away all the letters from Windy, Miller, Ben, & Don—am keeping George Gustafson's and Tuve's because they are from the Great War." On November 13 of the previous year she had burned all the letters from Sam Lang, a strong contender for her hand until she met my father.

Although telegrams had long been used for fast communication, particularly over great distances, and the telephone had become a regular fixture in offices and even in many private homes, people depended heavily on the U.S. mail to keep in touch during the period covered by Rayline's diaries and letters. Mail was delivered twice a day during the week and once on Saturday. Within the city, it was possible to receive a letter in the morning and get a reply in the mail quickly enough for it to be delivered in the afternoon of the same day. Even letters between Milwaukee and Canton, Ohio usually took only two or three days as mail traveled and was sorted in special railway cars on cross-country trains. It was only the rare delay and jam-up when several letters would arrive at once that elicited complaints about the postal service in my parents' correspondence.

What I found strange is that with so much writing going on, I had to deal with so much indifferent to really poor handwriting among reasonably well-educated people. My mother's writing matured somewhat over time but didn't become any more legible and I suspect she used it to camouflage her admitted lifelong problems with spelling rather than bother with a dictionary. My father's penmanship was not much better and his letters were often written in haste with the usual tendency to leave out words and confuse the spelling of homonyms such as they're, their, and there. The letters from Gustafson were pages of almost straight lines and faint to boot. Frances Roberts had serious eye problems, discussed in her letters, but her breathless style of expression and what my mother told me about her suggest her writing would have been slap dash even if she could see well. Lalla gets an A, as does Ragna, for what used to be called "a fine Spencerian hand" and Floden rates an A-. Mary Ball's rather vertical hand was undistinguished but fairly easy to read. Mary's letters are usually signed with her nickname, Mernnie, and she is referred to in Rayline's diaries by that name, sometimes spelled Mernie.

The diaries occasionally advert to "helping Daddy with his letters," his business correspondence, which puzzled me at first since I had seen his writing and it was much like Lalla's. My father once told me, however, that my grandfather never caught on to punctuation and his letters started with a capital letter and ended in a period, even going on for several pages in this way. A few references in the diaries to "typewriting letters for Daddy" reminded me that since my grandfather was enamored of technology of any kind, he probably had a typewriter from the time he began his business in the early 1890s—after all, the first practical typewriter was perfected in Milwaukee by C. G. Sholes in the 1870s. Possibly the typewriter was already contributing to the deterioration of handwriting although even in my youth it still was considered impolite to type personal correspondence. Besides some misspellings, Rayline occasionally used incorrect verb tenses (she never did when speaking) but since she wrote in her diary just before going to bed she probably was sleepy. I like to believe that she was grammatically alert when she typed business letters for her father and, dictionary at hand, proof-read them too for spelling. Although not mentioned in the diaries, I know my grandfather also had an early model adding machine. Rayline evidently checked figures on it when she refers to helping her father with estimates in bidding for building contracts.

Not surprisingly, my grandfather is supposed to have had the first automobile on the south side, a ten horsepower 1903 Cadillac, but it took a long time for modern automotive jargon to evolve. Rayline notes in her diary on January 7, 1918 that because of a heavy snowstorm, "All cars stopped running and no one has gone down the boulevard in a machine or with a horse." Right up through 1921, "cars" meant streetcars and the once vast network of interurban trolleys, while automobiles were called "machines."

I was particularly glad she had kept her collection of letters in their envelopes that preserved the dates in the post-marks. Although Carl meticulously dated his letters, the other writers had a tendency (shared by my mother in her letter writing throughout her life) to simply note in the upper right hand corner, "Friday," "Tuesday Morning," and the like.

Out of habit, I jotted brief notes as I read the letters and diaries, having allowed for the possibility at the outset that maybe some pages were of historical interest and should be saved. Carl often adverted to the fact that he was in Canton, Ohio when Jim Thorpe played football for the Canton Bulldogs and I had the impression he was a close friend of the famous Indian athlete.

He probably did have at least a nodding acquaintance but, as I learned from his letters, his free seat on the sidelines was because his friend Howard Buck, who had been captain of the University of Wisconsin team in 1916, played tackle for the Bulldogs when Carl was living in Canton. By the time I finished my reading, to my disappointment, Thorpe had not been mentioned once, but by then I knew everything should be archived with other family papers I had already given to the Milwaukee County Historical Society. These concern the Janesville Plank Road, the Layton House, and my grandfather's business that all figure in the story to follow. Although occasionally intimate matters were mentioned with frankness or suggestive playfulness, there was nothing in the letters and diaries that sharing them with others for their historical interest would be an embarrassment to my parents' memory, and some entries are just too thought provoking to keep to myself, e.g., diary, November 18 and letter, November 16, 1919:

"Had a wonderful letter waiting for me when I got up this morning. Carl does say the funniest things—he is going to love me until we have a colored president."

I realized, however, that the maximum usefulness of the papers as a source of social history depended on information only I could provide—identifying people, places, events, and circumstances and filling in essential or illuminating details that the writers took for granted. Rather than undertake tedious footnoting, I decided to provide contextual underpinning in the form of a narrative, sometimes chronological, sometimes in regard to particular topics over a period of time. In the course of writing clarifications and pertinent details, I was reminded of other germane but unrecorded family stories that really deserved inclusion to show the whole picture, and I found myself with a book on my hands that I couldn't put down, at least at first. Another writing project intervened and so several years separate the first drafts of the first four chapters and the rest of the book. It was hard to pick up the story where I'd left off and I finally found it necessary to re-read all the letters and diaries several times. And a good thing, too! In my eagerness,

I had missed a lot on the first go-round, like the significance of the "colored president," that as late as 2004 I had overlooked as just another, albeit original, way of saying, "Until hell freezes over."

The letters and diaries offer a rare, if sometimes random and fragmentary, perspective on a momentous period as it was experienced and remarked upon by a small but representative sample of middle class Midwestern Americans: World War I, the "Spanish flu" pandemic, the Russian Revolution, nation-wide labor unrest and major strikes, the transition from horse to automobile, prohibition, women's suffrage, even the inception of air travel, and lots more. The documents also demonstrate the error in popular thinking and even some purported history as presented on TV that the "Roaring Twenties" followed immediately on the heels of repressive Victorian propriety when women gave up corsets and long skirts for the skimpy garb of free spirited flappers. The "Edwardian Period" following Victoria's death in 1901 and lasting scarcely a decade launched the trend toward liberation in manners and dress that continued beyond the reign of Edward VII and was reinforced by women's roles in World War I. The diaries are particularly charming in illustrating the accepted patterns of flirtation, dating, and courtship of my mother's generation—by an adept participant. Naturally, diaries and letters concentrate on personal, day-to-day issues but I was surprised that, in addition to "the Great War," other global and national events commanded attention and mention. Besides these familiar historical contexts, I also was reminded of or introduced to what were once major public concerns or common customs that are now all but forgotten.

I am resigned to the fact that the full names of some people and the meaning of a few private jokes and allusions along with the outcome of some passing but tantalizing references will never be known. Also, my stock of oral history might not be entirely accurate as I discovered in a few instances where my received versions of given incidents did not exactly jibe with accounts written at the time they occurred. Generally, however, I was astounded at the persistent accuracy of family stories, including quoted remarks.

Besides expanding on the incidents within the period of the letters and diaries, my account of family saga *qua* social history includes essential narrative information leading up to and following the period, 1915-1922.

As I have already detailed my mother's father's family, the Danielsons, it is now necessary to sort out my mother's maternal relatives, the Martins and Schuettes, who also are mentioned frequently in the letters and diaries. The following is not required reading; the information is provided simply for reference as desired, either in reading this account or in using the archived papers for further research. On the other hand, the genealogical information has a certain appeal looked at as a whole, like a tapestry that does not require remembering the color or course of each thread to appreciate an interweaving of distinctive details and recurrent patterns of family ties.

There are many more Schuettes, Martins, and their affines (as we anthropologists call in-laws) than Danielsons. They began emigrating from Europe a generation or more before Bernhard and Caroline came from Norway. They also had an unfortunate proclivity to name their children after themselves, their parents, or their siblings, so I must distinguish among the several Williams, Victors, Edwards and others. Few members of the family moved away from Milwaukee, or even the south side; many lived within easy walking distance from Rayline's home. They visited each other regularly and got together for big family gatherings of 30 people or more on birthdays and holidays, as duly recorded in Rayline's diaries. Carl had grown up on Milwaukee's north side and his kindred, with whom I had minimal interaction compared to my maternal ties, will be discussed after he and Rayline are introduced in 1919 although information from his letters will be included when it is particularly germane to a topic of the moment.

Rayline enjoyed the special status of being the oldest and in some ways the favorite grandchild to both sets of grandparents. At least, with all of her first cousins being considerably younger she knew their grandparents better and I had the advantage of hearing her recollections. By the time the diaries begin, Pa Martin was living with my grandparents following the death of his wife, Emma (Ma) Schuette Martin, in 1916. Pa died when I was nearly thirteen and I was privileged to grow up hearing his stories of early Milwaukee and his descriptions of the countryside where he and his father fished and hunted and visited villages of Potawatomi Indians who managed to linger in the Milwaukee area until the 1860s, although most of the tribe had been forced to remove west of the Mississippi River after 1833.

He was born in Passaic, New Jersey in 1848. About two years later, his parents moved to Milwaukee, their journey expedited by the rapid western expansion of railroad lines since the early 1840s replacing the slow water routes via the Erie Canal and through the Great Lakes. His father, William J. Martin, Sr. was an Englishman from the Devon region who, with a partner who remained in New Jersey, had invested in building a plank road from Milwaukee to the city of Janesville, a distance of 65 miles. Milwaukee was a center of such entrepreneurial road building, the first and best known being the highway still officially named the Watertown Plank Road. Although my family's story had it that the planks were black walnut, as a matter of fact they were three inch thick oak planks, eight feet long, set on a bed of oak logs. By 1854 only the first 24 miles of the Janesville Road were completed and the whole idea of plank roads was proving inefficient as the planks soon wore out with use and rotted in damp soil. Since my family's contract with the state allowed planks or their equivalent, most of the distance was maintained with gravel. My mother said that the first toll station was on Milwaukee's south side near the site of the present Modjeska Theater on Mitchell Street where the Martins first settled, with toll gates every ten miles or so all the way down to Janesville near the Illinois border. A historical marker memorializing the Janesville Plank Road was erected in 2000 at the corner of Forest Home Avenue and South 92nd Street. Twice a year, my great great grandfather went with a pony and wagon to check on the condition of the road and settle accounts with the various toll keepers, mainly farmers, paying them and collecting his and his partner's share. An original placard from the plank road surfaced when Rayline was packing to leave Layton Boulevard that we donated to the Milwaukee County Historical Society. It lists fees per mile for various categories of users: an animal led, ridden or drawing a vehicle cost one cent; a score of sheep or swine cost three cents; a score of "Neat Cattle"—neat signifying a herd—cost four cents, and "Penalty for Passing Without Payment, $10.00." The state eventually bought out these private toll roads.

Lalla always made claims to aristocracy through the Martins who, she said, had been listed in *Burke's Peerage*, the regularly updated guide to titled families in the United Kingdom, and were here before the American Revolution but, being Tories, they sent the women and children home when war broke out. The men joined them back in England after the Americans won. She also claimed her grandfather had been destined for the clergy but was estranged from his family and left in a huff for America after some kind of falling out with the local bishop. I inherited a rectangular gold and black enamel "mourning pin," containing a tiny braid of hair under glass with the name "Margueretta Martin" engraved on the back along with the date of her death, 1835, at the age of 55, presumably a memento of William J. Martin, Sr.'s mother. Another heirloom is a gold watch fob enclosing a large topaz with the Martin family crest engraved in the surface to mark the hot wax used to seal letters and certify documents. That was all I knew about the Martins until a comment popped up in Rayline's diary, November 30, 1918: "Mother and I have been reading some things of great-grandparents Martin. They both must have been very well educated, but grandpa sure was stubborn when he refused his inheritance."

Of all the things Lalla and Rayline saved, why didn't they preserve those papers!

Pa's mother, Wilhelmine Wendt Martin, had emigrated to New York from Saxony (she never said Germany) with her mother and stepfather, Franz Hoffmann, when she was quite small. I never thought to ask my mother if she knew how Wilhelmine met Pa's father although I know they were married in New York's St. Thomas Episcopal Church. Wilhelmine's mother's first husband had owned a furniture factory. After she was widowed and later married the factory manager they emigrated to America rather than put up with the ostracism and gossip that resulted from her marrying beneath her class. When Pa's parents moved to Milwaukee in 1850, the Hoffmanns accompanied them and opened a grocery store in the city. After Pa's parents moved to Hales Corners, he lived with his grandparents in Milwaukee where he attended the German English Academy, the equivalent of a high school and junior college. He used to tell me how he helped with work at the store that entailed, among other duties, making "tutes" of brown butcher paper—a corruption of the German *Tüte*, before paper bags were manufactured.

Pa was an only child, and his oldest child, born in 1876, was named William for his father and grandfather, though Ma Martin wanted to call him Independence in honor of the nation's centennial. She seemed to have a penchant for unusual names, as witness Lalla Rookh. Son William is referred to in the diaries as Uncle Will. He and Aunt Alice (nee Muetze, pronounced Mitzi) had one child, another William called Billy in the diaries and letters. Will and Alice lived only three blocks away from Lalla and Daniel. Lalla was two years younger than Uncle Will and eight years older than the last two siblings, identical twins named Raymond and Royal. Roy never married but Ray married Clara Koch and named his only child Florence for his sister. "Little Florence," as she is referred to in the diaries, was born in 1913, three years after her cousin Billy. These much younger first cousins spent a lot of time at Rayline's home, particularly Florence. Rayline comments frequently in her diaries that Clara neglected to keep her only child's clothing neat and clean. After Ray died in 1923, Florence spent practically every weekend with Lalla and Daniel and was like a younger sister to Rayline. After she grew up and married, she named her second daughter Nancy Rayline.

The Schuette sisters, ca. 1875-1880, from top to bottom, youngest to oldest: Hattie (Harriet), Jennie (Eugenia), Tony (Marie Antoinette), Emma, Bertha, and Louisa.

Although my great grandmother, Ma Martin, had died before the story opens, seven of her eight siblings were still living and many of them were still around when I was growing up. Louisa and Bertha were the oldest and actually half sisters to the rest but their mother had died when they were so small that the only mother they really knew was Cathrine (as spelled on her gravestone) Nunnemacher Schuette, second wife of their father, Victor Schuette, Sr. His oldest daughter, Louisa had died in 1906, many years before the diaries and letters begin, but she is part of the story too. Her sister Bertha (Mrs. Anton Grueninger) had three children: Nettie (Antoinette), Clara, and Antoine, Jr. Nettie was Lalla's close friend as well as her cousin and is mentioned frequently in the diaries. My great grandmother Emma (Martin) was the oldest of Cathrine Nunnemacher's children, followed by Marie Antoinette (Aunt Tony) a school teacher who never married and died before I was born, and *THE AUNTS*, Hattie and Jennie, always so distinguished collectively from their sisters who were simply aunts—in any case, pronounced "ants." They had married late but very well and although they had no children they were a formidable family presence (particularly Aunt Jennie, tall with an eagle beak and commanding eyebrows), taking it upon themselves to instruct all their nieces and nephews and their spouses and children and grandchildren how they should run their lives, particularly regarding the virtues of thrift and habits of refinement. Aunt Hattie's husband was Sherman Spurr who, I believe, was a stockbroker.

Louisa's husband Charles Kuehne (pronounced Keen) was a wealthy produce broker, I believe originally from Milwaukee but for many years based in Kansas City, Missouri. Their oldest child, Meta (Mrs. Walter) Carroll, had a daughter, Louise, who went to live with *THE AUNTS* after her mother died. Their son Carl never progressed mentally beyond the age of four or five and died in 1914 at the age of 25.

Aunt Jennie had lost no time rushing to Kansas City when her sister Louisa died in 1906, ostensibly to help look after "poor Carl," but really, according to my mother who had heard it from her mother, she had set her cap for her brother-in-law. Widowed in 1917, Aunt Jennie was still living in Kansas City when my mother began her first diary in 1918 and several times expresses the hope, to no avail, that Aunt Jennie would invite her to visit and pay for her train fare. Lalla, Daniel, and Rayline had visited Kansas City when Rayline was much younger.

By 1920 Aunt Jennie had moved back to Milwaukee and she and Aunt Hattie and Uncle Sherm', who had been living on the south side, bought a large house together in Shorewood, at that time Milwaukee's most fashionable suburb. They had a live-in cook/ housekeeper, daily maid, and chauffeur. *THE AUNTS* periodically invited their grand- and great grandnieces and nephews, two at a time up to about the age of ten, to spend a weekend at their home as a kind of socializing experience. In later years we compared notes and realized the house was neither so large and elegant nor *THE AUNTS* so rich and aristocratic as we remembered them or were led to believe they were. I must note in their defense, however, that while their names really were Eugenia and Harriet, they chose to be called Jennie and Hattie, even on their headstones.

Besides the Schuette aunts, there were three Schuette uncles. The oldest, Victor, named for his father, was married to Augusta Schmidt, and they had Victor III, Alma, Jeanette, and Edward. Uncle Victor's wife was Roman Catholic and their children were raised Catholic, a matter the Protestant in-laws privately deplored but tolerated because everyone liked Aunt 'Gusta. Jeanette was about Rayline's age even though she was of Lalla's generation and she and Rayline were close friends throughout their lives. Jeanette is mentioned often in the diaries and my father's letters. She was a pretty child in the pictures of her playing with my mother when they were small but she was afflicted with kyphosis and her deformity became progressively more obvious as she grew up, a misfortune Rayline adverts to from time to time in her diaries as Jeanette's "burden," "cross," or "affliction." Jeanette was destined to be "an old maid" and earn her own living while my mother was enjoying the attentions of many suitors and expected to marry and be supported by her husband.

Otto married Aletta Rostad (of Norwegian descent—her mother had come to this country as the pianist who accompanied a once famous Norwegian violinist, Ole Bull) and they had four children—George, Antoinette, Lawrence, and Jane (Eugenia). Jane was a minor when her mother died and was raised by *THE AUNTS* along with Louise Carroll over whom she was clearly favored and indulged. George married Meta Roloff and had George, Jr., Jack, Betty, and "Little Jane," named for her father's

The Layton House located on the Janesville Plank Road, now 2504 Forest Home Avenue, as it appeared when this picture was taken ca. 1880. Photo courtesy Wisconsin Historical Society, # 9489

sister. Betty and I were about the same age and best friends when we attended the same grade school. Antoinette, whose elopement with Robin Middlemas is reported in the diaries, belonged to my grandmother's generation, like Jeanette, but was only two years older than Rayline and also her close, lifetime friend. Her children, Catherine and Bobby (Robin Jr.) also were my childhood friends.

My great great grandfather, the progenitor of the Schuette clan in America, was originally from Germany, Stuttgart I believe, and owned a restaurant, The White Bear, in what is now the old part of downtown Milwaukee where the Milwaukee School of Engineering is located. About 1870 he took over the management of the Layton House at the request of the owner, Frederick Layton, an early entrepreneur who got his start in the meat packing industry and became a well known philanthropist. Layton Boulevard is named for him. The offer appealed to my great great grandfather, I was told, because he had health problems and looked forward to fresh air and a less hectic pace of life than running his restaurant in the city. Also, by this time, his children were old enough to do most of the work required at the Layton House.

The hotel, built in 1849, was out in the country on the then far southern outskirts of Milwaukee on Forest Home Avenue, a segment of the Janesville Plank Road. It was across from Forest Home Cemetery that was established in 1850 and was assured a steady income in part by its location since it was customary for bereaved families to feed people who had to come a distance by horse and buggy from Milwaukee to attend funerals. Arrangements would have been made in advance so sufficient food could be prepared but last minute tasks were timed to the cemetery bell tolling the number of years of the deceased that marked the end of the burial ceremony. By the time the cortege exited the cemetery gate, practically at the door of the Layton House, piping hot food would be on the tables ready to be served.

The Layton House also was a favorite stop-over for farmers bringing produce many miles to market in Milwaukee since they could get a good night's sleep and still get to "Commission Row" when it opened for business early in the morning. Family tradition says that supper, a bed, breakfast and horse fodder cost $1.00. Unfortunately, by the late 1860s the place was getting a bad name for rowdy parties and who knows what other hanky panky, which prompted Mr. Layton to ask Mr. Schuette, a man of good character as well as experienced in the restaurant business, to run the establishment. His first managerial decision was to close the dance hall on the top floor, a regular feature of such country inns, and turn it into a play and recreation area for his children. The three story building still stands across the street from the cemetery but is barely discernible behind an architecturally unfortunate addition across its front.

As the Schuette children married and left home, most of them settled within a few blocks of the Layton House and Forest Home Cemetery where Pa was a co-director and a regular visitor at the Layton House. The senior Schuettes thought he was interested in one of the older sisters, Louisa or Bertha, but it was Emma, nine years his junior whom he asked to marry him. They lived in

The "haunted" Cotswold style cottage that stood at the entrance to Forest Home Cemetery where the Martin family lived from ca. 1890-1899.

various places until my grandmother was about twelve years old when they rented the large Cotswold style "cottage" that stood just inside the cemetery next to the gate. It had been built for the cemetery caretaker but the incumbent at the time had decided rather suddenly to move to a farmhouse he owned nearby. Pa was pleased with the convenience of the location and the good deal he got on the rent because he agreed to assume one of the caretaker's occasional but essential winter duties. The cemetery maintained a large greenhouse to supply ornamental plants for its own landscaping and sale to the public. If the temperature dropped in the greenhouse, threatening the valuable assortment of plants, an ingenious mechanism was rigged to ring a bell in the cottage to awaken the caretaker so he could run over to the greenhouse and stoke the furnace.

As soon as the Martins took up residence in the cottage, they heard strange thumpings at night emanating from the closed space between the ceiling and one of the gables. My great grandmother is supposed to have said to my great grandfather, "Billy, I am sure there is some perfectly natural explanation for that noise but if you don't find out what it is I'M NOT STAYING!" They opened the ceiling and found a colony of flying squirrels that returned from their nocturnal foraging through a small hole under the eaves, landing with a thump on the upper side of the ceiling. An easily exorcised "ghost" that had driven out the caretaker and his family!

I guess it is remarkable, now that I think about it, that a cemetery figures so importantly and affectionately in the recollections of my extended family and even in my own memories. Among other things, Forest Home is where I learned to ride a bike and drive a car. When I was very small, Pa used to visit former colleagues after his retirement and took me along. A Mr. MacGregor was in charge of the greenhouse and I would search around surreptitiously while the men were talking to see if I could find the blue coat with brass buttons that Peter Rabbit had left behind in escaping from Mr. MacGregor's clutches.

Lalla and Daniel enjoyed startling newly met acquaintances with the information that they were married in a cemetery. Not among the tombstones, the image that seemed to spring to people's minds, but at the bride's home just inside the entrance to the cemetery. Now they rest at Forest Home, along with the Martins, the Schuettes, the Danielsons, my parents and paternal grandparents. My plot is there too, and I even had a choice. One of my distant Nunnemacher cousins sent me a note shortly after I changed jobs in 1972 and left the university to become head curator of anthropology at the Milwaukee Public Museum. The Nunnemachers, originally from Switzerland, made their money in the distilling business and have a long association with the museum since it was established in 1882 and were among its first benefactors. Cousin Hermann said it was nice to have a family member again associated with the museum and praised me highly for all my scholarly achievements. Then he informed me he was just going through his late father's papers and discovered there was one last grave still unspoken for on the large Nunnemacher lot and he would be honored to let me have it. I explained I already

Victor Schuette and Cathrine Schuette ca. 1899.

was accommodated beside my parents and while I thanked him I couldn't resist the opening his offer gave me: "Oh, Hermann, you men are all alike. You compliment a girl for her mind but all you're interested in is her body."

Apart from family associations, Forest Home is an interesting place to visit, a sort of landscaped museum of changing times and tastes with roads winding through its 200 acres among soaring obelisks, mausoleums derived from many styles of architecture, headstones ranging from modest and austere to large and flamboyant, and Victorian era monuments heavy on symbolism— broken pillars or mighty oaks carved of marble, grieving angels, draped urns. In the oldest sections, weather worn marble lambs and cradles remind us how many children did not survive infancy in the 19th and even early 20th centuries. Here and there one sees crosses of various sizes and patterns, almost always indicative of Catholic graves. Although established by St. Paul's Episcopal Church, the cemetery is non-denominational, even including pioneer Jewish family graves and, a legacy of Milwaukee's history as an abolitionist

Four generations, 1899: Rayline at about a year and a half; her mother; her maternal grandmother Emma ("Ma") Schuette Martin; and her great Grandmother Cathrine Nunnemacher Schuette.

stronghold, it was integrated almost from the start. As the Latino population of Milwaukee has grown and prospered over the last few decades, their departed family members rest beneath ethnically distinctive kinds of markers. Crypts set one above another in stone walls have become popular since about the 1960s.

While *THE AUNTS* might have abandoned the south side for a fancy suburb on Lake Michigan north of Milwaukee, as soon as Aunt Jennie moved back to Milwaukee, she bought a big lot in Forest Home Cemetery, across the road from the Nunnemacher lot, where she had the bodies of her husband, his children, and her sister Louisa moved from Kansas City. A large granite marker with a simple laurel motif and bearing only the name Kuehne stands in the middle of the lot. Now Aunt Jennie is buried there beside Aunt Hattie and Uncle Sherm' along with her brother Otto and his wife, her brother Victor and his wife, their daughter Jeanette, and sons Victor and Edward and their wives. All the graves have small no-nonsense headstones, obviously mandated by Aunt Jennie, but when I visited there to check on dates in connection with this book, I noticed for the first time that a small concession had been made to Catholic Aunt 'Gusta and her children and their spouses: tiny crosses are incised above the names on their headstones.

Finally, certain close friends of my mother's mother are mentioned with such regularity, that they too must be identified. Like *THE AUNTS* and most of the other relatives discussed, I remember many of these people very well from my childhood and beyond. What I know of their stories also sheds interesting light on the era of the diaries and earlier.

Jennie Walters, sometimes called Jane, and my grandmother started in school together and remained friends throughout their lives. Jennie's grandparents had come from Holland and her mother was orphaned along with some older brothers when their parents left their farm to buy supplies in Milwaukee and never returned. It is quite certain that they were unclaimed victims of a cholera epidemic in 1849-1850. The brothers continued to run the farm but arranged a marriage for their sister with a fellow Hollander. The Walters had 13 children of whom Jennie was the youngest. My mother's diaries often mention Jennie's visits (sometimes with her sister Anna) and her helpfulness with sewing and other family activities; she wondered why Jennie never married as she certainly was good looking and personable. About 1935, when I was in high school and Jennie was around sixty, she surprised us all with the information that she had been keeping company with a gentleman, Alfred Haas, whose wife had long been confined to an institution because of brain deterioration of some kind. For all that, when the wife finally died, they waited a year to marry in deference to her memory. Jennie, who had lived on a small income from her sewing and helping at the rooming house her mother ran, moved to New Jersey where her husband was a very successful sales representative for a textile company. He called her Jeanette with a French pronunciation, although of German birth himself, and showered her with luxuries—jewelry, furs, a beautiful apartment. Alfred was debonair, wearing his fedora turned up along one side in the style of John Barrymore, and courtly. He had a sly sense of humor and was very generous, always amused that Jennie could never quite overcome the penny pinching habits of her spinster years. Both Jennie and Alfred were blessed with good health and enjoyed more than 20 years of marriage. Jennie is buried with Alfred's ashes in Forest Home Cemetery.

In some cases my mother refers to such friends as "aunt" or "uncle" as a matter of respect as was still the custom in my early life if they were too close as family friends to call them Mrs. or Mr. but too old by a generation to be called by their first names, the fact that I called my immediate elders by their first names, notwithstanding. Sometimes one's parents' or grandparents' older cousins were also called "Aunt" or "Uncle." Thus I called my grandmother's cousin, Nettie Riemenschneider, "Aunt Nettie."

Minnie Wieseman was another of my grandmother's lifetime friends whose story is far less happy than Jennie's but she prevailed in the end. Her family originally came from Canada and there was kind of a mystery about them. Her mother was institutionalized with some sort of mental disorder but visited home occasionally, always beautifully dressed, and died when Minnie was quite small. Minnie's father was well-to-do, owning a park where people gathered and paid to eat, dance, and listen to concerts. He arranged for Minnie to marry a widowed friend, about his own age, with grown children. When her father was dying and it appeared Minnie would have no children he said it was just as well as he would not have to tell her the real history of the family. Minnie was so modest that she could not bring herself to tell her father immediately that she was carrying her first child, and then her father died. She had three children: a son Theodore, a daughter Jessie, and another son Frederick. While her husband apparently earned a good living, he had debts and never invested in life insurance. He died when the children were quite young and Minnie was left destitute, inheriting only a poor little farm about 35 miles from Milwaukee that barely supported the family.

On Thursday, November 18, 1920, my mother wrote in her diary:

> Poor Aunt Minnie Wieseman. She seems to have more than her share of hard knocks. But this last is the worst. Her house and every solitary thing in [it] burned up Tuesday night. Mother has been busy all day collecting things & money & she is going out [to see her] to-morrow. It is almost incomprehendable [sic] to imagine not to have even a handkerchief to your name. They ran out without any stockings or shoes and if they had stayed a few minutes longer they all would have been burned to death.

The fire was generally believed, although never proved, to have been set in spite by a mentally disturbed man whose romantic overtures Minnie had rebuffed. With the help of friends and neighbors, the Wiesemans moved to a small house (equipped only with a privy in the back yard) in the town of Palmyra, Wisconsin where Minnie clerked at the general store and the children worked at various jobs when not in school. They all earned college degrees, Theodore in engineering and Jessie in education. After a stint of teaching in Alabama, Jessie eventually found employment in the Whitewater, Wisconsin school district where she and Aunt Minnie then made their home. Frederick, the youngest, was a career officer in the Marine Corps, rising to the rank of Lt. General. During WWII he served with distinction in the Pacific Theater and at the time of his retirement in 1966 was commandant of the Marine Corps Schools at Quantico, VA. When he enlisted right after graduating from high school in 1925 he was scheduled to take the entrance exam to the naval academy at Annapolis, but was sent off to China instead. Among my father's papers archived at the Wisconsin Veterans Museum in Madison is a 1926 letter from his friend Senator Robert La Follette assuring him he had followed up on his request to look into the matter of "young Wieseman" and that he had been tracked down in the Philippines. He was allowed to take the exam there and entered Annapolis in 1927.

Never one to complain, Aunt Minnie met adversity with wit and humor, noting in her later years that she lived long enough to realize her two fondest dreams during the hard times: grandchildren and an indoor toilet. Her grandson Ted, Fred's son, and I still keep in touch and cannot help but continue to ponder the family secrets Minnie's father took with him to the grave.

Another of my grandmother's friends from childhood, in fact, her maid of honor at her wedding, is mentioned briefly in the diaries. Her name was Cora Washburn and her family moved to Paducah, Kentucky where Cora married a man named Jesse Nichols. Their only daughter, Josephine, about my mother's age, is mentioned in passing now and then in the diaries and my father's letters. "Aunt" Cora and my grandmother stayed in touch by letter and occasional visiting that continued through my childhood.

Then there were the Alberts, Oscar and Hattie and their son Warren (their second son, Roy, was born later) with whom Daniel entered into business ventures. The Alberts did not live in Milwaukee and were frequent overnight guests. Many other friends appear in the diaries and letters, but their particular roles do not require the depth of context of the relatives and quasi relatives noted here.

As I began sharing information about my project with various family members and was well into the third chapter, Betty Danielson O'Sullivan's daughter, Mary Eleanor, my second cousin who got Rayline's hope chest, remembered that along with my mother's wedding veil, some trousseau lingerie, dress patterns and other items, the chest contained "some old newspapers" and she wondered if I'd like to see them.

Would I!

They date from 1916 through 1918 and include the first issue, Vol. 1, no. 1, Feb. 8, 1918 of *The Stars and Stripes*, the official newspaper of the AEF, the American Expeditionary Force in France, along with nos. 41, 44, 45, 46, and 47. My mother noted in her diary that Tuve Floden sent her *The Stars and Stripes* from time to time and on December 13, 1918 she expressed some annoyance that she'd rather he'd write her a letter. Earlier he had sent her the *Fort Sheridan Reveille* (Vol. 1, no. 6, July 20, 1917).

Despite having destroyed Sam Lang's letters my mother had kept the copies of the YMCA sponsored *Trench and Camp* (Vol. 1, no. 30, April 29 and no. 33, May 30, 1918) that he sent from Fort Oglethorpe, Georgia, but noted in her diary on May 10, "It can't compare with the AEF paper." Later, he sent her the *Paris Edition of The Chicago Tribune* of March 8, 1919 that she received on April 8. A final item, possibly sent by Sam, is a page torn from an undated French publication, apparently a slick paper magazine, *Fantasio*, with an anti-German propaganda cartoon on one side and a satirical but otherwise obscure cartoon on the other labeled, "Les Parvenus."

A single sheet of newsprint, the front page of the Social Section of The Birmingham News, Sunday, October 15, 1916, shows a picture of Mary Ball, Rayline's closest friend, along with pictures of six other debutantes, "to be formally presented to society." The earliest paper consists of "Part Two, Women's Features" and "Part Five, Magazine Features" of the *Chicago Sunday Herald*, April 9, 1916. I have no idea why Rayline saved these pages although they are fun to peruse, especially the ads showing women's clothing.

The papers are not in very good condition, yellowing, dog eared, and tearing at the folds, with pieces torn and cut out of some of the later issues of *The Stars and Stripes*, but it is remarkable they survived at all. They add a dimension of "being there" to the hand written letters and diaries, a kind of time warp, letting me share, if only to a tiny degree, what my mother and her contemporaries at the time saw and literally feeling something they felt. In addition to the news and features relating to another time, what is strikingly different is the sensation of holding these pages in my hand. They are huge, generally 18" x 24," compared with current newspapers that are barely a foot across and well under two feet deep; even the smaller *Trench and Camp* is larger than today's tabloids. Although I'd relinquished any claims to the contents of the hope chest, my cousin did not hold me to this agreement and gave me the papers when she saw my excitement about their relevance to the letters and diaries with which they will be archived. A hope chest, by the way, is referred to in my mother's diaries and her girl friends' and my father's letters in the slang of the day as "the God knows when box," or just "the box."

A number of other documentary items surfaced here and there among my mother's things when I was getting ready to move that I just put in a large plastic envelope as I went along, not knowing what to do with them—old greeting cards, family snapshots, Rayline's wedding invitation, a letter she wrote to her parents from Downer, a telegram from Aunt Lou from Colorado Springs on the occasion of Rayline's wedding, and the like. Two are of special interest in connection with the bag of letters and the diaries. One actually is a surviving letter to Daniel from Lalla in Norway, August 11, 1906, that she speculated would reach him around the 25th of the month. The context indicates that both she and her mother-in-law received money by check from their respective husbands while they were away, but because they would be starting home early in September and they needed money again it should be cabled rather than mailed as checks to be sure to reach them. It gave real substance to the Edison cylinder record story!

The other is a theme Rayline wrote when she was enrolled at the Milwaukee Normal School, "My Auto-Biography," that explains why she went to the Downer Seminary rather than a public high school. Her parents indulged her whim. When she was in grade school she and several other girls formed a club, of which she wrote:

> At our club meetings we always read boarding school stories, and each of us dreamed of the day when we would be boarding school girls.
>
> I was the only one who had this dream realized, and at the age of fourteen I entered Milwaukee Downer Seminary.

She also wrote that when she graduated from Downer she looked at a lot of catalogs and brochures for different colleges and then decided to go to the Normal School. Maybe she thought this would curry favor with the instructor because she very much wanted to go to the University at Madison and her diary makes clear she soon "hated" the Normal School and dropped out in her sophomore year. The theme, handwritten on both sides of nine pages, offers clarification of a number of details in the letters and diaries to be discussed. It also contains the completely unfounded claims that part of her ethnic heritage was French and that her father "lost" their luggage in Boston.

Another set of documents I had on hand that proved very useful in writing this account is the detailed descriptive inventory and in some cases actual copies of items I assembled when I donated my father's papers to the Wisconsin Veterans Museum at Madison. Included among these materials is Robert La Follette's letter, cited above, records of my father's military service, and the University of Wisconsin Faculty Resolution prepared in his memory in 1956, a few months after his death.

I am grateful for John Gurda's encyclopedic and engagingly written book, *The Making of Milwaukee*, published by the Milwaukee County Historical Society in 1999 that sometimes intersects with the oral history I learned from my elders. It has provided both verifying information and occasional corrections of significant details. Finally, when the manuscript was finished and I was assembling illustrations, Kara Thomas, a Schuette family relative, happened to show me her great aunt Jeanette's photo album with snapshots from 1916-1917. Thanks to Kara, I am able to include clearly identified pictures of Rayline's early beaux Karl "Windy" Windesheim and Sam Lang, and one I am confident must be of Gladys Boerner, all taken at Phantom Lake. The originals of all other illustrations unless otherwise noted are archived at the Milwaukee County Historical Society.

2

Layton Boulevard and Phantom Lake
School Friends and Boy Friends

Consideration of the family's association with Phantom Lake is as important as the Milwaukee background to fully savor my mother's diaries and collection of letters, but it also requires some review of people and events antedating the earliest documents in the collection. Phantom Lake is about 25 miles from Milwaukee near the town of Mukwonago, Wisconsin, and is entirely spring fed. It derives its name from mysterious mists rising from its surface in early September, the result of the configuration of the land surrounding the lake and the interface of markedly contrasting temperatures of air and water. An "Indian legend," embellished upon in the course of re-telling over the years, concerns rivals for the hand of the chief's daughter (the tribe variously identified as Potawatomi, Sauk, Winnebago, and others). Eloping with one "brave" in his canoe, the "princess" was pursued in a canoe by the other suitor. The two men struggled with each other and fell into the water, drowning together in a death grip. As the fair maiden watched in horror, the lake's resident spirit, aggravated by all the commotion, rose up and claimed her as his bride. Thereafter, it was said, the Phantom claimed the fairest maiden on the lake every September. Rayline always knew the legend was hokey because she was the only maiden around in the fall before other homes began springing up and the legend gained currency.

Rayline, about four years old, in her new hat that she
remembered had special rosettes to keep her ears warm.

My grandmother bought the Phantom Lake property in 1910 as a surprise for my grandfather, and he decided they should camp for a summer or two to establish the best location and orientation for a house. Once the house was built, as my mother's diaries make evident and in the recollections of my own early years, the family really lived more or less simultaneously in Milwaukee and "out at the lake." They spent weekends from early spring to summer and from early fall to winter in the country and week days in the city, but they sometimes spent extended periods at Phantom Lake in the winter and at Layton Boulevard in the summer depending on weather and other considerations, so it is almost impossible to discuss one home apart from the other. In fact, it is sometimes hard to tell whether my mother is writing her diary on Layton Boulevard or at Phantom Lake.

The family home in Milwaukee, across from open acres of celery fields when it was built in 1902, had gas lighting.

Although electric lines were extended to the area a few years before World War I—much sooner than expected—the family delayed converting to electricity until 1920 because of the investment that had been made in costly gas chandeliers. A large bay window on the second floor of the home was designed to watch horse drawn sleighs called "cutters" race down the street in front of the house on winter Sundays. Behind the home a good sized barn housed draft horses needed for Daniel's contracting business, along with my mother's Welsh ponies, Dandy and Prince. Apart from the fact that Daniel's parents and parents-in-law lived on the south side, he chose to build there in a still undeveloped area where he could buy a number of lots to store building equipment and supplies.

Daniel's business kept him in the city much of the first summer they owned the Phantom Lake property, so the ponies

On the left: Rayline and to her right, her cousin Jeanette Schuette playing at Rayline's home, ca. 1903. Note barn behind the house.

On the right: Lalla, Daniel, and Rayline, ca. 1905, in front of the house at 874 22nd Ave. (later South Layton Boulevard). The Knox automobile was steered with a tiller rather than a wheel. Note unpaved street and gas lamp streetlight.

became essential transportation to pull the two-wheeled buggy for my grandmother to go shopping in Mukwonago and on other errands. The ponies made the long trip between Milwaukee and Phantom Lake in the spring and fall. The first time it was tried, the plan was for my grandmother, her friend Jennie Walters (who was to spend the summer at Phantom Lake) and Rayline to take two days and stop overnight with relatives en route, but even after visiting various people along the way and a leisurely picnic lunch under the trees, they made good time and decided to keep on going. My grandfather had already gone out with some of his work crew in his "machine" (a Stoddard Dayton, gray with red leather upholstery) to put up the tent. When the women came trotting down the driveway, he was furious.

"Well, now you've done it! You've killed the ponies! I TOLD you they aren't strong enough for such a long trip in one day! Now you're stuck here for the summer!" (Normally easy going, his occasional outbursts were awesome and the family referred to him as "The terrible tempered Mr. Bang," a character in the old Toonerville Folks comic strip—behind his back, of course). Still ranting as he unhitched the ponies, Daniel was astonished when Dandy kicked up his heels and was almost halfway to Milwaukee before they caught up with him, and then he had to be led back. Welsh ponies are notable for their strength and stamina; Dandy was notorious for his willful, mischievous nature and getting the well-behaved Prince into trouble with him.

The custom-made tent was gabled and big enough to hold two double beds, chairs and other furniture. It had a canvas floor sewn tightly to the walls, a feature Lalla insisted on because of her fear of snakes. For all that, one day when the family came back from an outing of several hours they found a neatly shed snakeskin in the middle of the floor, almost a defiant gesture by the snake proving it could get in if it wanted to. It had completely disappeared despite a thorough search of the tent when the family returned.

A screened extension, dubbed the *Affenkäfig* (monkey cage), with a hinged door, extended across the front of the tent where

Tent at Phantom Lake with screened "Affenkäfig" (monkey cage) entrance
where the family lived while the new summer home was being built, 1911.

cooking was done on a camp stove when rainy weather precluded
cooking outdoors; an auxiliary tent served as a dining room in
bad weather. The tent was almost as secure and comfortable as a
cottage except for offering little protection from the neighboring
farmer's cows that were strangely drawn to it at night, stumbling
into guy ropes and uprooting tent pegs. They also blundered into
the clotheslines, pulling clean wash to the ground, and leaving
calling cards of fresh cow plotches. The farmer who owned the cows
responded to repeated complaints with promises to repair the fence
that was supposed to confine the animals but never got around to
it. The women frequently had to shoo the cows away, shouting
and waving dish towels. On one occasion they set off a stampede
causing a full grown heifer to crash into a fence post and knock
herself out. "Throw it over the fence," my mother is said to have
screamed, "don't let it die on our side!" As if they could! The cow
recovered and departed on its own power, but Lalla and Jennie
decided to take action.

Leaving my mother asleep the next time the cows came
around, they took up the sturdy poles they used for walking sticks
and, like avenging angels in their voluminous white cotton night

gowns, they rounded up the cows, herding them out the driveway, down the one lane right-of-way to the county road and all the way to the main road where they took them several miles more toward the town of East Troy. It was well after midnight when the women got back to the tent. There was no night traffic in those days so they carried out their mission unobserved. If the farmer ever suspected why his cows had wandered so far that it took several days to find all of them, he never mentioned it, but he did mend the fence.

Toward the end of that first summer, Daniel had a large garage built where the family lived while the house was being built during the second summer. Instead of following the custom of giving summer cottages romantic, funny, or faux Indian names— "Whispering Pines," "Last Resort," "Me-Ma-Kids-n-Pup"—our place had a rather grand and certainly original name, Floraydan Lodge. It was a fairly large, year-round house intended, though never used, as my grandparents' eventual retirement home rather than simply for vacations. Architecturally, Floraydan Lodge was patterned on the style of an English hunting lodge. My grandmother created the name, after many less mellifluous attempts to avoid giving herself top billing, from her name Florence, my mother's name Rayline, and my grandfather's name Daniel. Although it was chalked in impressive Gothic letters across the red brick front of the large living room fireplace, it was mainly guests who used the name. We just said we were going to or had been out at "Phantom," "the lake," "the country," or "Muk'" (for Mukwonago); the house was only part of the total experience. Furthermore, many people, myself included during my early childhood, did not even make a connection between "Flo" and my grandmother because she always was called Lalla or Lally.

Of course, there is a story behind my mother's unusual name too. She was supposed to be called Eileen but went nameless for nearly two years. Her parents had moved to Chicago when they were married in 1897 and shared a duplex with a family whose Eileen was such a brat that my grandmother came to hate the name during her pregnancy. She didn't consider an alternative, believing the baby would be a boy to be named William after her father. My mother was still just "Baby" when they moved back to Milwaukee in 1900 where my grandmother's brother Raymond was so attentive as a first time uncle that my grandfather suggested the name Rayline, like Pauline.

By the time I came along, my mother had decided on Nancy for a girl's name although my father had strongly favored Rayline. "This kid is going to have *one name* everyone knows how to spell and pronounce," she said on the basis of her experience with Rayline compounded by having married a man named Carl Oestreich ("that's pronounced A-Strike, as in baseball or bowling, not ostrich," we would explain.)

Floraydan Lodge was located on more than four acres of wooded land overlooking the lake from an elevation approaching 30 feet. It had two stories with low, curved dormers. The walls, covered with gray stucco, sloped out from the roof—barely perceptibly but giving an effect of the house being comfortably settled into the land around it. There was a large open porch supported on pillars facing north across the front of the house with a panoramic view of the lake. The most prominent feature on the lake's far side was what the family called the "Inn Hill," so symmetrical that it looked like a huge, overturned soup bowl. A luxury resort once graced the top in the days when well-to-do mothers and their children enjoyed carefree summers in the country and fathers joined them on weekends and during their own vacations, commuting to Mukwonago on the Soo Line from Chicago or the interurban trolley from Milwaukee. Such summer retreats lost their appeal with the growing popularity of automobiles and ease of travel. The grounds served briefly as a Campfire Girls camp in 1918 according to my mother's diary, and on August 9, 1919, she noted, "The Inn burned to-day. Goodness, the good old Inn is really gone." It was rumored, though unproven, to have been a case of arson for insurance when the inn ceased to be profitable.

The Floraydan Lodge porch had a long wooden swing hanging by chains from the ceiling. It provided me with a world of make-believe—pirate ship, train, stage-coach, even an airplane, still so rare in my very early childhood that we ran outside when we heard a motor overhead to gaze up and wave. It also was a wonderful place to swing gently during summer storms and bet with Carly where the next flash of lightning would streak out of the sky and then count the seconds between the flash and the crack of thunder.

There was a large screened porch along the east side of the house where we ate most of our meals and enjoyed watching birds and chipmunks go at the stale bread we threw on the ground for them. When it was too cold to eat outside we ate in the kitchen, warmed by a big wood burning range. The dining room, with beamed ceiling, built-in cabinets and room for a day bed, side-board, and desk besides a large table and more than a dozen chairs, was used when the number of visitors exceeded the capacity of the screened porch or kitchen. And we had lots of visitors. The dining room was usually filled on Sundays when family and friends came out from the city to swim and, of course, had to stay for supper. Lalla's hospitality also meant frequent overnight and weekend guests as well as friends or relatives simply needing a place to stay for several days to several months. There were overnight visitors in Milwaukee, too. Since the house was not as large as the place at Phantom Lake, Rayline occasionally complains in her diaries about having to sleep on the living room davenport or a folding cot in Daniel's office when the volume of guests extended to having to give up her bedroom.

Having grown up in the same houses, I marvel now that with so many people we managed quite well with the then customary single bathroom. A toilet in the basement on Layton Boulevard was used mainly by my grandfather's workmen and at Phantom Lake my father had a sequestered outhouse with a Dutch door where he "communed with nature," but these alternatives were used by others only in dire emergencies. Rayline's diaries indicate that in the city she also monopolized the bathroom for long leisurely baths. The lake served as bathtub in all but the very coldest weather in the country. A graceful stairway of wooden blocks built into the earth stretched from the top of the hill to the lakeshore, the work

Floraydan Lodge at Phantom Lake shortly after it was built in 1911, and as it appeared ca. 1928. Child at pool is the author.

of one of Daniel's employees who had learned this special skill in the mountains of his native Norway.

At Phantom Lake, there were two large bedrooms, each with a fireplace, on the first floor. Eventually, four bedrooms were partitioned off upstairs along with the *Rummpelkammer*, a low ceilinged walk-in storage closet where books, odds and ends of furniture and a lot of other things were as jumbled together as the name suggests.

The foundation was the most unusual but least obvious feature of the house. The entire first floor was poured, reinforced concrete supported on a single pillar about two feet in diameter located in the middle of the basement. Metal rods radiated from the top of the pillar into the concrete that formed the basement ceiling and the first floor of the house. My grandfather had invented this "beamless" support system that he patented in 1907. Family lore insists he was ahead of his time and while the system was used in the big multi-storied Kunzelmann Esser Furniture Company store that my grandfather built and still stands on Milwaukee's south side, architects generally feared specifying it as possibly unsafe. Years later, after Daniel's patent ran out, Frank Lloyd Wright came up independently with a similar and widely acclaimed concept. That Wright described his design in terms of lily pads and other graceful plant analogies might explain why his idea prevailed in comparison to my grandfather's turgidly titled "Musculous System Reinforced Concrete Construction." It is illustrated in the letterhead of his business stationery that my grandmother used to write to my mother in Dallas in 1922.

My grandfather typified his generation of dedicated tinkerers whose heroes, such as Edison and Ford, changed the world with

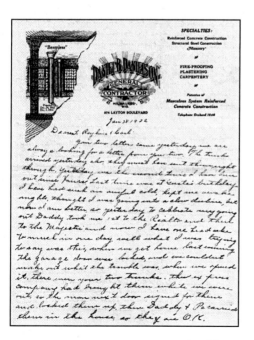

Letterhead illustrating "Musculous System Reinforced Concrete Construction" that supported the house at Phantom Lake.

their inventions. His friends included fellow Milwaukeeans Ole Evinrude, and William S. Harley and Arthur Davidson. He too might have gone on to wealth and fame, but bouts of poor health interfered with developing and marketing a number of patents he held. His one real success, Tie-To Inserts, were used to attach metal laths to walls and ceilings or to anchor brickwork or stone siding in poured concrete construction. Patented about the time I was born, the inserts in various lengths were produced in the barn behind the house in Milwaukee. His contracting business was mechanized by then and he didn't need the barn for horses; he sold his extra lots on the block in the 1920s. The first floor was converted into an assembly factory and the loft into office space. My grandfather cut back on contracting as he expanded his Tie-To business, employing an office manager-salesman, stenographer, and truck driver along with hourly workers as needed to assemble the inserts made of heavy gauge wires encased in wood molding.

When the Great Depression began in the fall of 1929, Daniel was optimistic he could weather it as he had previous hard times, but it had not abated and he was deeply in debt by 1934 when he suffered a massive stroke and lingered helplessly bedridden for nearly a year before his death in 1935. My grandmother took over management of the business during his illness and, thanks to specification of Tie-To Inserts in some government construction as the country moved toward World War II, she paid off the debts and made the company profitable again. My mother continued the business after my grandmother died in 1953 and finally sold it when the barn burned down in 1966 and zoning laws prevented rebuilding and manufacturing in a now fully residential area. Records of the company are archived at the Milwaukee County Historical Society.

At Phantom Lake, besides the main house, there were two small square buildings of gray stucco close to the shore. One had a diagonal partition forming two rooms for changing into and out of bathing suits. The other housed a gasoline powered generator to pump water up to the house from the lake for wash water and flushing the toilet. Drinking water was carried by the pail-full from a spring, orange with iron. Like my mother before me, I got the job of water carrier as soon as I was able to handle it. Among the many routine matters Rayline never mentions in her diary were her several daily trips to the spring, although it was more than the distance of a city block away and, as I well remember, entailed coming back with a full pail of water *up hill*.

The spring was at the foot of the hill below my great grandfather's substantial, two story clapboard cottage that stood a hundred yards or so to the west of the main house. He had bought a strip of land adjoining my grandparents' property and built his cottage about the same time the main house was built in 1911. It was simply called "Pa's house." Although Pa had lived with Lalla and Daniel on Layton Boulevard after his wife died, he lived in his cottage at Phantom Lake during the summers and spent a lot of time there off and on all year until he was well into his eighties.

The spring bubbled into a basin that had been dug near the lakeshore. It was about a yard square, lined with boards with a hinged wooden cover, and overflowed through a curved iron pipe, some four inches in diameter, that gushed out its icy water for us to fill our pails. Flights of migrating ducks passed over the point of land where the spring was located and when I was very small I sat long hours with Daniel and Pa in the blind that stood there, looking out at the wooden decoys and watching as the men raised their guns getting a bead on a passing flock and firing away, KABOOM! KABOOM! Daniel would retrieve the birds in his sleek Dan Kidney skiff while smoke and the smell of gunpowder still lingered over the blind. Both men were avid hunters and fishermen. Pa confined these activities to Phantom Lake by the time I was around, but Daniel hunted deer "Up North" and various game birds in season at different locations. I was cautioned at an early age always to chew roast duck and the like with great care lest I crack a tooth on a piece of shot. I learned on my own not to take a swig of cold milk before I had fully swallowed a mouthful of venison if I didn't want a film of tallow sticking to my palate.

On the left: Lalla's friend, Jennie Walters, ca. 1911

On the right: Daniel (left) and his hunting partner, Frank Fuller of Mukwonago, with skiffs and dog in Daniel's Stoddard Dayton automobile ca. 1911. Note steering wheel on right side.

Rayline mentions puppies in her first diary, offspring of hunting dogs that lived in the barn behind the house on Layton Boulevard, but my grandfather had not owned dogs for many years until I was about seven when he brought home a puppy, a liver and white English springer spaniel, "Spot of Floraydan." Since she was never called anything but Poochie, it was the only name she responded to. Because Daniel's deteriorating health soon curtailed his hunting, Poochie never served as the hunting dog he intended but happily chased rabbits in the tall brushy grass on the hill leading down to the lake. First a rabbit would jump high above the grass to elude Poochie and then Poochie would fling herself into the air to get her bearings, her long ears rising up like those of the rabbit. They really are *springers*!

Another, smaller cottage stood at the entrance to Pa's land that had been built by his old friend and hunting and fishing partner, Ernie Wegner, referred to in Rayline's diaries as "Uncle Ernie." I barely remember Ernie who had moved into the Lutheran Altenheim in Milwaukee when I was quite small. While we continued to call the place Ernie's house, during my childhood it was occupied by an elderly Swedish couple, parents of my grandfather's friend and foreman from his building contractor days, Emil Sjodin (shoDEEN). Sometimes Emil took me with him when he brought groceries and other supplies to his parents in the winter and I skated on the lake. All my life I have searched unsuccessfully at Scandinavian bakeries and church bazaars for Swedish rye bread that even approaches Mrs. Sjodin's wonderful *limpa*. After both Sjodins died and I'd left home for college in 1941, my mother's aunt Elisabeth spent her summers there— widow of Daniel's youngest brother, Charles, of the "C.B.s" who are mentioned frequently in Rayline's diaries.

As the family spent more and more time at Phantom Lake, Lalla realized it was lonely for Rayline and encouraged her to invite friends to stay with her for extended periods. They included cousins Jeanette and Antoinette Schuette, a neighborhood friend, Ada Kroening (pronounced KRAYning) and especially friends from her high school years, 1913-1917, when she attended Milwaukee Downer Seminary. Frances Roberts and Mary Ball, whose letters are part of the collection my mother saved, were Downer friends, along with Margaret Breed, Gladys Boerner and others whose names appear in the diaries.

According to Downer custom, each freshman was assigned a kind of mentor from the sophomore class. Mary was put in charge of Rayline and they remained best friends throughout their lives. While Rayline's diaries are sometimes critical of other girls and mention disagreements and reconciliations with them, particularly Ada and Gladys, and occasionally Antoinette, Mary is always true, dear, and dependable. Mary came from a socially prominent family in Birmingham, Alabama, as shown both in the newspaper clipping of her presentation as a debutante and the whirl of parties and entertainments described in her letters after she had graduated. She was a frequent visitor at Phantom Lake because she spent her summers in Milwaukee. Her mother had some family ties to the city and maintained a spacious apartment on the east side, cooled by Lake Michigan, to escape the heat and humidity of summers in the deep South. Mary's 21 letters from September 22, 1919 to May 28, 1920, including a penny postcard, detail her life in Birmingham and are better understood in the context of the diaries and my father's letters during that period.

The letters from Frances Roberts are the earliest documents in the collection, apart from Ragna's letter, and relate to the period when my mother was still a Downer student. Somehow, I was not surprised Rayline had saved them. Frances was "special." I knew from my mother's occasional comments that Frances was cute, somewhat scatter-brained, and very witty but had an unusual family life. Her marriage to an Englishman was marked by a tragedy that was still able to command popular interest at the very time I began work on this book.

Frances spent only her freshman year at Downer, 1914-1915, but her letters more than suggest it was one of the happiest and most stable periods of her life. Rayline spoke of Frances taking special pleasure in "Just us" eating at the family table at Phantom Lake, a novelty compared to the usual student dining rooms when she was in school and restaurants when she stayed with her mother. The dozen letters Rayline kept are all signed "The Child," a nickname reflecting the fact that she was in the class behind Rayline and two classes behind Mary and another mutual friend, "Babe" Anderson, with whom, according to Frances's letters, she also continued corresponding after leaving Downer. Although her handwriting, spelling, and punctuation are atrocious, her handling of language and humor are far from childish. In a letter, post-marked Nov. 19, 1915, she refers mischievously to her disregard for school rules: "I don't know what Mernie and Babe do without me to lecture—am being a very good little girl this year but really miss my lectures."

She seems to have gravitated naturally to the older girls. In her third letter to Rayline, postmarked Nov. 27, 1915, she asks for "some sophmore [sic] news" even though she admitted not being in touch with any of her former classmates. As best I can piece the story together, her mother was single—probably divorced because Frances speaks of having her picture taken and sending one to her father—and appears to have been in show business. In her letter post-marked March 23, 1916 Frances writes, "I am going out on the road with my mother for the rest of the year." Between October 4, 1915 and February 25, 1917 the post-marks and return addresses include Baltimore, Annapolis, Washington, D.C., two addresses in New York City, and Wyoming, Delaware. There seems to have been no shortage of money as she and her mother stayed at fine hotels and had a very active social life. Frances was quite taken with the midshipmen at Annapolis, and they with her, as she chatters about clothes and attending formal dances and "hops" and going to football games. She attended the Army-Navy game of 1915 that Navy lost: "Well, its over an[d] Oh such a tragedy—14 – 0 !!!" For all that, she had "a <u>wonderful</u>, <u>wonderful</u> time!" As Frances and her mother moved around and she attended different schools, she continued writing about going to dances and games and restaurants with different boy friends and then the letters stopped until September 4, 1918 when Rayline wrote in her diary, "Had a letter from the 'Child' Frances Roberts."

The letter has not survived but Rayline paraphrased it: "She is living in England and has been married over nine months. The Child, of all people to be <u>married</u>. Her husband who she met in the U.S. is of the Royal Flying Corps and comes from a noble family. Well, I only hope that she is happy, for she has had a queer life so far." There possibly were other letters and news of Frances exchanged between Mary and Rayline, now lost, as suggested by a diary entry of January 20, 1919: "Received a letter from Mernnie & she enclosed a letter from the "Child. Well, she sure had a little romance in her life. She knew her 'Ronnie' 2 months & had only met him 7 times before they were married. She seems to be blissfully happy and expects the stork in April. She thinks they'll live in the colonies & that he'll be in the Areo [sic] Mail service. Her whole life has been extraordinary. My how I wish something exciting would happen to me."

Nearly a year elapses until we hear about Frances again. On November 27, 1920 Rayline wrote, "Heard from Frances and she has a little son 18 months old. She lived a year in W. Africa and then went to Wales for a time and now she is in Sussex. Her life has been like a story and from what she writes she is ideally happy. How I wish I could see her and have a good old talk. Maybe that will all take place too." In the Memoranda pages at the back of the diary we find the address, "Mrs. Ronald True (Frances Roberts) Abby Cottage. Old Bosham (near) Chichester, Sussex, England."

On January 10, 1921, there is a brief and puzzling reference to Frances, "Heard from the 'Child' this morning. A letter and a card. Conditions must be awful from the way she writes." This is followed by a final entry on Jan 17, "Received the promised photo from Frances [now lost]. He[r] baby is the cunningest young one I've seen in ages. But Frances looks rather tired and worn. Of course, she was just a carefree school girl when I last saw her and now she is a mother."

Later, I learned from Rayline that there had been some kind of criminal proceeding against Frances's husband that was rehashed in an American publication when I was quite young. I didn't know the particulars but remember my mother's concern and sorrow for Frances with whom she had long since lost touch. Thanks to the special effort of my friend and museum colleague, Dawn Scher-Thomae, who was among the proof readers for this book, we learn from Wikipedia that Ronald True had already been mustered out of the Royal Flying Corps in 1916 for erratic behavior and morphine use when he visited the United States in 1917 where he met and married Frances Roberts. By 1921 he had abandoned her and their child. He was clearly mentally deranged when he murdered a prostitute in March of 1922. Tried and found guilty of a capital crime, he was reprieved and confined to the Broadmoor Prison Hospital by the Home Secretary, causing a controversy that English justice at the time protected a titled man who murdered a street walker but hanged a working class man who murdered a titled woman. A book by Donald Carswell (ed.), The Trial of Ronald True, published in 1950 and a play inspired by the True story, Lullababies of Broadmoor, presented at London's

Finborough Theater in 2004 indicate the enduring interest in the case.

What struck me about Frances's and Mary's letters were the effusive expressions of affection: "Dearest dearest," "Dearest Rayline," "Please write to me soon I love you so," "All and all my love," "Give my love to all the folks with a heap for you dear," "I love you oceansfull dearest," "I love you heaps," and so on in every single letter. Letters from fellows, even from my father after he and my mother were engaged, are affectionate but the wording is almost restrained and calculatedly funny compared with the way girls wrote to each other. If all we had were girls' letters, contemporary analysts might well misconstrue them.

Rayline and Mary, who married a Milwaukee man, remained close friends throughout their lives. Sometimes Mary's older daughter Pauline and I went to lunch with our mothers. On one occasion talk turned to homosexuality—I think it probably was about the time the "Kinsey Reports" appeared. The older women were amused as they speculated how the behavior of best friends in their day would be viewed: their "crushes" on girls they admired and exchanging gifts of candy and flowers. Mary said something to the effect that, "I suppose now people would think we were queer," and Rayline agreed, also finding it funny.

Pauline and I were astounded, as adult children always are to learn their parents were once harebrained adolescents too, when our mothers reminisced about Rayline sneaking into Mary's room at Downer, risking her life by climbing outside from window sill to window sill to share her bed. Boarding students were not supposed to visit each other's rooms after 9:00 P.M. but they had so much to talk about, and they could chatter and giggle under the covers together without being heard. What did they talk about? *Boys*, of course! When I joined the faculty at UWM and showed Rayline my office, she recognized the building immediately as the old Downer Seminary dormitory and pointed out those neighboring windows *on the second floor!*

Another Downer girl who, like Mary Ball, remained a lifelong friend, was Margaret Breed, variously called Marga or Margie, from Racine, Wisconsin. She was a frequent visitor at Phantom Lake and Milwaukee and Rayline often visited her in Racine and was very fond of her parents whom I also remember well. Margaret's young brother, "Bow," had a crush on Rayline. Rayline's diaries mention letters from Margaret but none of this correspondence survives. The Breeds were of old Quaker stock, and Mr. Breed was a descendant of the Breed who actually owned the hill of Revolutionary War fame that has been misdesignated Bunker Hill. They were quiet people but Margaret was "high spirited" and given to sudden enthusiasms and spontaneous projects. My grandmother was impressed with Margaret's genteel ancestry but found her exhausting compared to Mary's easy fit into the household routine, as revealed in Rayline's diary entries regarding the two girls' visits.

Then there was Gladys Boerner, "Glad," also a Downer girl, whose story is almost as enigmatic as that of Frances Roberts and, like Frances, a year behind Rayline in school. I knew Gladys had introduced my parents and that her doctor father delivered me, but apart from these two facts I cannot recall my mother ever talking about her as she did Frances and other girls. I had no idea how close she and Rayline were until I read the diaries. She was a regular visitor at Phantom Lake—her parents also made at least one trip there, and Rayline was a frequent overnight guest at Gladys's home. I never knew Gladys personally as I did Mary and Margaret and a number of other Downer girls whom Rayline saw regularly throughout her life and whose names pop up in the diaries and letters—Irma Sichling, Grace West, Viola Reckmeyer, Thyra Wiethaupt, Helen Klann, and others. I didn't know if Gladys died or moved out of town, or if some irreconcilable falling out terminated their friendship. I'm sure my mother would have told me whatever happened to Gladys Boerner but I didn't realize there was a question to be asked until I read the diaries and Rayline was no longer alive to answer it. It was not until I re-read my father's letters that I began to understand how and why Rayline and Gladys might have drifted apart, but those insights are meaningful only in connection with the discussion to come of my father's family and neighborhood background.

Likewise, I never knew why my mother went to Downer rather than a public high school until I read her "Auto-Biography." The Downer campus was located in fashionable and moneyed Shorewood where *THE AUNTS* lived after Rayline graduated. Downer drew most of its local student body from that area as well as from prosperous families far from Milwaukee. Beginning as just the high school department of Downer College whose origins reach back to the 1850s, the Seminary was established with its own buildings, faculty, and boarding facility in 1910. The consequences of the Downer years are obvious in material longings, comparisons, and outright envy expressed in Rayline's diaries, and the fact that many of her friends lived in Shorewood. I was frequently amused while reading the diaries that this frivolous, sometimes even snobbish girl turned into the sensible woman who was my mother.

For example, each Downer Seminary girl had to bring her own complete and marked flatware set for use in the school dining room. Rayline's set was still in a sideboard drawer when I was a child and I asked about it. She laughed as she recalled how annoyed she had been when Lalla bought silver plate, considering the sterling flatware "all the other girls had" a foolish extravagance for only a few years' use insofar as it did not match Lalla's "wedding sterling" that the family used for all our meals.

As I read and reread the diaries, I became increasingly aware of the significance of what was NOT reported. Things that were simply taken for granted often represented the most marked differences between everyday life during my mother's youth and her later adulthood when my recollections begin to kick in. The lack of electricity at Phantom Lake affords a striking example.

I remember what it was like because we used kerosene lamps until 1930 when I was six years old. My mother never once mentions in her diaries that it was her job *every single day* to gather up the dozen or so kerosene lamps used throughout the house and deal with them at a special work area on the small, screened in back porch.

This meant removing the chimneys and wicks in their adjustable holders, adding kerosene (or coal oil as some people called it) to fill all the fuel containers as needed, and expertly "trimming" the wicks with a wooden matchstick. Besides removing any loose char, trimming was done to create a straight surface for an evenly shaped flame so smoke went up the chimney without touching the sides. Finally, the chimneys were washed with warm suds and rinse water and dried with newspapers that impart a special sheen to glass. This was simply a household routine, like making beds, washing dishes, and going to the spring for water, that also went without saying.

Even if a lamp had not been lighted the chimney had to be washed because kerosene "creeps" and forms a film on the chimney that reduces the lamp's brightness. On the other hand, Lalla employed an old trick taking advantage of kerosene's volatility to keep our wind-up, pendulum clocks oiled by placing a bottle cap full of kerosene inside each clock case.

After Rayline came to live with me in 1970, she would express amusement and exasperation about movies, TV productions, museum exhibits and the like devoted to the 19th through early 20th centuries that showed (and still show) kerosene lamp chimneys black with soot, a calculatedly quaint but ludicrously inaccurate device to suggest the ambience of the times. Oil lamps were an enormous improvement over candles in the use of flame for illumination and it was pointless as well as wasteful of fuel to get less than the maximum amount of light possible out of them by letting chimneys get sooty. A further step was to place a strip of flannel in the kerosene container, usually a recycled piece of long red underwear. I don't know if this really helped prevent any impurities in the kerosene from traveling up the wick but it indicates that people went to special lengths trying to achieve bright light.

Also left unmentioned in the pre-electricity days were precautions against the ever present threat of fire, from storing flammable fuels in isolation from living areas to ingrained motor habits in the carrying of lighted lamps and setting them down on assuredly stable surfaces away from any materials that might catch fire. Even children, too small to appreciate logical explanations of the dangers of fire, including the handling of matches, were routinely, if illogically, conditioned with fear of that most humiliating of childhood experiences: "If you play with fire you'll wet the bed!"

While it is well known that rural electrification in the South gained momentum in the 1930s with the development of the Tennessee Valley Authority, the fact is that many rural areas lacked electricity at that time. We got electricity in 1930 because the Hotpoint Company that made electrical appliances had decided to build a summer resort for its employees on Phantom Lake and shouldered the considerable cost of erecting poles and stringing power lines from Mukwonago that could then serve other residents along the way. I really don't recall the house being any lighter at night after we got electricity. The big difference as far as the adults were concerned was the convenience of light at the flick of a switch and the use of electrical appliances—curling irons, flat irons, space heaters, electric fans, radios.

It was a while, however, before we got our first refrigerator. Iceboxes were still common at that time, even in the city. I always enjoyed going with my father to the "ice house" on the outskirts of Mukwonago, a chilly, barn like structure built over a pit piled full of huge blocks of ice, insulated in layers of sawdust. The owner would chop out a block to the desired size with an ice pick, fifty pounds or more, and dexterously haul it up with tongs and swing it into the newspaper lined trunk of the family car. Our icebox stood in the same back porch where my mother took care of the kerosene lamps. My father would back the car to the door and with tongs would wrestle the block into the ice compartment that opened from the top like a chest. A few years before we got a refrigerator, the ice house owner's sons bought a truck and made home deliveries, just like ice was delivered in the city. I don't remember how often we had to buy ice but I do remember that morning and evening someone had to empty the pan under the icebox that the melting ice dripped into, or the porch would be flooded.

A technological curiosity was that while Floraydan Lodge lacked electricity for many years it had access to a party line telephone almost from the start that doubtless helped coordinate family activities between their Milwaukee and Phantom Lake homes. We could relate to the many jokes and true stories people told about operators and party line subscribers listening in on other people's conversations. Once when my grandmother was talking to a friend she heard a clock chiming and remarked, "Oh, I didn't know you had a chiming clock." There was an audible click as her friend replied with annoyance, "I DON'T!"

The family's closest neighbor along the Phantom lakeshore was the YMCA Camp to the east, located on the road on the way to our property. Established in 1899, it is the second oldest Y' camp in the country and was to figure prominently in my mother's social life from the time she entered her teens until she was nearly 21 and met my father. Extrapolating from my mother's diaries and letters, I learned that by 1914 counselors from the Y' camp were regular visitors at Floraydan Lodge during their off time and occasionally even after "taps" when their charges were asleep and they snuck away to visit with Rayline and her girl friends for marshmallow roasts around a campfire at the lake shore or impromptu parties up at the house where Lalla always had good things on hand for the young people to eat.

Rayline made candy, her cinnamon drops being particularly favored, and sent it as gifts to fellows with whom she corresponded when the camp season ended. The girls were invited to the camp for special occasions such as amateur theatricals and seem to have wandered over there regularly during lulls in the regular camp routine.

Some of the stories from the Y' Camp years are the bitter-sweet stuff of romance novels. Rayline's very first real love was "Windy," and he was similarly smitten, but she then seems to have thrown him over. She notes in her diaries more than once that he was "wild" about her and admits that she had not treated him well. Frances Roberts, in a letter postmarked Oct. 25, 1916, adverts to Rayline's "cruelty" to Windy. In time he became just one of the "Y' boys" who collectively paid court to Rayline and her guests. When I began reading the diaries, I was not sure if this was "Windy" Wilcox, the camp bugler, or another "Windy," Karl Windesheim, but he is definitely identified as the latter when Rayline became serious about my father and wrote of disposing of earlier boy friends' letters.

A number of years after my father died, Windesheim, by then an emeritus professor in the Speech Department at the University of Illinois, got in touch with my mother. He too had been widowed for several years. On one of my visits home when I was living in Michigan in the late 1950s, he came with my mother to meet me at the airport—a tall, good looking and easily likable man. Renewed friendship and visiting back and forth turned to courtship and Rayline was seriously pondering his proposal some months later when, tragically, he died in an automobile accident.

Windy wasn't the only Y' boy who carried a torch for Rayline as her diaries and correspondence demonstrate. Most of them did not come from Milwaukee but visited and wrote to her there. By the time her diaries begin she was considered as good as engaged to one of them, Sam Lang; at least Sam and Lalla thought so. Sam came from Racine and was a student at Lawrence College at Appleton, Wisconsin. While Rayline enjoyed Sam's attentions and gifts she was not eager to date him exclusively or talk seriously of a wedding date after he proposed to her in 1917. When Sam was away, she went out to dinner, the movies, and dances regularly with nearly a dozen other fellows and received cards, flowers, candy, and other gifts from them on special occasions. The names of Hans Jennings (who would disappear for months only to appear suddenly and briefly with lavish gifts and expensive outings to dinner and the theater), Ben Egan (a med' student and the Y Camp "doctor" for several summers), Don' Morey, Miller Mureson (whose frat' pin she wore for a while), Ben F. Carstairs (referred to as "Ben F." whose good looks she compares to movie stars), "Gerb'" Gerber (his first name remains a mystery), George Schultz, Bob Craig,

Charles Knudson, Irving Hansen, Bill Fritsche, Tuve Floden and others surface with varying degrees of frequency in her diaries.

Tuve had only a brief association with the Y' Camp, but made a profound impression during his short stay, and caused Rayline to express increasing doubts in her diary about her feelings for Sam. He also had the nicknames of "Pete" and "Big Six," and was rather vain about his height, referring in several letters to the fact that he was six feet tall. Twenty-one letters from Tuve cover the period from July 13, 1916 to August 21, 1917 and February 13 to April 1, 1919. The only correspondence for 1918, when Tuve was in France during the First World War, is a card from Tuve's mother, dated March 9, saying she was sending a photo of Tuve as he requested (now lost) and that "Tuve told me of the lovely Christmas box you sent him and I thank you for your kindness."

Although Rayline complains in her diary about not hearing from Tuve as frequently as she wished, I am sure that some letters got separated from the rest and were lost because Rayline's diary and information in George P. Gustafson's letters discussed in Chapter Three indicate Tuve did write to her a few times while serving overseas. Tuve met Rayline late in his tour of duty as a YMCA Camp "leader" (counselor apparently is a more recent term) in 1916. I gather from his letters and Rayline's diaries that the job paid little if anything, and was considered a kind of summer vacation with free room and board while doing good for society through working for the YMCA.

The summer was broken into four periods when new campers replaced those of the previous period, and the camp director always had trouble finding leaders interested in remaining through the entire summer. Two matters, never spelled out but adverted to frequently as simply hilarious, concerned Tuve "rescuing" Rayline and rowing her back home when the Evinrude motor on her boat ran out of gas, and Mrs. Wones, wife of the camp director Walter "Daddy" Wones, suggesting Rayline run the camp store on a voluntary basis and mistakenly calling her Genevieve. Some of Tuve's letters begin, "Dear Genevieve...."

Tuve expressed regret in his first letter that he only met and "rescued" Rayline after he had already decided to leave camp, which he had found boring up to that time, to take a five day canoe trip up the Rock River. He and a friend, Elmer Holmes, left Tuve's hometown of Rockford, Illinois and paddled to Lake Waubesa, northeast of Madison, Wisconsin where they stayed long enough to establish a post office address. The second letter sent from Lake Waubesa on July 20 includes thanks for the box of cinnamon candy that Rayline had made and sent with her reply to his letter. Tuve's letters are amusing with a kind of self-deprecating style that indicates he was anything but lacking in self-confidence, yet clearly likable: "If I only were a little bit more forward and not quite so modest I would get along better."

He and Rayline exchanged letters about once or twice a month until April 2, 1917. We learn from the correspondence that he is 23 years old, a high school teacher but has other ambitions, his favorite movie actress is Blanche Sweet but Rayline outshines her, he is active in his high school alumni athletic association, and he responds to her pondering where to go to college by suggesting (April 2), "You ought to come down and try Rockford [women's] College for a while. It has a good faculty and a fine reputation. And you would have a perfectly hilarious (?) time. One or two dances every year, and young men may call Friday evening, and once in a while a man takes someone and a chaperone to a show." Obviously, it was old fashioned according to standards then in vogue. By the time of his next letter, begun on April 24, 1917 but not mailed until May 1, the country is at war and Tuve is headed for the Army Reserve Officers Training Camp at Fort Sheridan, Illinois.

3

World War I, Overseas and at Home

Personal glimpses of the diverse army experiences of Tuve Floden, George P. Gustafson, and Sam Lang in World War I in Rayline's letters and diaries convey a sense of the human reality of that now long ago conflict. By chance, my father also documented some of his military experiences. Although my parents did not meet until shortly after the war, the record of his service is included both for its comparative relevance and because of the on-going importance of his army affiliation after my parents met, courted, and married. Throughout the more than 500 love letters he wrote, he refers to himself regularly as "your little shavetail," old army slang for a recently commissioned officer, usually a Second Lieutenant, because the tails of unbroken mules were shaved at the base for quick identification to avoid trying to use inexperienced animals.

Floden had joked in a letter post-marked April 2, 1917 that he hadn't seen Rayline in so long (there had been a visit after he returned from the 1916 canoe trip) that he could hardly remember what she looked like so she had sent a photo of herself with some other Downer girls that he acknowledged on April 24. "You and your girl friends," he writes, "can make camp life much pleasanter by writing bushels of letters to hard-working soldier boys this summer. I am trying to persuade all my lady friends (both of them) to lay in stocks of stationery." On May 24, he wrote about life at Fort Sheridan, noting mail was appreciated even if it was hard to find time to answer.

Camp is a wonderful place. Just like a big university, only better because the work is all out-of-doors. Nearly every fellow is a college student or graduate and most of them athletes and a fine bunch. The life here is much nicer than I expected. The food is excellent and we are well quartered in wooden buildings, electric lighted, and with good shower baths. No dishwashing or anything like that for the embryo officers, but we leave that to our colored servants.

If there were unexpected amenities, camp life also entailed hard training as described in a subsequent letter (date indistinct):

Literally 'in the trenches' as eight blisters on my left hand and four on my right hand bear witness to that fact. We have an exact reproduction of a sector on the Somme front in France, dug by us with our picks and shovels (oh for a job weeding a garden!) The ground is clay and some other hard stuff and a trench 5-1/2 feet wide and 5 feet deep is a very big hole to be dug. The sun was blistering hot yesterday for the first time, and there are many pink arms, shoulders, and necks.

I had my first swim in Lake Michigan yesterday afternoon after work. It is rather chilly but we have an excellent beach all along the camp for sun baths in the nice warm sand. The water will probably be warm about the middle of August. Speaking of water, while we were digging trench yesterday a fellow was standing in a puddle of water and another fellow shouted, 'Get your feet out of that water; I have to sleep in it tonight.' Evidently he was thinking of those poor French who lived for days in trenches with water up to their knees. Everyone is cheerful here under all conditions. Woe to the Kaiser if this bunch is ever turned loose on him.

As in his earlier letter, Tuve sheds some wry light on racial attitudes: "We had a little trouble the other day. An Irishman named O'Mara wanted to lick one of our colored cooks for singing 'Ireland must be heaven for my mother came from there'."

In almost weekly letters throughout June until July 23 he reports on camp life and finally that he passed the physical exam to qualify for overseas duty: "I'm keeping a list of young ladies who send me candy (a very short one) so that I can send them souvenirs from France." Rayline had sent him her cinnamon specials and stuffed dates. He writes about invitations to dinners and dances extended by well-to-do families on Chicago's North Shore and other entertainments arranged by the Red Cross, and describes marching in parades. Reminiscing about a brief visit to Phantom Lake, he chides her jokingly about things in her letters, including her handwriting.

Most of the Fort Sheridan letters are written on stationery bearing the YMCA logo and letterhead with its New York address and the statement, "The *Association Follows the Flag on Land and Sea.*" A dotted line to fill in the location follows the phrase, "Public Correspondence Table at." At one point Tuve apologizes, tongue in cheek, for using this free "charity paper." He reported news of mutual YMCA camp friends and managed to plan a visit to Phantom Lake with his friend Elmer Holmes, also stationed at Fort Sheridan. In answer to her question he said "llth P.T.R. means Eleventh Provisional Training Regiment."

Augmenting Tuve's correspondence is the issue of *The Fort Sheridan Reveille* (Vol. 1, no. 6, July 20, 1917) that was preserved in Rayline's hope chest. It contains not only news about Fort Sheridan but military matters across the country and overseas along with commentaries, cartoons, poems both humorous and serious, and many advertisements, dominated by clothiers. Most of them were in the Chicago area but companies as far away as Kalamazoo and Milwaukee competed for the custom of "embryo officers," as Tuve termed them, who would have to buy their own uniforms when they were commissioned.

In his letter of July 23 he notes, "There is much excitement in camp. Fellows are being let out continually and the men who are to get commissions will soon be picked. No one has the least idea as to who the lucky 47 out of each company of 150 will be and there is much worrying and conjecture."

His letter post-marked July 31 details maneuvers:

> Work is interesting now. Every evening instead of study we have trench warfare in the dark. To-night our battalion attacks the trenches. Searchlight and flares such as are used in Europe make it a pretty scene. The only thing that we don't like is the cleaning of our rifles after firing the blanks which have poor powder in them. Think of us poor boys cleaning our rifles after 10 o'clock tonight."

By August 13, his training is completed, and both he and Holmes are commissioned First Lieutenants. A note on August 21 from Rockford explains he will not be able to see her because

The "Carte Postale" Tuve Floden sent to Rayline, challenging her to find him in this group of American and British officers.

he only has time for a brief visit with his family before leaving for Hoboken, New Jersey and from there he is to be sent to France. Among the miscellaneous items that were not part of the shopping bag collection is a group photo of about 40 men in uniform. It probably was taken in France as it is on a "Carte Postale." On the back Tuve scribbled: "Find your old friend 'Big Six' This is a bunch of Irish, Scotch, English, and Welsh officers of the school I was at. We used to eat together at the same mess." There is not much chance of ever identifying "Big Six" in that photo.

No letters from Tuve survive from his overseas experiences during 1918 but that he did write is shown in Rayline's diary entry of April 26, 1918: "Had a long letter from Tuve. He was caught out between the lines in No Man's Land and had a real exciting time of it from what he says." It is impossible to establish the particulars of this incident, but the issue of *The Stars and Stripes*, Vol. 1, No. 36, Dec. 20, 1918, that she must have received from Tuve, contains a concise review of the entire course of the war thus far. He bracketed two paragraphs covering the period March 28 through May 28, 1918, underlining two references to the 1st Division: that it had been transferred on March 28 "from the Toul sector to a position in reserve at Chaumont-en-Vexin," and then, on April 26, it "had gone into the line in the Montdidier salent on

First issue of Stars and Stripes, official newspaper of the American Expeditionary Force in France, February 8, 1918.

the Picardy battle front. Tactics had been suddenly revolutionized to those of open warfare, and our men confident of the results of their training were eager for the test." The paragraph concludes with a description of the Division successfully demonstrating its "fighting qualities under extreme battle conditions."

If Rayline complained in her diary that Tuve did not write as often from France as she wished, he did make good on his promise to encourage correspondence between girls he knew and fellow soldiers, as witness a small packet of letters from Lt. George P. Gustafson who came from Sycamore, Illinois, not far from Tuve's hometown of Rockford. They appear to have known each other before the war but information is lacking as to how Gustafson ended up with Floden in France.

This packet puzzled me when I first emptied the bag of letters because I could not recall my mother mentioning George Gustafson among her many beaux. The fact is that Gustafson represented a brief but memorably poignant chapter in her life and I understand now why she saved the letters but never spoke of him.

Gustafson had seen Tuve's picture of Rayline with the other

George P. Gustafson, with whom Rayline corresponded but never met.

Downer girls and apparently wrote to one of them before writing to Rayline, perhaps in deference to Tuve having a prior claim on Rayline. Since Tuve had been writing to other girls besides Rayline, Gustafson found an excuse to begin writing to her by showing her how to solve some kind of puzzle Tuve had sent her. His first letter, dated France, December 17, 1917, received January 5, 1918, starts off fairly boldly,

> Dearest Rayline:
> When I saw your big heart breaker Tuve putting that first line on the enclosed card I knew darn well some fair little dame way back in God's country would be worrying her head off trying to solve the puzzle. So to pull the good fairy stuff I am going to help you out and give away the secret.

Since Tuve's letter, the puzzle, and enclosed card are lost, Gustafson's discussion followed by detailed directions for solving the puzzle don't make sense, but they served their introductory purpose as he goes on to say,

> Anyway Rayline I have had the pleasure of seeing your picture and hearing all about you. Judging from the picture and reports I have concluded that you are a wonderful girl and have a wonderful way. Am I right? Now don't be too timid or modest but just frank. I know that I have never seen you but that is my misfortune for I surely would enjoy the occasion very much. Maybe some day when I come back to old Chgo [Chicago] I'll take a stroll up to Milwaukee where you make the famous beer and look you up.
> But we can't afford to take a chance on getting back so some sweet day when you are lonesome and haven't a world of things to do drop me a few cheery lines. They are always welcome in this forsaken region

of the earth you know and help us along very much.

Give my best to Sister Sue [I have no idea which of the Downer girls this is] and tell her I haven't heard from her either. Maybe the letter was lost so she had better right [sic] again. (I mean the girl friend in the picture).

Sincerely Yours
Gus

All of the envelopes containing Gustafson's letters are stamped, "A.E.F. PASSED AS CENSORED," but it appears that formal regulations were not stringently enforced. Only the first envelope bears the statement: "Censored by Geo. P. Gustafson, Lieut. Inf. U.S.R. B Co. 26th Inf. Amexforce [American Expeditionary Force] France Approved by Tuve J. Floden 1st Lieut. Inf. U.S.R." Except for Floden's name and rank written in his own hand, the rest was all written by Gustafson himself. Floden barely outranked Gustafson who was still a 2nd Lieutenant.

On March 18, 1918 Gustafson wrote:

Dear Rayline;

I had just gone back into my dugout for a minute's rest when a runner brought your letter. I sat there and read it while our artillery exchanged a few shells with Fritz, and thot [thought] what would she think if she knew where her letter found me.

However, we are out for a rest now so I am taking a day or two off to write letters. Naturally yours will be answered with the first because your letter meant so much to me. Coming as it did when I was pretty tired and had just pulled through some stunts that were exciting but dangerous, it gave my thots [sic] a chance to come away from this bloody struggle. Both the letters cheered me up, and I went back out to my lads who were tired, wet and cold with a smile and a pleasant word for all.

One can only wonder if Gustafson's offhand references to the dangers he faced on the front were expressions of manly bravado or restrictions on communicating information that would be useful to the enemy if inadvertently leaked. His letter continues:

Rayline, I will beg your pardon for writing so freely to you, because it is my nature. I feel as tho I had known you for a long time and that you were one of my old time pals instead of Floden's. Anyway I know you will forgive me because from your picture I see that you are a good scout. That alone [of] all other traits in a woman counts as far as I am concerned.

Someone who becomes a pal, who is there for a good time when it is present and who can be otherwise when the occasion demands it.

What you say about not having seen me and that I have seen your picture is perfectly true. I have a small picture here which I shall enclose for your special benefit. At first I felt that it was a h— of a kiddish trick but I'll do it anyway! The reason I am doing it is this. I expect you to do likewise when you write to me. And furthermore if the Hun doesn't get my name on one of his shells I expect to simply jump up to Milwaukee after I get back to old Chgo. And say Chi is a regular place after all isn't it? Or perhaps you might wander down to the smokey city and if you should just look me up. Easy to find of course for I live right in town. But to be more definite you could get me at B.F. Goodrich Rubber Co. on Michigan Ave. Remember that will you?

Now don't wait until you are lonesome before writing again, but send me a letter any old time plus that picture of course. I'll try to answer your chum's letter today too. However, if I don't get a chance give her my love and I'll do it some other day. [I can't identify the "chum"].

Cheery Ho and best wishes to you and all your sweethearts.

Sincerely
George
(alias)
Gus

Diary entry, Saturday, April 13, 1918: "This morning I received a letter from George P. He also sent his picture and wants me to send mine. It is real exciting and thrilling to get a letter from Over There from someone I don't know. I wonder how far this affair will go. From his picture he looks to be about thirty. Oh joy, a real man."

Gustafson's picture is included in the envelope with the letter, along with two snapshots of Rayline. He looks very serious but certainly not thirty. Rayline adds that she went to "the Liberty Loan Parade" that afternoon with three of her girl friends, and completes the entry: "I can't stop thinking about that letter. I'm beginning to believe that everyone has a little romance in his life."

France, May 12, 1918

Dear Rayline;

This letter will not be written in installments, but might be made pretty short. You see I am being [indecipherable] these days and have very little time for letter writing altho I always manage to have enough time to read them.

Your letter which came yesterday was very interesting. The picture was good although it surely made you look rather young. I am waiting to see the picture of you which you say shows you as you are now and see how great will be the change.

At present it seems almost impossible to write a letter that is worth reading. We are more or less 'fed up' on war subjects and telling about the scenery and weather over here so those subjects are banned. Then I don't feel it is worth while to say anything about myself in present conditions because they are far from interesting.

Just for fun I might say that you would be more than interested in our place of abode at present. Our men are around here in hay lofts, and Lt. Holmes and I have a nice pile of straw here in the barn. It makes a cracking good bed when you are all in and far from home. Of course the darn horses make a lot of noise most of the time, but we manage to overlook such small troubles.

Liberty Bond parade, Milwaukee.

No doubt Floden keeps you well posted on what we are running into here. I don't know exactly what he usually writes about or how his line runs but I feel that my letters must be poor when you compare them to his. However, he has one over me for he knows you and is able to adjust his letters so as to make them fit.

I am at more or less of a disadvantage. I hardly know which way to go. Yet if I am not too poor a judge I think I know you pretty well already. You are after my own heart I think. That is you are one of these happy, good scouts a fellow likes to know. Some day when I come up to the town that made Schlitz famous, I'll see if I am right.

He ends with further romantic bantering and his usual, "Cheery Ho."

Rayline continued writing to Floden as well as Gustafson as shown in Gustafson's Letter of May 25, 1918. The playful tone of his letter makes one wonder what she wrote to him concerning the fact that all the boys were going off to war.

Dear Rayline

Last night I received your letter of May 1, and it did almost tickle me to death. I surely was surprised to hear from you because I felt sure that Floden had a monopoly on your letters, and that I could only expect one at rare intervals.

I don't remember showing Floden any of your letters but I guess I did. Anyway I know I told him how pleased I was to hear from you.

You probably know that we are not in the same camp any more. He went to D company when it was organized and I stayed with the old outfit. We are still in the same battalion, however, so every once in a while I see him.

A few nights ago he had an accident and was shot in the hand. Nothing very serious I hear, so he was quite lucky.

Actually, Tuve's wound was more serious than Gustafson realized as he went on at light hearted length responding to comments in her letters concerning the dearth of men at home and its effects on girls' social life, his opinion of French girls as "all right in their way," but he was too shy to approach them, and other expressions of pleasure and amusement in receiving her letters. Still maintaining his cheerful tenor, he made a brief return to the realities of war and the dangers he faced on the front line.

> Would give a lot of francs for a picture of this place. You would laugh perhaps and perhaps not. The scene is funny. On the side of a hill my men have dug several caves or dugouts. This one of mine goes back in almost twenty feet. It is not exactly shell proof for a direct hit would knock it in, but at least it is fairly safe. Shells are bursting mighty near right now and even as I write this letter the earth shakes and seems to quiver. Fritz is pretty wicked, and doesn't care just where he sends those messages of death. Although I haven't an assumed name, I guess it is too hard for him to pronounce so as yet he hasn't sent my shell over. If he does I'll bet the dirty crooks give me a 210 [the huge 210 mm. German mortar shell] and makes it direct.

The letter closed with references to Rayline's school work, news from a friend in Illinois who, like Rayline, complained that the fellows still around were "only youngsters," and concluded, "Well Rayline I have some business at the company P.C. [*Poste de Commandement*, i.e., Headquarters] so I must quit and go up. Write to me real soon again, and don't hesitate about it," adding he looked forward to a rest when "I can forget about war."

The final three envelopes in the packet, post-marked May 29, June 21, and June 22, 1918 were from Rayline and had been returned, stamped, "DECEASED verified by STATISTICAL DIVISION HAEF," along with handwritten notations to that effect. According to army records, Gustafson died June 6. Although Rayline only notes the return of the first letter in her diary of August 7, she had known of his death since July 2:

Well, I now realize what an awful thing war really is. I was just running upstairs to write George P. Gustafson when I stopped to read the casualty list [apparently in the newspaper] and there was George's name among those who died of wounds. It doesn't seem possible that he is dead. Life certainly is an uncertain thing. I'm hoping against hope that it isn't 'my George.' Yes, I feel as if he were just a little mine. There's no telling how this affair might have ended. I simply cannot make myself believe that it is he. No. No, it can't be.

In the margin at the top of the page, she added that she planned to write to him anyhow in case he wasn't really dead, that there might be two George P. Gustafsons, but evidently accepted the fact of his death after her first shocked reaction to the news.

Filed with the packet of letters is a 3x5 card with the newspaper notice pasted on it and in her hand, "The end of a war time Romance.'What might have been can never now be'." The packet also contains a newspaper clipping, unidentified as to source and date, perhaps sent to her by Tuve, reporting that a letter from Major Theodore Roosevelt, Jr. to George's mother, dated June 19, 1918 was read at his memorial service. Roosevelt praised George's courage and leadership and, as his commanding officer, was planning to recommend him for promotion.

Details about both Tuve and George finally reached Rayline on September 7, when she wrote in her diary, "Had a letter from Tuve. He has been in a hospital for three months because of his hand. A rifle grenade went right thru it. He said that George Gustafson was gassed. A gas bomb broke right on him and before he could get his mask on his lungs were filled with gas." Although it is almost unbearably sad knowing that George never saw Rayline's last letters, their playful, flirtatious style and perspective on major news on the home front indicate what a welcome break her earlier correspondence must have been for a young man in the midst of combat, even though she had misgivings that she might be too flippant under the circumstances. She confided in her diary (May 28) "[I] wonder what he will think when he gets that letter—it sure was a nutty thing."

Dear Georgie—

Why the 'ie' I don't know, but I like it like that (that last is my pet expression). I have just finished doing my duty for the Navy—I have knitted a pair of socks [she knitted prodigious numbers of socks, sweaters, caps, and scarves for servicemen during the course of the war, both directly for men she knew and donated to various organizations]—and now I'm going to do some thing for the Army, which is writing to you— but it is far from being a duty. Nay, it is a pleasure. You see I'm following your orders by writing some times besides when I'm lonesome. I'm about the happiest and cheerfulest person on earth just at present. The dearest friend I have [Mary Ball] came to-day from the South to spend the whole summer with me.

To be continued in our next—I have to go with Mother some place or other in the machine.

Well, I have 'been' and returned and nearly froze in the going and coming. Here it is the 27th of May and to be comfortable I have to wear a fur coat, ear muffs and over shoes—yesterday it was so wonderfully warm and summer-like I that I went in swimming.

A week ago Saturday we had a great big parade for the Red Cross—and it sure did look great to see all those women dressed in their Red Cross outfits—I don't blame the soldiers for falling in love with their nurses and singing 'I don't want to get well.'

Can hardly believe it, school [Milwaukee Normal School] will be out by next month at this time—but between now and then I have so much work to do that I nearly go insane thinking about it.

I just heard someone mention downstairs that the family is going to eat, so as I am nearly famished, I guess I'll join them—

As ever—

Rayline

Again unsure about the tone of her letters to a man at the front, Rayline wrote in her Diary on June 17 regarding the letter postmarked June 21, "I started a letter [to] George P. A real nutty one. That man will think that I haven't any sense 'atall'."

Dear Georgie—

Here a whole week has passed and your most welcome letter not answered. Now the first thing I want to get out of your head is that your letters aren't interesting and you can't imagine how thrilled and flattered I am to receive letters from a strange soldier man—Oh, I forgot we have gotten past the stage of being strangers, nevertheless, I am more than pleased to get letters from 'Over There.'

I'm afraid that if you don't get back soon there won't be any famous Schlitz Beer, for the way things look now it seems as if we are going to have universal prohibition. However, I'll still be here, and expect to be until I die. Well, there [are] some places worse than Milwaukee, for instance Germany or the Congo River.

The latter, rather strange reference probably relates to a diary entry of January 25, 1918: "Vashel Lindsy spoke today at school," spelled as she heard the name, Vachel Lindsay. She was deeply moved by the recitation of his poems that doubtless included his most famous, though racially controversial, work, *The Congo*.

Her letter continues:

George it seems as if I simply can not get a picture that looks 'perfectly' like little 'me,' here's hoping this picture is more to your liking—Maybe some day I'll send you a real [undecipherable] one. But remember 'turn about is fair play.'

The number on the back [26 written in pencil] is not my Age!!! [These pictures were still in the packet of letters.]

I have been reading so many autobiographies, and had to write my own for a final English theme that it has be come quite a habit with me of telling certain essential facts of my past history— Maybe you too would be interested to know the kind of human being I am. Well, here goes, if you think that you'll be bored with the details why just skip this part.

I sign all official documents such as exam papers— Rayline M. Danielson. The 'M.' stands for Martin [her mother's maiden name—she was christened Rayline Emma for her maternal grandmother but since neither of them liked the name, she settled on Martin]. I'm just five feet tall and every one teases me about the fact. I'm, oh well, if the women get the vote I can vote for President [apparently she is being coy about her age, almost 19 at the time, but she would be almost 22 by the time the 19th Amendment to the Constitution was passed to enfranchise women]—I have never been engaged [although she sounds definite here her equivocation about the exact nature of her relationship with Sam Lang is a recurrent theme in her diaries], married or divorced. Have never served a jail sentence and never hope to. My favorite colors are Red, White and Blue and, of course, olive drab—No one has ever died from my cooking, but sometimes I get mixed [up] and put salt in things instead of sugar. Just at present I am a little peeved because the dean of the school from which I graduated, Milwaukee Downer Seminary, has one of those good looking bead chains made by a wounded French soldier. I have been dying for one almost and then that 'old maid'—I know this sounds disrespectful, had to go and get one before I did.

Rayline's diaries indicate that souvenirs from overseas were highly prized, shown off and compared among the girls back home. She mentions little French dolls she received from Tuve and a beaded bag, jewelry, and other items of adornment from Sam.
[Her letter to Gustafson goes on]:

Please excuse the slant of this letter but I hurt my wrist the other day and as a result I have it bandaged up so tightly that I can't move it, so I'm writing under difficulties—I'm surprised that I didn't kill myself the other morning than just hurting my wrist. I fell down a whole flight of stairs and when I came to the turn, I turned a complete summer salt [sic]—I'm sure that the neighbors for blocks around thought that the world was coming to an end, I made so much noise. I was so stiff and sore after my tumble that I felt like an old woman of ninety. I was late to history class that memorable morning and when I gave 'falling down the stairs' for an excuse for tardiness to the 'history prof', I thought that the dear man would die from laughter. He said of all the years he had been teaching he had heard some pretty good excuses, but mine beat them all.

I'm sure that you must be tired of my raving so I'll close. Do write soon.

As ever just
Rayline

She noted in her diary of June 14 that she bought three lucky charms to send to Sam and Tuve as well as Gus. Gus's was among the returned correspondence, a pathetic piece of patriotic kitsch consisting of a copper medallion about the size of a quarter with a four leaf clover embossed on one side and, on the other, the message, "GOD BE WITH YOU TIL WE MEET AGAIN," tucked into a little folder printed in red, white, and blue and tied with a tricolor ribbon:

> Good Luck
> May this Lucky Piece be
>   your companion and charm
> Until the last bugle of
>   Warfare shall cease
> May it keep you, God willing,
>   from danger and harm
> May it bring you back
>   soon to a nation at peace.

Lucky charm Rayline sent to George P. Gustafson.

Inside, Rayline had written, "Even though we haven't met I feel sort of that back in the days of Egyptian mummies you and I were good friends—you never can tell—Rayline." Since this item antedates the much publicized discovery of King Tut, Rayline apparently was inspired by her course in ancient history, a favorite subject.

Sam Lang's army career differed markedly from those of Floden and Gustafson. Because Rayline destroyed his letters when she finally broke off her relationship with him in 1919, we don't have his personal correspondence giving details on the date and circumstances of his enlistment in the Medical Officers Training Corps, but the outline of his military career from the beginning of 1918 is discernible in her diaries. His plans to become a doctor posed a problem from Rayline's point of view as she soliloquizes occasionally in her diary. He wanted her securely and exclusively committed to him for five years or so to complete his education and become established before they would get married. He comes across as humorless and a whiner, but Rayline's increasing doubts about her affection for him might have had a subconsciously negative influence in her references to him.

By 1918, he was stationed at Fort Oglethorpe, Georgia. On January 30, Rayline wrote, "Had a letter from Sam and the poor kid has been sick. This grand and glorious country of ours is treating its volunteered men very shabby. He was in the hospital tent and his bed stood in four inches of mud. Refused to give him any water when he asked for [it] and the food was only cold left overs. How can a person be patriotic when someone you know is being treated in such a shameful manner."

February 11: "Wrote to Sam and thanked him for the insignia that the medical men wear that he sent me." On March 9 she received, by special delivery, "a beautiful silver pin with his insignia in the middle." By April 1 he has been transferred to a hospital in Chattanooga, "quite an advancement," and on April 9 she learns he has been made a corporal. "He sent me [a] codouse [she finally takes a stab at writing caduceus instead of insignia] of khaki to wear on my coat. Real good looking it is." Underlining in the issues of *Trench and Camp* that Sam sent from Chattanooga indicate that he was assigned to the 13th Evacuation Hospital and the teams he coached in "weekly interbarracks field meets" swept the field.

Rayline corresponded regularly with Sam but her diary makes no reference to the content of their letters until May 15, 1918 when a telegram from him informs her he is about to leave for France. Five days later his orders are changed and by June 5 he is transferred to Camp Gordon, Georgia. On the 28th he has a brief furlough and pays her a surprise visit. She is less than thrilled but unable to bring herself to tell him that she has serious doubts about ever marrying him, noting in her diary that, "Of course, I was glad to see him, but I'd be glad to see anyone I hadn't seen for six months."

On July 8, her diary points up an all but forgotten footnote in the history of World War I. "Had a short letter from Sam. The poor kid is all upset because he might have had a job with the Redpath as managers [sic] of one the Liberty Theaters of the Government's. He'd [have] gotten $225 per mo. with a 1st Lieut. Commission and I might have had a 'Mrs.' before my name. Well, maybe it is just as well as it is for he is getting good medical experience." Redpath refers to the Chatauqua organization that began at Lake Chatauqua, New York in 1874. It fielded tent shows all over the country well into the 20th century, offering programs ranging from inspirational and educational lectures to a variety of dramatic and musical productions. Redpath was the major Chatauqua "Bureau" that set up itineraries and booked performers. I recollect my mother mentioning that Sam had worked for Chatauqua before the war so he would have been well qualified for this government supported endeavor. Also in his favor was his affiliation with the YMCA that went beyond a mere counselorship at the Phantom Lake camp—he is referred to in passing here and there as a YMCA secretary.

The Y' was the primary civilian organization devoted to the welfare of military personnel during World War I, setting up its "Huts" and canteens at military installations at home and overseas to assist service people and their families in myriad ways. It gained enormous respect for its efficiency and lack of sectarian bias in cooperating with other religious and secular service organizations, coordinating their efforts to serve the individual and group interests of the men in uniform. The Y' provided the model for the United Service Organizations, the USO, that was established almost at the outset of World War II. While the USO performed many functions, it was most familiar to the folks at home and is remembered particularly today for bringing top name performers to military bases all over the world. Rayline's chance diary entry reminds us that this kind of organized entertainment of the troops had its origin in World War I.

The Liberty Theaters operated only at bases in the U.S., but the Y' brought stage performances to as many locations as it could "in France and beyond." In an article headlined, "ARMY'S HAM ACTORS WILL GET TO TRY OUT," *The Stars and Stripes* of December 6, 1918 reported that the Y' had launched a plan to expand its talent pool by auditioning amateur and professional "vaudeville artists." Finalists would be "sent over the A.E.F. entertainment circuit" to assure "every hut as many shows as can be secured and of as much variety as possible." The final paragraph is almost prophetic of a scene in the musical *South Pacific*:

> Special emphasis is to be laid on the formation of small companies at various posts to play simple one-act plays, the A.E.F. itself furnishing the male members of the casts and the Y furnishing the female, although that does not mean that the art of female impersonation on the part of the hairy Yank will be discouraged.

On August 7, 1918 Sam wrote from Newport News, Virginia, "expecting to sail any day," and a few days later sent her his Corporal's chevron as he has become a sergeant. He returned all the letters she had sent for safekeeping until his return and on August 13 he embarked for France on the transport ship "Martha Washington." References to their correspondence continued but Rayline fails to note Sam's specific whereabouts or activities in

France, only complaining at times that his letters aren't very interesting. She received a letter on November 12: "Heard from Sam again today and also got a French letter from a friend of his [Rayline studied both French and German at Downer.] Sam thinks he is going to be made a Lieut. & I hope so for his sake. Wouldn't it be wonderful if he would be for he would have worked his way up from the ranks."

As the troops began streaming home after the Armistice on November 11, 1918, Sam was still "Somewhere in France" when Rayline began her second diary on January 1, 1919—a suede bound volume, incidentally a Christmas gift from Sam. She received a letter from him on February 3 but notes only that he was then in Luxembourg. His letter of March 10 included "three packs of cards," apparently picture post cards, because she adds, "He sure is going to see all there is to see while he is there," commenting, "How different he is from Tuve in that respect."

Tuve simply wanted to get home and forget the war. On February 13, 1919 he visited Rayline after his discharge and while she enjoyed their date of a movie and dinner, she writes, "but he nearly broke my heart because he wasn't in uniform. He is so queer he says as long as he knows he was 'Over there' and no one else need know about it. The two fingers (little one & next) are stiff from his wound. I didn't find much out for he is secretive about his stay in the war."

By March 22, 1919 Sam apparently is back in France: "Heard from Sam this morning and he is either desperately in love or he is a nut. I told him how wild I was about the 'C.B.'s' baby [Betty] and now he would like to buy baby clothes in France for me to put away." She comments that if anyone but Sam had made the suggestion she and her parents would have been "shocked and horrified" but they all took it "as a big joke" even if Sam was dead serious. During this same period Sam sent her the March 8, 1919 issue of the *Paris Edition of The Chicago Tribune*, dominated by responses, mostly outraged, to an article in a previous edition that contended the servicemen still in France did not want to go home since they were no longer in danger and leading an easier life than they could as civilians.

By Easter of 1919 Sam was in Germany, somewhere, and sent her holiday greetings via cablegram, the first she had ever received, but she really wished he'd arranged with his sister to order her a corsage instead. The date of his return was as fraught with uncertainty as his being sent overseas. In May, he thought he would be home by mid-June. Then he expected to leave Wolferdinger, Germany on July 1. On July 18 she read in the newspaper that the 5th Division—the first indication in the diaries of his service assignment—was going to land on July 20. On that day she received a telegram, courtesy of the Salvation Army, that he had arrived in New York; a second telegram two days later told her he was headed for Camp Gordon, Illinois (another Camp Gordon was located in

Carl Oestreich and sailor, cover illustration of the (University of) Wisconsin Engineer, May, 1918 that carried Carl's article about his experiences in the Quartermaster Corps.

Georgia where Sam had been sent earlier). On July 30 he finally arrived in Milwaukee in uniform with gifts of roses and a cameo. I deduce that he had received his commission because Rayline thinks he is not as "cute" in uniform as Carl whom she had met in the meantime. Carl had worn his lieutenant's uniform at her request for a social occasion and she would have commented if there had been any difference in rank reflected their uniforms.

Carl was finishing his senior year at the University of Wisconsin when war was declared in April of 1917. He registered for the draft in Milwaukee, Ward 9, and was issued his certificate, #230, on June 5, 1917. He had completed his B.S. in Civil Engineering and intended to seek a commission in the Army Corps of Engineers but ended up enlisting in the Quartermaster Corps. This classic military mismatch of training with job assignment is explained in an article Carl wrote for *The* [University of] *Wisconsin Engineer*, "Experiences in the Quartermaster's Department" (Vol. 22, No. 8, May, 1918: 323-325).

> After leaving school last June I was employed by the McClintic-Marshall Co. at their Pottstown plant... about thirty miles from Philadelphia...fabricating steel for government contracts only. However, I was anxious to get into the third officer's training Camp. This camp was to be for enlisted men only, and with this requirement in mind, my partner, a Cornell '17 man, and myself enlisted at Philadelphia on the 17th of August. At that time the quartermaster department was the only one taking recruits. But our well laid plans for getting into a training camp never materialized, for Congress finally decided that seventeen men out of every thousand were to be taken from the ranks, and, to make matters still worse, our particular detachment was not even given application blanks.

He was called to active service on October 1, 1917 and ordered to report to Old Point Comfort for equipment and then proceed to Newport News, Virginia where he was assigned to the subsistence branch of the Quartermaster Corps as a deliveryman (although he had enlisted as storekeeper) taking care of all the ice and beef deliveries to three camps near Newport News. By the time he wrote his article he was a sergeant and had been "transferred as clerk to the issue department" that entailed complicated and tedious computations of procuring and distributing rations for troops at home and overseas. He comments, "My slide rule was my best assistant in this work and if ever I find an Iron Cross I'm going to tack it on to the rule for saving many a weary hour of figuring." Not mentioned in the article but a familiar bit of family history was the fact that the slide rule kept him stateside while the rest of his outfit went to France. When Carl's commanding officer learned he knew how "to run one of those things," he didn't want to lose him and changed his orders.

Every family has spooky stories they love to tell even when dismissing them as coincidence or mere chance. Carl's occurred when he was still in Pottstown and called on his aunt Emily, his mother's sister, who lived nearby, and had dinner with her family. Fortune telling with tarot or ordinary playing cards was a popular home entertainment, and Emily was supposedly very good at it. She agreed to tell Carl's fortune and informed him he would be in the army but would never leave the United States. He smiled to himself as he had not told his aunt he had already enlisted and his orders to report for service to go overseas were in his pocket. Not serving abroad was an enduring source of disappointment throughout my father's life.

Newport News was a major embarkation port but when my father arrived it was in a chaotic state:

> ...ships were lined four and five deep along the Newport News shipyard docks, waiting to have their guns mounted, crews assigned to them, and to be

generally refitted... Some of the interned German boats were badly damaged by their crews, but, thanks to a new welding process, the broken parts were repaired, the ships rechristened, and they are now part of the fleet that is spelling doom for Germany. The Dutch ships that were held here are all flying the American flag now. In fact, everything is moving along so smoothly, and the ships come and go with such regularity, that it is hard to believe that there are actual dangers in store for the boats when they get out on the ocean.

He had an admittedly cushy assignment with permissive officers, a great deal of free time and "no drill, guard duty, or manual of arms," but, he concludes, "there is no excitement, and quite a few of us are trying to get transferred into outfits that will see more active service. The difficulty is to get a transfer."

He used to tell how he took matters in his own hands when he learned that exams to qualify for a commission were to be held in Washington, D.C. There is a pass among his papers, issued in June of 1918 although the day is not clear, that he might have obtained to go to Washington. Possibly it expired before he was able to return because he always said he went AWOL to take the exam but by the time a disciplinary hearing was scheduled for Sergeant Oestreich, he was 2nd Lieutenant Oestreich and the matter was dropped. He received his commission in the Quartermaster Corps on July 25, 1918 and took his oath at Newport News two days later.

It is possible that, coincidently, both Sam and Carl were stationed briefly at Newport News at the same time but as the war progressed Carl was sent to Camp Dodge, Iowa where he availed himself of the opportunity to take an exam as an army interpreter. Although born in this country, like many Milwaukeeans of his generation, Carl spoke German as his first language. He and a professor of German at the University of Iowa tied for top score on the written exam but Carl claimed he beat out the professor on the basis of the oral interview with the officer in charge of the exam; Carl could swear as well in German as he could in English, and in a variety of dialects, at that. His father came from the Prussian area of Germany and his mother from Bohemia in what was then part of the Austro-Hungarian Empire. Besides knowing their different "accents," he picked up other linguistic nuances among the variety of German speakers where he grew up on Milwaukee's north side.

As fate would have it, this was just days before the armistice was signed on November 11, 1918 and Carl's hope of serving in Europe was again dashed as the demand for interpreters for interrogation had come to an end. He received his honorable discharge at Camp Dodge on April 21, 1919 and shortly thereafter enlisted in the Reserve Officer Corps.

The country had been at war nearly ten months when Rayline's first diary begins in 1918. It is a truism that technologically World War I was the first "modern" war foreshadowing World War II in ordnance, communication, and transportation, and particularly in the introduction of aircraft. Not so commonly noted, it was a precursor on the home front as well. I was sometimes momentarily confused in the course of reviewing the documents at hand that this was my mother's war, not my war of 1941-1945 when I was an undergraduate student at the University of Wisconsin-Madison. The ordinary business of life goes on in the diary but comments about the war are regularly sandwiched in among discussions of clothes, beaux and the like. For example, after writing about friends and school she ended her entry on January 8, 1918 that, "Wilson gave out his peace terms to-day, if not accepted [it] may mean three more years of war." Three days later, she wrote, "Germany answered our peace terms and withdrew all former terms. Got 90 in English. Saw Glad this noon and she gave me a letter for Geo. P. Another storm starting." On March 2 Rayline speculates facetiously that she might end up "an old maid" what with all the eligible men in military service because of the Kaiser's "world power ambitions."

A few days later she writes, "The folks got me out of bed at 10:00 to see the Aurora borealis which Pa says are [sic] the most wonderful he has ever seen. The sky was one mass of red and greenish white streaks. The Enc. [encyclopedia] says that a crimson Aurora means war, famine or calamity or the death of a great chief. Well, we surely have the war." She comments on April 6, "We have been at war just a year. I wonder what this next [year] will bring. I surely hope peace." The pervasiveness of war talk is reflected in an amusing incident that occurred in early May. Rayline, her mother, and Rayline's four year old cousin Florence were on their way to Phantom Lake and noticed a church steeple had been knocked to the ground. The women wondered if it had been caused by wind or lightening when Florence piped up, "No, Germany did that."

Besides attending Red Cross and Liberty Bond parades, my grandmother was actively involved in the sale of Liberty Bonds and training other workers. A brief diary remark on May 3 indicates other home front service: "[Went] down town with mother and then went to the children free hospital [sic] and later to the city hall to get instructions for the welfare work."

Mention is made throughout the diary of friends and family members entering the service as volunteers or conscripts, and of wives, sisters, and sweethearts traveling to visit them at various camps. Rayline's prodigal Uncle Ben, though beyond draft age, ended up in the Navy for less than patriotic reasons. His mother had been ailing for several months and when she died on May 11, 1918, Ben, true to form, expressed his grief by going on a massive binge. Hung over and contrite and before he could offer much resistance, Rayline's father forced him to enlist hoping the discipline of military life would finally straighten him out. All this is recorded in Rayline's diary. Unrecorded but preserved in family memory is that he cut such a fine figure in uniform and, with his con-man's charm when sober, was put in charge of a group of younger recruits to shepherd to the Great Lakes Naval Station near Chicago. To Daniel's relief, he carried out the assignment and managed to ride out the war without incident and earn an honorable discharge.

Ben's fortuitous military service led, at least indirectly, to his tragic death in 1932 when he fell off a freight train while en route to Washington, D.C. with a group of "Bonus Army" marchers. Although scarcely remembered today, the demonstration was a major and controversial event at the time. In 1924, Congress had voted to issue "Service Certificates" to World War veterans. Something like bonds, they would mature to face value after 20 years, when they could be redeemed. The face value varied, averaging about $1,000; the individual certificates were based on a complicated formula regarding rank, days of service and other considerations.

With the onset of the Depression of the 1930s, many veterans sought immediate payment and, according to some estimates, possibly as many as 40,000 men (some with their families) descended on Washington in May of 1932 to present their demands. Although the House passed a bill in their favor, it was defeated in the Senate. President Hoover also strongly opposed the bill and toward the end of July, ordered the forcible removal of the marchers and destruction of their shanty towns and camps around the city. The Bonus Army dispersed and fled, suffering a few casualties in confrontations with the combined forces of the Washington, D.C. police supported by detachments of infantry, headed by Douglas MacArthur, and cavalry, headed by George Patton. The army also sent six tanks to the scene. Although I did not know the details about the Bonus Army, I remember hearing the term as a child when my grandfather and his brother Charles were called to some place in Illinois to identify and claim Ben's body. He is buried at the Veterans Administration Cemetery in Milwaukee.

Some items in Rayline's diary, such as the Liberty Theaters, are surprising little revelations of experiments that would figure significantly in the next World War. Rationing is another case in point. On September 9 she mentions being regularly inconvenienced by the law forbidding the use of automobiles on Sundays "as a movement to conserve gasoline." Apart from gasoline, rationing in WWI did not affect the range of goods, from butter, canned food, sugar, and meat to stockings and shoes, that were rationed in WWII. Nevertheless, some items were in short supply and a familiar note is struck when Rayline goes on to say, "Pa and Daddy are getting to be regular socialists in their views and one can hardly blame them with all this profiteering and high prices." Daylight saving time also was introduced briefly during World War I as Rayline noted on October 27, "We got back the hour we gave [up] last April. It will seem to get dark early now."

It is not until late September that Rayline mentions the "Spanish influenza." A double date with her friend Gladys had to be cancelled because the two fellows, wherever they were stationed, were under quarantine and could not leave camp. On October 2 she comments that Dr. Boerner, Gladys's father "has more cases of Spanish influenza. I didn't realize there was so much around." In fact, the incidence of influenza was relatively low in Milwaukee because its department of public health instituted and enforced rigorous measures of prevention and isolation early in the course of the epidemic. She noted on October 13, "This sure was a queer Sunday. Not a machine on the street because of the gasoline conservation order. All places of amusement closed because of the 'Flu' and so we just stayed home and read and knit all day. Couldn't even go to church because they were closed because of the 'Flu'."

There were, nevertheless, deaths among people Rayline knew, including an elderly neighbor and the head of the Red Cross of her ward. A number of family members contracted but recovered from the disease. I had been led to believe that my mother's college career ended with her sophomore year because she had been sick with the flu. Her diary makes clear that the Normal School did not close, something of an exception compared to other institutions, but though she remained well she used the flu as an excuse to stay home and eventually she quit school altogether.

Rayline was a faithful diarist, but the pages for July 26 through 28, 1918 are blank with no explanation. The blank pages from November 3 through 6 are in all probability due to the distraction of rumors that the war was winding down. On November 7 she exclaims, "Oh, glorious day, war is ended!!! So the papers say. The city has gone mad, simply mad. The streets were packed down town. It was like ten New Year's eve's combined. If it is only true is my only thought. When I heard the great news, the first idea that came into my head was, if only George P. were coming back. I wonder what the future holds for me." Rayline's phrases, "So the papers say" and "If it is only true..." surprised me. Evidently, there was some question about the news at the time it was publicized; I had always been under the impression that almost everyone was completely misled by the "False Armistice" of November 7.

Understandably, her diary is blank until the announcement of November 11:

> The whistle started in at 3 A.M. & this time the report of peace is official; so we are sure it is true. Oh, great, grand, and glorious. I wonder if Tuve or Sam will come home first. Everyone out parading. Went down again in the after-noon & all traffic on the Ave. was stopped. Toward evening the crowd started to get rough so we didn't go down in the evening.

The diary resumes with her usual everyday reporting except for December 1 to 7, 11-12, and 16-17 when, again there are unexplained blank pages. The war is all but forgotten in her diary after the armistice apart from mention of correspondence with Sam and a letter from Tuve who enclosed copies of "French & German proclamations that were posted in Germany by the AEF," apparently announcing the armistice—unfortunately now lost.

A kind of strange parallel to the Americans' experiences from the "other side" shows up among my father's letters to my mother. On September 28, 1919 he wrote:

I just finished a four page German letter to my cousin Hans, from whom I received a letter yesterday. The poor kid was in since April 1ˢᵗ 1915. He started out on the Russian front, was slightly wounded, sent to Galicia, Italy and wound up opposite the 27ᵗʰ Division in Flanders. He ended up a shavetail in the Artillery. It runs in the family [reference to his commission as a 2nd Lt.]—only he's got a bunch of decorations. He intends to study medicine.

It is clear from the context that they had been in communication prior to the war and that the relationship was through Carl's father who came from Germany rather than his mother's family who identified themselves as Austrian.

My father's next letter contained a snapshot (now lost) and a reference to American propaganda about alleged German atrocities during World War I. "I'm sending you a little picture of my cousin Hans taken in 1915. That ribbon he wears is an iron cross ribbon. He doesn't look as brutal as the papers would have us believe. One year younger than I." Hans would have been nineteen when the picture was taken. Apparently, Carl and Hans continued to correspond but my father does not mention his cousin again until a year later, writing on October 17, 1920 that, "I sent Hans his carton of cigarettes. Hope they arrive safely cause from what he says there is nothing like a good smoke in Germany. He is at the U. of Jena now."

4

Hard Times, Good Times, and Changing Times

The War was already under way when Rayline graduated from Downer Seminary in the spring of 1917; in the fall she began her college education at the Milwaukee Normal School. That Christmas she received her first diary—for the year 1918, leather bound with a tiny lock and key. By the time I got the diaries, the keys were lost and the hasps, fortunately, hung open. At the start, here and there, she indulged in a custom of the time, addressing the diary as "You," or "Little you," like a confidante, but soon settled into straightforward reporting, juxtaposing the

Rayline when she was a student at the Milwaukee Downer Seminary.

interesting with the mundane and sometimes venting her feelings and opinions. She was a faithful recorder, leaving less than a dozen pages blank in the first diary, and only a few in 1919, 1920 and up to June 11, 1921—the day she was married. My father had asked her to give up keeping a diary because even in the best of marriages misunderstandings and arguments occur and since she was in the habit of re-reading past entries (as she notes in the diaries themselves) they both recognized that recall might re-kindle anger after they'd kissed and made up.

At the end of all the diaries there are a number of blank pages headed "Memoranda" followed by double spread pages of columns for each month's "Cash Account." The first three diaries were Excelsior publications while the 1921 diary was published by the Standard Diary Company. Rayline occasionally used the Memoranda pages for addresses or to continue daily entries that exceeded the allocated daily space, but she ignored the cash account pages after a few brief entries in 1918. The 1921 Memoranda pages, however, detail the menus of half a dozen bridal showers given in her honor in May and early June and that same year, perhaps in preparation for her

Sam Lang, a Phantom Lake YMCA Camp counselor who proposed to Rayline when she was still in high school. He considered himself her fiancé but her diaries indicate her ambivalence about the romance almost from the start

role as a homemaker, she kept assiduous accounts of her expenditures from January through June 10.

Unless otherwise identified, the figures in the "Paid" columns of the Cash Account section of the 1921 diary are the source of any prices cited throughout this book. They total less than $100.00 and Rayline gives no inkling as to the source or total amount of funds she drew upon since the "Received" column is blank, but doubtless it was "spending money" she notes receiving from "the folks" from time to time for everyday expenses and small luxuries. She also hoarded her "own" money to use as she wished—cash gifts recorded in her diaries from her parents, grandparents, other relatives and close friends for birthdays, Christmas and other occasions. Pa found various reasons to indulge his first grandchild with gifts of money as he did me, his first great grandchild. His retirement income derived in part from bonds and he "paid" Rayline $1.00 to $10.00 for carefully clipping the coupons for him although she would have done it gladly for nothing as she notes in her diary after every expedition to the bank where the bonds were kept in a safety deposit box. He also paid her small sums for trimming his hair—not much of a chore as he was quite bald by an early age. At one point Rayline began saving her "own" money to visit her friend Mary Ball in Birmingham but the flu epidemic there interfered with her plans.

Another noteworthy feature of the 1921 diary is that unlike the others, it carries no gratuitous printed information on weights and measures, important historic dates and the like, but devotes the last two pages to a form for "Summary of Receipts and Allowable Deductions, For Income Tax Returns." I don't know if this reflects a difference in the two diary publishers' format policy or increasing concern about income taxes. Wisconsin and some other states had already enacted income tax legislation before the federal income tax was established under the 16th Amendment in 1913.

Along the tops of the pages above the dates, Rayline noted the birthdays and wedding anniversaries of family members and friends as well as anniversaries of important events such as the November

11 Armistice. She also kept track of her "monthly visitor" with an X in a page corner. On September 8, 1918, the cryptic entry, "T. 27" appears on the left side and "S. 6" on the right that turned out to be Tuve Floden's and Sam Lang's initials, subsequently written "T.J.F." and "S.J.L." followed by numbers referring to the number of letters she had sent each of them since the beginning of each year. Letters to other fellows and girls and letters received were mentioned in the diary texts. As I worked my way page by page—chuckling, shaking my head, mumbling "I never knew that," and realized I had a book in the making, I began creating categories and indexing entries on 3x5 cards for future reference. The last sentence in the entry for March 13, 1920, however, brought me up short. Following a humdrum account of domestic activities, Rayline wrote, "Have been reading Ruth [indistinct]ndall's diary in the paper. She killed herself and married lover- - I wonder if any strangers will ever read my **diaries – Hope not!**" For a moment I was ready to abandon the whole project, especially with the final words emphasized, and return to my initial plan to burn the diaries and letters. That is, until I realized, as in other instances of increasingly faint writing, Rayline's fountain pen had begun to run dry and would start with an initial gush of ink when she refilled it. I am confident if she were in my place (and she *does* contemplate the possibility of strangers reading her diaries) her reaction would be, "Well, if she didn't want anyone to read them, then she should have destroyed them!" So, I continued.

Besides their intrinsic interest as a glimpse of another era from a personal perspective, the diaries and letters happen to cover a generally overlooked stage in respect to many significant changes in American society in general, a time when once new and even awesome things were becoming commonplace but the old was still well entrenched. For example, horses no longer bolted at the sight, sound, and smell of an automobile but it would be a long time before there were no horses at all on the streets. I have heard that bird feeders came into vogue when the last dray horses clip-clopped off the scene leaving starving sparrows with no "horse apples" with undigested grains to pick at in their wake.

The letters began during a time that the family enjoyed growing prosperity, but financial difficulties had set in when Rayline began her first diary. The serious crises were long over when I heard about any of them and the sense of desperation was sufficiently blunted by time that some incidents were even recalled with amusement, such as my grandfather's bursts of extravagant self-indulgence when he was close to insolvency. I never gave much thought to the fact that my mother became a day student, commuting from home, rather than continuing as a boarding student at Downer Seminary during her junior and senior years. I might have figured there were monetary reasons but since I never heard her complain about the hour long ride each way by streetcar, I accepted that it also was her own preference, just as I had assumed she chose to attend the Normal School, located next to the Downer campuses, rather than go to Downer College or the university at Madison after she completed high school at Downer Seminary. Isolated entries scattered in ordinary and even upbeat information in the 1918 diary make painfully evident that Rayline had to economize on her education because her parents were in deep financial trouble that continued off and on well into 1919. Things began looking up in the mid-1920s and by April 19, 1921, Lalla's 43rd birthday, Daniel could again afford to give her expensive presents, in this case, "a wonderful platinum and diamond dinner ring."

The sentiments expressed on February 26, 1918, however, pop up now and again throughout the next year and a half: "Mother had a face on about a mile long…always how hard up we are. I almost feel as if I'm depriving the folks of food because I go to school." Or, October 1: "Long faces on Mother and Dad because of business worries." On Jan. 2, 1919, she reports a New Year's resolution: "Mother and Dad seem more cheerful, not that anything has turned for the better, but they are going to look at the 'silver lining of the dark cloud' hereafter." By Jan. 22, however, Lalla had slipped back into despair while Daniel's reaction must have done little to relieve her anxiety: "Mother had one of her 'pessimistic' spells again to-day. Of course, it would be terrible if we lost everything but talking about it and roaming around the house half of the night and not looking for a brighter side and a better time won't help matters one bit. On the strength of it Dad went out and ordered a forty dollar suit."

The diaries give substance to family stories that my grandfather, like his father, had weathered national economic "panics," and that his career as a general building contractor in many ways resembled that of a professional gambler. He took enormous risks that sometimes paid off prodigiously and sometimes brought him to the brink of bankruptcy. The fact that he liked to live lavishly when the money rolled in left little cushion for the hard times and took a toll on my grandmother's sense of security.

Generally, however, his luck and acumen paid off. He was only 29 years old in 1902 when he built the substantial home on Layton Boulevard with its formal and informal living rooms, dining room, kitchen, and Daniel's office on the first floor, and bathroom and three large and one small bedroom on the second floor. In 1911, he built the even larger house on Phantom Lake that became his ace in the hole when serious reverses began to occur about 1917. Throughout the diaries, whenever there was an economic set-back or just the fear of one, there is talk of renting or even selling the place at Phantom Lake, sometimes extending to prospective buyers coming to see the property, but somehow the family managed to survive without sacrificing the summer home. On April 9, 1919 Rayline wrote: "Had the [cleaning] woman here [Phantom Lake] and Mother and I worked like troopers to get everything done. Had hopes that we'd sell the place but that is all off." Even my father's letters that begin in the spring of 1919 refer regretfully now and again to the possible necessity of selling the Phantom Lake home.

As I understand it, although I do not know the details, by 1918 a series of miscalculations on bids and bad luck like inclement weather resulted in my grandfather making less than he anticipated and even losing money. He also was embroiled in a major lawsuit to collect a debt. The litigation dragged on and the final settlement of $3,200 awarded on February 27, 1918, while a lifesaver, was less than the $4,800 he had expected; then there were further delays until he actually got his money. All this affected domestic life as my mother complains repeatedly about her parents being "cranky," "grumpy," and bickering, as well as indifferent to and dismissive of her problems and needs during this period. She complains of undiagnosed chest pains, head aches, and weight loss, and severe cramps she always suffered with the onset of her monthly "visitor." October 29, 1918: "Came home from school dead tired, and Miss White [one of her teachers] suggests that I drop a subject for she thinks I don't look well, goodness knows I sure don't feel well, but the minute I say anything about [my health] the folks begin telling me that I shouldn't think about it. They are the best Christian Science followers when I'm sick but the minute there's anything the matter with them they're nearly dying." Domestic dust-ups between Rayline and her parents were sometimes followed by a ritual of reconciliation when Rayline would crawl into bed with her mother and Daniel brought them breakfast in bed. That's the phrase she used, but I suspect only because she wasn't sure of the spelling of the Norwegian equivalent, *kaffe på seng*, literally coffee in bed, the only term I ever heard for the custom that was still observed as a special treat in my childhood.

Rayline's diaries indicate that at this time my grandmother, never exactly sylphlike, began having serious problems with her weight. Some years before, she had fallen and broken her kneecap leaving her with a stiff leg and a limp that made her more sedentary and, with less exercise, she gained more weight and so on in a vicious circle. The family's financial problems also might have spurred some compulsive eating. Before I could read, I simply took it for granted that Jack Spratt and his wife as shown in my nursery rhyme book was a picture of my grandparents. Lalla cooked rich food to fatten up tall, skinny Daniel but he had health problems of his own that resulted in a poor appetite, so she ended up eating a lot of it herself. "Waste not, want not." An entry on January 19,

1919 verified a family story that I had heard as a child. Lalla tried a product that guaranteed weight loss, but it had distressing side effects her doctor immediately recognized and prescribed a remedy accordingly. Its literally active ingredient was tapeworm eggs. "Mother took her medicine to get rid of her friend—the tape worm & she was frightened to death. For a while she was pretty sick tho."

Throughout much of 1918 and 1919 Rayline makes exasperated references to what today we would recognize as her mother's classic symptoms of depression: periodic indifference to her appearance and neglect of housework and other daily routines. Rayline tried to help but it wasn't easy. Immediately following the tape-worm incident, she notes:

> I worked so hard to have a nice dinner this evening and then the roast wasn't done. I felt so badly [sic] that I came upstairs and cried & Pa was wonderful to me. Poor Pa, Ma [as a newly wed] experimented cooking on him & now I. But in one way it really was mother's fault, for she insisted I turn the flame down as she could smell the meat burning. I'm all dressed up in cap & kimono & curls—the way I would always like to look. Oh, how I wish that I could have heaps of pretty dainty things—oh well, why sigh for the moon.

The last phrase typified Rayline's personal philosophy of get over it and get on with it, and was expressed in various ways in her diaries in the face of disappointments or unrealistic expectations, from the cliché that "you can't have your cake and eat it too" to my favorite, June 10, 1919, when she decided Tuve Floden really wasn't seriously interested in her, "Oh well, why cry over spilt milk. Call the cat in."

Rayline was enrolled in the newly established Home Economics program at the Normal School and writes several times of wanting to put her learning about efficient household management into effect, but while Lalla was dilatory and careless at times and depended on Rayline to fetch and carry, she was not about to turn over her authority. She was smart and knew how to manage very well. She simply did not like housework and the need to economize had meant doing without the daily or live-in maid she had become accustomed to. Her usual sources of such help were the Catholic House of the Good Shepherd and what Rayline calls "the Industrial School," in either case, places where "wayward girls" might end up. My grandmother had a strong sense of social responsibility and also was a good judge of character. She realized that some perfectly trustworthy girls were institutionalized simply because they had no families or means of caring for themselves, and that both she and they could benefit from their employment. Throughout most of the period covered in the diaries, however, Lalla's only household help consisted of a weekly nameless "woman," for major cleaning. Rayline was expected to help with dishwashing, cleaning, and the like. She expresses gratitude and relief on April 29, 1921 when, "Mother got a maid from the Industrial School and Nellie seems to be a real nice girl."

When Lalla could afford daily help, she taught these young women the basics of house keeping and took a continuing interest in their welfare even after they left her employment. On Oct. 7, 1918, Rayline wrote, "Ethel, one of the maids we had in the past, was here. Her husband is lying around with other women and the poor girl came to mother for advice," adding that Ethel by then had "a darling baby." As her domestic situation did not improve, Ethel again turned to Lalla. Rayline notes on September 5, 1919: "Ethel's case came up to-day & so mother left early this morning with her for the court where she spent the day." Four days later: "Ethel's case came up again today & so Mother was gone all day— Ethel's husband got it in the 'neck' from the judge & I'm glad of it." I know from later family references to the case that, thanks to Lalla's testimony, Ethel got a divorce and a substantial settlement to make a new start on her own.

Rayline mentions Lalla buying specialty items such as lace

from sales people who came to the house. One reported instance affords a further glimpse into spousal abuse and the vulnerability of women. On December 18, 1919, Rayline wrote: "Meta Sweeney was out today selling stockings. Mother bought six pairs of silk and two pairs of lisle for me. [Meta's] face is terrible looking. It seems terrible that there isn't some way that a man can't [sic] be punished for giving a woman a thing like that. It gives me the creeps to think of it."

My grandfather's business gradually picked up and sometimes even flourished, particularly in pursuing building opportunities at places outside Milwaukee with his friend and associate, Oscar Alberts. In 1919-20 they seemed to be spending a lot of time in Two Rivers, Wisconsin, but it wasn't until I went through my father's letters that I learned they planned to open a door factory there; I have no idea what became of the venture. As noted earlier, the Alberts were frequent houseguests.

Often what is left unsaid or said so casually as to nearly escape notice at first is particularly productive of unexpected insights on the early years of the 20th century. For example, people *walked*! It was a matter of both necessity and sociable recreation. "We took a walk," Rayline would sometimes write when she paid informal visits to the homes of her friends or relatives or they visited her home just to chat—no particular destination nor distance nor duration is given for these walks. She also refers to her mother, weight and limp notwithstanding, taking long walks with friends. Walking was just something people did to make casual visiting more interesting, like playing cards or doing needlework together, and probably contributing unknowingly to neighborhood security.

Few people had cars when the first letters begin and most people in urban areas didn't have horses as they have cars today, so they walked. Having grown up in the same neighborhood, I know how far Rayline and her friends and family walked from one place to another, taking several miles literally in stride. What she does mention was when they didn't walk what were normally walking distances, when they took the streetcar or, extravagantly, took a taxi any distance.

It was not until I read Rayline's diaries that I really understood her initiating walks together after she came to live with me. It was not just for exercise as I assumed. We observed, remarked on, and wondered about the odd architectural detail of a particular house, toys left in driveways asking to be swiped or run over, the shade that was always drawn, the neat yard, the messy yard, the cat in the window, the new dent in a neighbor's car. We never met other strollers, only occasional solo walkers or joggers energetically concentrating on their health, music plugged into their ears, and looking neither to right nor left.

Rayline makes a number of passing references in her diaries during the winter months that Pa had gone out to Phantom Lake, these trips deserving mention because he brought back freshly caught fish for supper. But it meant that a man, by then in his seventies, took the interurban trolley from Milwaukee and then had to walk well over a mile from the stop nearest his cottage, to say nothing of the exertion of going out on the lake and jigging for fish through a hole he chopped in the ice, and returning by the same route with his catch.

Rayline with her cousins Jeanette and Antoinette on either side of Gladys Boerner at Phantom Lake.

Lalla and Daniel sometimes entertained family and friends at the house on Phantom Lake during the winter. On February 28, 1918, Rayline and her cousins Bernard Nelson (Inga's son) and Carl Riemenschneider (Nettie's son) walked to Mukwonago and back on the ice just for a lark, a distance of well over two miles each way across Phantom Lake and the adjoining Howitt's Lake (now called Lower Phantom Lake). Her only complaint was getting wet feet because of the deep, wet snow covering the ice that also prevented the popular sport of ice boating on the lake.

Meanwhile, more people were acquiring automobiles. Historians have pointed out the enormous social and economic ramifications and unexpected consequences of its invention, but Rayline's diaries and collection of letters illustrate how easily ordinary people took to the automobile with young people, at least, immediately bent on seeing how fast they could go. Even the proverbial white horse gave way in Rayline's romantic fantasies: "Oh how I wish that some prince charming would come racing along in his roadster and fall in love with me and I with him" (March 2, 1918).

Also generally overlooked in studies of the impact of the automobile is how readily and fearlessly women took to the road. A number of matter-of-fact references in the diaries indicate that well before the U.S. entered World War I, my grandmother was driving although Rayline claimed to be "terrified" whenever her mother was behind the wheel. After they drove out to Phantom Lake on May 2, 1919 she referred briefly to an incident that had occurred several years earlier. I know the details because they were still good for a laugh during my childhood whenever we passed the farmhouse where it had happened. By this time, the ponies had been sold and my grandmother was driving her own Model T Ford, or "Tin Lizzy." On this occasion, with Rayline and her cousin Jeanette jammed next to her on the front seat, my grandmother got too close to the soft shoulder of the road. "Children, children," she announced calmly, "We're going over." The farmer and his wife who had been looking out the window when they drove by rushed out to help. No one was hurt and the Model T suffered no damage as the five of them got the machine up and back on the road. The farmer's wife reported, however, that she had been after her husband to teach her to drive and just as she said, "See, now there's a woman driving," the Model T slowly keeled over on its side.

Rayline was eager to drive and by April 1, 1920 got her way thanks to the fact that her Downer and Normal School associations meant her social life centered on club meetings and friendships with girls living on the north side of town. "Daddy started to teach me how to run the Ford. I guess he is tired of carting me around." But Daniel was an impatient teacher and she was driving regularly when she only knew how to shift gears to go forward (it would be nearly a decade before Wisconsin instituted drivers licenses and testing). She recalled when she was teaching me to drive, that it wasn't until she found herself in a situation where she absolutely had to back up that she finally learned to shift into reverse from a friendly cop. Rayline noted several times in 1920 that her friend Gladys had her own car, a "roadster" of course. Another friend, Margaret Flett, whom I have not been able to identify further, also had her own car and Rayline and Margaret Breed went joy riding with her on May 3. "Hit 55 mi per hour on one stretch."

Because the patterns for manual transmissions were not standardized among the early automobile companies, Rayline became adept at handling her mother's and father's succession of cars. When she and my father were married and bought a second hand Scripps Booth, she had to learn yet another system. Driving remained one of Rayline's greatest pleasures throughout her life, clocking thousands of miles all over the country. She was a good driver and when her only serious accident resulted in her being sued, the jury found the other driver, the plaintiff, fully liable for his injuries.

After she came to live with me she said that if I saw she was becoming a menace to herself or others I should tell her it was time to stop driving. I made a point of riding with her on occasion. She was always attentive and careful and certainly didn't dawdle

108

indecisively in the manner of some elderly drivers, but about a month before she turned 94 she handed me her car keys. "I got lost on the south side where I grew up," she said matter-of-factly, "It's time I quit driving."

In a totally different realm, a major revelation in the diaries concerned church attendance or, rather, not attending church. It is hard to shake the habit of expecting older generations to have been more strait-laced and conventional than one's own, but the fact is that Rayline's family and their contemporaries certainly were not very concerned about observing the Sabbath. I paid little attention to Rayline's comment of Sunday, February 17, 1918, soon after she began keeping a diary, that "Don [Morey] called up this morning and asked if he couldn't take me to church, but as I wasn't dressed I said no." I gradually realized that was about the closest she came to going to church at all throughout the course of her diaries. The first clue I noted was on Sunday, October 13, 1918: "All places of amusement closed because of the 'Flu'…. Couldn't even go to church…." Well, it turns out they didn't go to church, anyway. She makes no mention of a formal lifting of the ban on public gatherings and by mid-November they are going to the movies again. Careful

Antoinette, Carl Windesheim ("Windy") and Rayline. The "Inn Hill" can be seen beyond Antoinette's right shoulder.

checking throughout the diaries reveals she never went to church. This is no mere oversight like not bothering to mention routine household chores; she accounts fully for her Sundays with dates, trips to Racine to visit her friend Margaret Breed, and family outings or simply reporting she slept until noon. Sunday was a day of rest but not worship as she notes on February 2, 1919: "We had a regular old time Sunday, just Mother, Daddy & me. We slept late and then just enjoyed each other's company." A side note to this final comment: the diaries and letters seem to indicate that people slept late every chance they got and they napped a lot more than is the case today.

I know from Rayline's stories of her childhood that she attended Sunday school, usually with her cousin Antoinette Schuette, at St. John's Episcopal Church, located at that time several miles to the east and north of her home. Although her parents were parishioners they just sent her off with money for the collection plate and carfare. The girls usually walked home to save their money to spend on candy. I still find it hard to believe, in view of the importance of church activities in my mother's life from the 1930s until her death, there is not one mention in the diaries of attending services, not even Christmas Eve or Easter Sunday. In fact, she had not even been confirmed, a deficiency remedied at the time of my confirmation when my father was "received" from the Lutheran church. She took special note of Palm Sunday, March 24, 1918, only because it was her Danielson grandparents' 43rd wedding anniversary—celebrated with a special family dinner; coincidently, their wedding day also had fallen on Palm Sunday.

I too began Sunday School at St John's but was too young to go alone so the family must have begun regular church attendance by then. Founded in 1847, it was the second oldest parish in the Milwaukee Diocese. Daniel served on the vestry and, as a general contractor, volunteered his talents and resources to keep the old building standing. By the 1920s it required cables with big turn-buckles across the nave some 12 or 15 feet above the floor to keep the walls from falling outward. When lightning destroyed the tall thin steeple, Daniel saw no point in replacing it and had it capped off with a little, pyramidal roof that Rayline dubbed "the candle snuffer." About 1930, the city condemned the property for public use and while many parishioners were outraged, Daniel was delighted. With the onset of what would become the Great Depression, the city's offer greatly exceeded what they could get on the open market at the time to build a new, stone church on property the parish owned closer to our home on Layton Boulevard. Daniel served as general contractor and the building was well underway when he suffered a stroke in 1934; I believe his was the first funeral held in the new church the following year.

After my mother came to live with me in 1970, she still faithfully attended St. John's, driving all the way to the south side where, as she put it, her mite made a difference that would not have been the case in the several more prestigious and richer Episcopalian parishes near our home on the east side. After the service, she always detoured before coming home in order to drive around Forest Home Cemetery and check on the family graves. She seldom got out of the car—just paid her respects.

There is a single mention of going to a church and while it hardly counts it raised my curiosity. On Sunday, September 22, 1918 she and her friend Mary Ball went to an evening lecture.

Had a beast of a headache all day, but even so went way on the other side of town to hear Cap. Hutchinson speak & it was worth it even though I did disgrace myself by having to very unceremoniously race out of the church with Mary tagging behind. For my supper and I started to part company. Met Cap. H. and he rode home on the [street] car. I saw him thru the car window after we transferred & he raised his walking stick and saluted to me. He surely is fascinating and won't Marg [Margaret Breed] be jealous that I met him. You'd almost think she had a mortgage on the dear man.

Although I decided at the outset that I would rely on the diaries, letters, and my own family recollections to add new perspectives to the historic record rather than turn to historical sources to expand upon my unique little cache of data, I did some computer searches to verify dates and other details. Captain Hutchinson eluded me and there was the chance that my generalization about church attendance needed revision; perhaps he was an army chaplain. So I checked the microfilms of back issues of the *Milwaukee Sentinel* at the Public Library.

According to the newspaper announcements for September 21 and 22, Captain S.J. Hutchinson "of the London Irish Rifles and the Royal Air Force" must have cut a dashing figure on the lecture circuit. He "served on the Western Front and also has been in charge of the protection of London against air raids." One of his venues just happened to be the Kingsley Memorial Church on the near north side of town where Rayline and Mary heard him speak. The next evening he spoke at a dinner at the City Club, the announcement noting that, "In private life [he] is a barrister, at present he is a candidate for parliament. His speech...promises to be both interesting and instructive." I have no idea how Rayline managed to cope with her nausea and regain her composure upon encountering the gallant Captain on the streetcar en route home, but her gloating at besting her friend Margaret Breed in attracting male attention was very much in character.

If my family and their circle of friends did not attend church regularly during the years covered in Rayline's diaries, they certainly patronized places of public entertainment, especially movie theaters, also closed briefly during the flu epidemic. Like transportation terminology, identifying the different kinds of performances took some time to figure out. Reference to "the bill" or "the acts" clued me in that vaudeville played at the Majestic and the Davidson. The latter, along with the Schubert, also was a venue for live drama or so-called legitimate theatre, as well as movies. When she wrote of going to the Merrill, Butterfly, Palace, Alhambra, Rialto, Strand, and Crystal it was to see first run films downtown at one of the fancy movie houses.

I was amazed to discover how many movies people attended. As in the case of the automobile, movies were no longer a novelty in Rayline's youth but were certainly still seen as a "modern" invention. She does not bother to describe the architecturally imaginative and grandiose movie palaces that had sprung up over the past few years before she began her diaries or the quality of the music scored for each film to fill the silence and set the mood— from humble pianos to orchestras to organs like the "Mighty Wurlitzer" with multiple keyboards and ranks of pipes that could imitate almost any sound short of the human voice. Naturally, she had no reason to comment on the commonplace of her time, but her remarks of August 29, 1919 are of special interest: "This evening Mother, Dad, & I went to the Alhambra [;] besides the regular picture, there were pictures as shown ten years ago. The moving pictures certainly have progressed & improved in such a short space of time. I wonder what ten years from now will be like."

As a matter of fact, between 1928 and 1930, the movie industry converted completely to "talkies." I once heard someone of Rayline's generation claim they were all good readers because of the skills honed by silent films requiring them to read the printed words of dialog quickly enough to be able to follow the action on screen as well. Both my father's letters from Canton, Ohio and Mary Ball's from Birmingham, Alabama show the same pattern of frequent movie attendance reported in my mother's diaries.

The first movies I saw and remember were at the very end of the silent era, at the Alhambra and Palace, that I attended with Lalla and Daniel when I was four years old. At that time there were vaudeville acts we called "stage shows" along with the films. This also might have been the case at these same downtown theaters Rayline refers to in her diaries, but she only mentions going there to see "movies" (the word usually wrapped in quotation marks). The many "movies" that Pa took her to generally meant the small, neighborhood theater "in the next block," the Layton Park, that showed second run films. While a week or so might go by without going to a movie, particularly when the family was at Phantom Lake, it was not unusual for Rayline to report attending three or four movies a week and two, sometimes even three, movies or a combination of movies and live productions in one day and evening with different family members or friends. Such outings might also include dinner at an elegant restaurant such as Tilleman's or The Gargoyle, or one of the downtown hotel dining rooms where couples also could dance. Some random examples from her diaries:

Saturday, January 5, 1918: Met Miller [Mureson] at five and went to the Wisconsin (hotel) for dinner, however, before the "eats" we went to the Merrill. After dinner went to the Strand, then met some more people and went to the Crystal Gardens and danced, from there we all went to the Plankington [Hotel] Sky Room and danced some more. Got home at 12:30.

Monday, January 27, 1919: [Ben Carstairs] came out [to Rayline's home] and we went down town to the Butterfly & then to the Merrill. Had dinner at the Badger Room (Hotel Wisconsin) & of course danced [where they met other friends]... We talked a long time and Ben tried to get tickets for the Maj[estic] but the place was sold out. However, Ben and I went to the Strand.

Friday, May 7, 1920: Took Glad [Gladys Boerner] to the Majestic and to Tilleman's to celebrate this great day [a year since Gladys introduced my mother to Carl Oestreich]. [later] Met Mother & she and I went to the Alhambra. After the picture met Daddy at the depot, & then the three of us went to the Strand.

Although she often mentions dining at "Charlie Toy's," a very popular and posh Chinese restaurant where there also was an orchestra for dancing, she does not mention Toy's movie house with its Oriental decor on the first floor of the Toy building below the restaurant.

According to TV documentaries, this was the great age of vaudeville and the slapstick movie comedy but, apart from one reference to "Vod Vill"—a spoof on the real thing for some kind of Boy Scout benefit, the word vaudeville itself does not occur in my mother's diaries although my father used the term occasionally in his letters. Likewise, the great majority of movies mentioned do not appear to have been comedies. More often than not, Rayline simply wrote that she went to a particular movie theater or just the "movies" with Pa, Mother and Dad, or other girls, or boy friends, and that the film was "punk" or "real good" without mentioning the title or naming the actors, let alone noting the plots. Where she does go into any particulars, she usually was not impressed by people who have become acclaimed icons of the era. On April 11, 1919, she says of Mary Pickford in "Captain Kidd," "Not very good," and dismisses an unidentified Pickford film on February 2, 1921 as "punk picture." On February 2, 1918, she merely records, "saw Theda Bara in Madame Du Barry" at a "downtown theater," but on March 19, 1919 she expressed her opinion about her. "Pa and I went to the movies this evening & saw Theda Bara in 'Salome.' Theda sure is a cow. How anyone can like her is more than I can see." Even the great Charlie Chaplin whom she saw in "Shoulder Arms" on November 15, 1918 rates no more than "real good," while an unnamed Buster Keaton film was just "very funny." On December 13, 1920 she saw Otis Skinner in his most famous role, Haji in "Kismet," and pronounced it a "wonderful production."

Earlier in the year she exchanged views in letters with my father about the "scandalous" film, "Aphrodite," starring Alla Nazimova. They concluded it wasn't really all that scandalous, and my father didn't find find Nazimova terribly attractive. I don't know if his closing of the letter in which he discussed the film was original or current slang: "Nightie, nightie, Aphrodite."

The reigning female star until the advent of "talkies" was

the now almost forgotten Norma Tallmadge. Rayline was among her fans and saw a lot of Tallmadge films that she didn't bother to name or discuss. On August 27, 1918, however, she went with her parents and her uncle and aunt, the "C.B.s," "to the Butterfly to see Norma Tallmadge and Eugene O'Brien in 'Her Only Way.' It was awfully good I thought, & Eugene O'Brien looks through his lashes the same as Ben. F. There is no doubting it, Ben is handsomer." She was briefly smitten by Benjamin F. Carstairs or, at least, by his matinee idol good looks, and, not surprisingly, he confided in her that he contemplated a stage career. But he was only one of many beaux and she considered him too much of a "kid" to be taken seriously.

On January 15, 1919, with two of her girl friends, she "went to the Butterfly & saw Norma Tallmadge in 'Heart of Wetona,'" but her only comment on what must have been a challenging role, insofar as Tallmadge (according to a Web search) plays the part of an American Indian, is, "Very good." An unidentified movie starring Tallmadge that Rayline saw with her parents on Jan. 11, 1920 is something of a harbinger of the social and cultural changes associated with the "Roaring Twenties." Tallmadge appeared for the first time with bobbed hair eliciting Rayline's response, "I'd really love to have mine cut if Carl would [wouldn't?] care so awfully much. It would be so easy to do up." I don't know exactly when my mother bobbed her hair. It was an occasional topic of debate in my parents' letters through 1920 and 1921, and her wedding picture is no help because the cloche cap holding the veil covers most of her hair.

While the list of named movies and actors is not long it would be tedious to enumerate them, but a few are worth noting. On January 22, 1919 she saw what was probably the first version of "Tarzan of the Apes," but gives no particulars, and on May 3, 1920 she saw another future favorite for re-makes, "Dr. Jekyl and Mr. Hyde," starring John Barrymore, that was sufficiently impressive to draw her reaction: "Wonderful acting, but horribly gruesome." On July 24, 1919, she wrote one of her rare extensive commentaries that hardly seems to refer to the film that according to a Web search was produced by the American Hygiene Association in 1918. It dealt with the diverging fates of two sisters, promiscuous Vera who died young and virtuous Mary who became a nurse and married a doctor. "Mary, Areline [no further identification and one of various spellings of the name], & I went to the Davidson and saw 'The End of the Road,' a picture dealing with venereal diseases. Goodness, I nearly wanted to swear I'd never see another man, but I guess there are some good ones on earth, besides the bad."

The Chaplin entry, above, indicates the movies reflected the fact that the nation was at war during 1918-1919, but only two other war related films can be identified among the movie titles or subjects Rayline bothered to mention, and these convey actual war news. November 20, 1918: "Went to the movies with Pa & saw Pershing's Crusaders." Apparently she had been alerted to see the film because she goes on, "Thought I would see Tuve but the part of the film he was in has worn out." On January 7 of the next year she was disappointed again that she couldn't discern Tuve in a film he had written about to her, "America's Answer," that showed "Major Roosevelt present Croix de Guerres to Lieut. Holund (George P.'s pal) & Sgt. Murphy." The parenthetical reference is to George P. Gustafson who died in France.

Rayline usually had more to say, but not much, about legitimate theater and vaudeville programs in comparison to movies. A memorable headliner, May 1, 1918: "Mother, Elizabeth & I went to see Sarah Bernhardt at the Majestic and she was wonderful and to think she is 74 years old and has a wooden leg." Evidently, "The Divine Sarah," as she was popularly known, was not appearing in a drama but vaudeville—one of her many "farewell tours," since Rayline notes the rest of the bill also "was real good." Besides seeing stars of their day on tour such as Annette Kellerman, the Dolly Sisters, and the Greenwich Village Follies, the family patronized local theatrical talent that prior to World War I in Milwaukee included both German and English speaking stock companies. By March of 1918, only an English company seems to have survived when Rayline "Went to the Schubert this after-noon with mother and Jennie [Walters] and saw the Stock Co play, 'Play Things,' real good. Lunch at some chop suey place"—obviously, not Toy's.

The high point of the theatrical circuit at the time was an early musical, "Chu Chin Chow," that played in Milwaukee in 1919. It was based on the Arabian Nights story of Ali Baba and the Forty Thieves with the introduction of a new character, a wealthy Chinese merchant, hence the title. Still not telling her diary what the play was about, Rayline positively gushes with enthusiasm on March 25. "Pa and I have just gotten back from seeing Chu Chin Chow & it was wonderful, marvelous, gorgeous, & well worth the $5.50 spent for seats. It sure is great sport to go out with one's grandfather - & he is a perfect dear too." Although Rayline provides no information on the usual cost of a theater seat, the price Pa paid for their sixth row seats must have been exorbitant for the time insofar as her 1921 diary reveals that admission to first run movies at downtown theaters such as the Butterfly, Alhambra, and

Rayline, ca. 1917, in stylish outfits of the period between the stiffly corseted Edwardian era that ended in 1910 and the short skirts that characterized the "Roaring Twenties."

others was forty cents and twenty two cents at the neighborhood Layton Park. My father's letters routinely note that balcony seats to theatrical productions in Ohio were fifty or fifty five cents, apparently cheaper seats because he mentions he and his friends passed around a pair of field glasses for better viewing.

Relative to the cost of movies and other items listed in the 1921 diary, women's ready-made clothing was surprisingly expensive. For example, lunches at restaurants were less than a dollar, streetcar transportation was seven cents a ride or only a nickel if you bought ten "checks" at a time. A round trip ticket, Milwaukee-Racine, on the interurban was $1.36. Even rent was cheap. Early in 1921, Rayline visited family friends at their two bedroom furnished apartment that she considered greatly overpriced at $135.00 a month. On the other hand, in 1919, she mentions shopping with her mother for winter coats that ranged from about $50.00 to $60.00 and suits from $30.00 to $35.00. Women's shoes, oxfords and "slippers" (pumps) are mentioned at prices of $8.00 to $12.00. In October of 1920, she hoped to get an "Australian opossum" fur collar for a new coat for $45.00 but later learned it really cost $85.00 and her parents weren't willing to pay that much.

As a young woman with an active social life and a keen sense of style, Rayline devotes a lot of attention to clothes and beauty aids throughout the diaries. Besides my surprise at the cost of women's ready-to-wear garments, I became aware that the diaries, along with family photos, document a brief but distinct and generally overlooked period in the history of fashion.

The cinched-in "hour glass" figure, leg-o'-mutton sleeved shirtwaist, and exaggerated pompadour to which dish-shaped hats with plumes or flowers had to be anchored with long hatpins—epitomized since the 1890s by the "Gibson girl"—had given way, briefly, to a stiffly corseted silhouette virtually devoid of waist line or hips and surmounted by a matronly bosom. By the time Rayline entered Downer Seminary in 1913 a more natural silhouette was in vogue featuring loosely belted dresses or suits with straight or pleated skirts, simple shirtwaists, and jackets. In one case an

"Eton jacket" is specified. Meanwhile, hemlines moved from floor to ankle to mid-calf.

Coiffures were no longer augmented with "switches" and "rats"—extra lengths and wads of hair—in the fashion of the "Gay Nineties," but long hair was still a woman's "crowning glory." Hats were flattering but practical, usually with relatively deep crowns and brims of equal width of a couple inches or so all the way around. Berets were also worn. The full-fledged flapper look—boyishly flat chested, bare kneed and low-waisted had not yet taken over and bobbed hair was beginning to be generally accepted by the time Rayline stopped keeping a diary when she was married on June 11, 1921.

Her white chiffon wedding dress was loose fitting without a defined waist, clearly trending to flapper, but reached well below her knees, while her veil, attached to a singularly ugly example of the new, 1920s cloche, trailed in traditional fashion on the floor. Because of her father's poor health and her mother's anxiety for him, Rayline chose to have a small wedding at home with Mary Ball as her only attendant. At the last moment as they were about to descend the open stair case to the parlor for the ceremony, she and Mary decided the veil looked incongruous and snipped it off to match the length of her dress. Lalla was the only one who noticed and concluded her memory was affected by the medicine she had taken to calm her nerves because she thought they had bought a floor length veil.

Apparently because store-bought clothing, including hats, was so expensive, Rayline's diaries document a lot of remodeling, recycling, and refurbishing, and making clothes from scratch, often as a sociable activity with the sharing of skills among friends and family members. The diaries indicate that while her friend Mary came from a well-to-do family and could afford expensive clothing and shoes, Mary's correspondence, 1919-1920, includes mention of her mother making over some clothing and Mary doing some sewing from scratch though admittedly confined to simple waists rather than Rayline's increasingly ambitious efforts. By this time

Mary is engaged to a man of apparently modest means and she is planning a wardrobe that is practical and durable.

Many of Rayline's forays into refurbishing concerned hats— replacing ribbons, pompoms, and other trim. In most situations, a hat was necessary to be properly dressed and so each year and seasons within the year required a new hat or at least a new looking hat for style conscious women. Hats of felted beaver fur were very costly and Rayline prized a "beaver hat" inherited from her maternal grandmother that she cleaned, brushed, and trimmed to look like new. Her father, ever the dandy, regularly bought expensive wool felt fedoras and Rayline appropriated one of his discards to be commercially cleaned and blocked to suit a feminine wearer. Broad brimmed woven straw hats called leghorns, an English corruption of the town in Italy where they originated, were absolutely essential to any stylish woman's summer wardrobe; like winter headgear, they underwent annual reincarnations with fresh ornamentation. The diaries reveal that milliners not only made and sold new hats but would retrim old ones.

Rayline's first attempt at sewing from scratch began in the summer of 1918, when she and Mary decided to make bathing suits. The project took nearly a month. On August 18, she wrote, "We got up real early & promenaded around in our new bathing suits but we didn't have the heart to get them wet." She thought the suits were "awfully good looking," with "bright yellow bloomers like riding breeches, and short black tops trimmed in yellow." Somehow, I see the girls as big bumble bees.

Rayline became increasingly adept at dress making despite her mother's consistently discouraging predictions as she tackled ever more complicated patterns that she would botch the work and waste money on yard goods. Lalla was not averse to remodeling where possibly ruining an older garment would not be much of a loss and helped Rayline take apart a wool jersey dress in order to wash and dye the pieces another color and then reassemble them. This seems to have been a standard kind of procedure to spruce up outfits that didn't rate the cost of professional dry cleaning and dyeing. Generally, however, Lalla considered work at the sewing machine drudgery better left to the professional "dressmaker," mentioned from time to time in the diaries, who came to the house or took work home and sewed curtains and other household items as well as dresses.

Throughout her life Lalla excelled and delighted in "fancy work," exquisite hand embroidery in satin stitch to monogram table linens or embellish them with colorful, cleverly wrought needlework of all kinds. She also crocheted endless yards of fine lace for edging sheets and pillowcases. As noted, Rayline's specialty was knitting: practical socks, "wristlets," sweaters and scarves for men in military service. In 1920, her dress making moved into high gear when she acquired a dress form she named Gwendolyn and the house had been wired for electricity. On November 4 she wrote, "Mother's electric motor came & it sure is fun to sew with it." This was an electric adapter that replaced the foot powered treadle. On March 7, 1921 she wrote: "Mother and I went to Aunt Inga's luncheon which was very lovely [a bridal shower for Rayline] and when I got home there was a big surprise waiting for me. Dad had gotten an electric sewing machine, & it is portable so it will surely come in very handy." I remember that "portable" machine with its bentwood carrying case. It weighed at least 30 pounds.

Rayline mentioned the dresses as she turned them out and the occasional store-bought ones but seldom described them in any detail except for specifying materials—some still familiar, some quaint, and some strange to modern ears: velvet, jersey (both wool and silk), organdy, organza, chiffon, crepe de chine (that she consistently and doggedly misspelled "crepe de chien"), taffeta, cretonne, georgette, dimity, pongee, wash corduroy, wash satin (especially favored for lingerie), voile, serge, "messeline" (messaline, a fine silk cloth), and tricolette, perhaps a brand name for tricot, a fabric woven to resemble knitting. More puzzling is charmeuse, whether a textile or part of a garment. It is mentioned in a newspaper clipping Mary Ball enclosed in a letter to Rayline dated November

1, 1919 detailing a high society wedding in Birmingham. The six bridesmaids "were gowned in orchid pink charmeuse with silver lace trimmings, made with panniers similarly planned but developed with the individuality of the wearer." (Panniers are an overskirt draped at the sides.) "The maid of honor, Miss Mary Ball wore a handsome pink charmeuse draped over a lace skirt."

Between December 9 and 29, 1920 we get references to the creation of Rayline's masterpiece, the black velvet dress, the account in the diary dovetailing perfectly with what I had been told about it. I knew it was for a special occasion and the diary supplied the detail that it was a party her friend Gladys gave at the Calumet Club, a private club located in downtown Milwaukee just north of the still active Wisconsin Club, called the Deutscher Club prior to World War I. An addition to the central library now occupies the site of the Calumet Club. Rayline had seen the dress at Chapman's Department Store and since her mother deemed it too expensive, she decided to use the amount of money Lalla was willing to spend for a dress to buy the materials and make it herself. She mentions taking her young cousins Billy and Florence downtown several times to see the stores' Christmas toys and it might have been on these occasions that she studied the dress in detail and made the sketches she told me she had drawn in lieu of a commercial pattern to guide her work. Lalla expressed gloomy prophesies that Rayline would ruin the expensive materials—lace and silver cloth besides the velvet. But she was determined although, as she recalled years later, she sat a long time, scissors in hand trying to work up the courage to make that first cut. She began work on December 17, emboldened by Daniel's assurances: "Dad certainly is lots more encouraging than Mother. Dad said I should start in on it, & if I spoiled it, just chuck it in the rag bag & start another," implying he'd pay for new materials.

And, after the ball was over: "I think my dress was the prettiest one there & Carl couldn't tell me often enough how nice I looked & he said he was so proud of me that I had made the dress all by myself." When I was a child, she still recalled with smug satisfaction how even her girl friends couldn't believe her mother hadn't relented and let her buy the dress. I don't know what ever happened to the dress but I remember playing "dress up" as a child with an accessory she carried with it, a Christmas present from her parents that year, "the most wonderful scarlet feather fan," of dyed ostrich plumes.

The diaries are rich in wardrobe details after Rayline was engaged and she enumerates items she made or acquired for her trousseau. Some of her creations put old dress materials to new uses such as ripping up a pink silk party dress to make a fancy nightgown. She also made a pair of pajamas from scratch of purple silk. The diaries are particularly informative about a topic that is seldom mentioned in reviews of changing styles—underwear. The multiple petticoats, voluminous drawers, and figure constricting corsets of the 19th century had been replaced by the first decade of the 20th century by bloomers (ankle or knee length in a variety of textiles and colors including black silk) and camisoles and chemises or, even more liberating, "teddies"—a single garment combining chemise and short panties, with the crotch conveniently closed with snaps. Rayline received many teddies as trousseau gifts, often hand made by the givers of silk and satin with lavish embroidery and ribbon trimming. Rich but tight fisted, *THE AUNTS* gave no-nonsense, store bought muslin teddies that Rayline considered "hardly worth taking home." A familiar contemporary item is mentioned only once, on January 14, 1920, but so casually that it obviously was no longer a novelty: "Went to town to-day & bought just lots of things" including "a lace brassier[e]" along with black satin pumps, two pairs of black silk stockings, and silver ribbon to trim a dress. She bought a lot of silk stockings in the course of the diaries as well as kid gloves but doesn't mention prices until her 1921 listings where stockings (described as brown or black but not specified as silk) were $1.95 a pair. A pair of "white kid gloves" cost $.39, but a general entry of "gloves" that cost $2.65 may have meant several pairs. Shirtwaists and bloomers each cost $3.98.

Besides references to such familiar items as gloves, scarves, purses, and jewelry, Rayline makes passing mention of two accessories peculiar to the period of the diaries that we tend to associate with outmoded male attire: spats and swagger sticks. Along with being fashionable, spats could help camouflage a woman's old and worn shoes, while swagger sticks, small canes at one time associated with military officers, enjoyed a brief vogue in a somewhat ornamental form among young women during World War I.

Women of Rayline's generation did not yet wear noticeably color enhancing cosmetics but powder to take the shine off one's face was an old story. In February of 1919 she mentioned receiving the gift of a "powder rag" that Mary had made from a silk shirt, obviously a more elegant object than implied in the word rag, perhaps the forerunner of the commercially made powder puff. A few days later, she bought a box of "Djer Kiss" powder. On October 16, 1920 she went shopping and "Bought [a] fancy powder puff contraption for Jeanette" that I assume was an early form of compact. In her list of purchases in 1921 we find various beauty products—powder, talcum powder, and cold cream. Rayline was particularly concerned about her hair, washing it and putting it up on curlers herself to save the beauty parlor cost of $1.25. Besides her continuing struggle with uncompromisingly straight hair until the invention of the "permanent" wave, she also never succeeded in imparting even a suggestion of red to her nearly black hair with the addition of henna leaves to her shampoos. She doesn't mention using a curling iron herself but by late 1920 she occasionally has her hair "marcelled", a then new technique named for its inventor, at the beauty parlor where a curling iron was used to create deep, natural looking waves. A shampoo and marcel cost $2.00.

By this time, Rayline is looking forward confidently to marriage and living far from Milwaukee, but her diaries reveal that this satisfactory state of affairs had been preceded by a lot of uncertainty, speculation, and reluctance to make decisions about her future until she met my father.

5

Marking Time, Leisure Time, Time to Decide

The two major personal issues Rayline brought with her into the New Year of 1918 were her diminishing affection for Sam Lang as she was increasingly attracted to Tuve Floden (along with an undercurrent of keeping her options open beyond these two front runners) and her growing dissatisfaction with the Milwaukee Normal School.

Her very first diary entry on January 1, 1918 begins with the phrase, "Sam just left. I wonder who'll be leaving next year at this time." The reference is to his imminent departure for Fort Oglethorpe, Georgia and only reflects the uncertainty of war time but by January 9 she begins to give voice to what will be (and probably has been) a recurrent theme of uncertainty as she soliloquizes about Sam: "I do, do, do love him if the feeling I have for him is love." February 28: "Got a letter from Tuve! My how happy I am. Have read it over three times. He doesn't say anything personal but anyhow I am wild about him. I am more excited by one letter from him than six from Sam." We can only wonder what Tuve had to say because, unfortunately and inexplicably, his 1918 letters are not among those she saved. After more agonizing about Sam's and Tuve's relative merits she writes, "I wish I could understand myself...I wonder how it is all going to end." Nearly a year later, February 22, 1919, outdoing herself in misspellings, she is still agonizing that she owes Sam a letter but doesn't feel like writing and concludes that "with Sam it is a case of 'Out of sight out of mind.' But conserning Tuve, it is 'Absents makes the heart grow fonder'." Such ponderings are interspersed among factual entries about the weather, washing her hair, shopping, going to the movies or club meetings, and other everyday events throughout her diary of 1918 and much of 1919.

She finally accepts that she really doesn't want to marry Sam but keeps putting off the unpleasant task of telling him, hoping that somehow the issue will resolve itself. She may have confided in Lalla, or Lalla was shrewd enough to see what was going on, as she notes on March 11, "Mother says that I'll have to marry Sam after leading him to believe that I cared for him. Every day that passes I feel more and more as if the affair between Sam and I [was just] a girl and boy affair. I was only sixteen and he nineteen and now what is it?" Meanwhile in the course of comparing her feelings about Sam and Tuve and exchanging letters with them, she dated other fellows—Don, Murray, Hans, Ben, Gerb', Irv'—and fretted when they or whoever else was not in town didn't write or call regularly.

Miller Mureson from Portage, Wisconsin and a student at Lawrence College was something of a special case. She didn't agonize over him as she did Tuve and Sam but he was seriously and unequivocally interested in her. On February 21, 1919 she wrote: " 'Speak of the Angles [sic] you hear the flapping of their wings' as the old saying goes. Mother and I were wondering what had become of Miller & lo & behold I get a letter from him this after-noon. He is in Hayti [sic] & expects to be out of the Navy by next September." Miller respected her presumed engagement but made clear he wanted to be next in line for her to consider if she ever broke up with Sam. When she finally did, September 7, 1919, on October 3 (as noted in the back of the diary where she sums up the year) "Miller came for his 'answer' which was No!" She returned his fraternity pin on this occasion, commenting, "& thank the Lord all thots [thoughts] of marriage have left his head," but couldn't resist noting it wouldn't take much to rekindle his interest. And she was right; he was still hopeful. On October 29 she wrote, "Had a great surprise this morning. Mr. Mureson, Miller's father, called up. He said Miller had asked him to phone to me—pretty bad when the fathers start trying to persuade a girl." By then my father had entered the picture, but Miller said he'd still be around until she was definitely married to someone else.

Initially, I was just amused, if a bit surprised, by the unabashed pleasure she took in counting the men who found her attractive. It wasn't just vanity that she was pretty; she knew exactly what she was doing and enjoyed the results of working her wiles (recognizing her expressive brown eyes and petite figure were particular assets). I also was greatly amused when she more than once expresses criticism of Margaret Breed in her diaries as "boy crazy." Who was *she* to talk, I thought, until I gradually realized that there were apparently unspoken but definite rules in socializing between the sexes in the first decades of the 1900s. This was not a gradual transition between the repressive, chaperoned formality, at least as an ideal, of the long Victorian era and the rejection of customary decorum, at least by the style setters, during the so-called roaring twenties. The system had a patterned identity of its own that maximized the opportunity for meeting and getting to know people on playfully but unmistakably romantic terms while minimizing the risk of premature commitment or inconvenient entanglements. Margaret was inclined to be impulsive and probably found it hard to play the keep-'em-guessing game with Rayline's finesse.

I tend to associate it with the word "vamp," used both as a noun and a verb in Rayline's diaries and the various letters she saved. Several times she wrote in her diary that she could easily have "vamped," that is, taken over some other girl's beau if she had a mind to do so. It is an old term. Early movie sirens like Theda Bara were described as "vamps." Although derived from the word vampire its use here antedates and is quite distinct from Bela Lugosi's 1931 portrayal of Bram Stoker's Dracula or even the first spooky movie vampire, Nosferatu, produced in 1922. And it applied to both sexes. "Vamp the little lady, vamp the little lady" was the peppy chorus and all I remember of a song on a player piano roll that was already old when I was a child. I was so small that my feet didn't reach the pedals. My father pumped the piano as we belted out the lyrics printed on the paper roll. The term appears to have signified something beyond casual flirtation but far short of serious seduction: "To beguile into admiration or attentions," according Webster's Dictionary in the 1920s and 1930s. By the 1970s, when the term had just about disappeared from common slang, a new generation of dictionary editors overstate the case, in my opinion, and confine the term to females: e.g., *American Heritage*, 1973, "an unscrupulously seductive woman" and as a verb, "to seduce or exploit (a man) in the manner of a vamp."

Although certainly not a statistically valid sample, there is a sociological reality in the similarities in behavior and attitudes described in my mother's diaries written in Milwaukee and the letters she happened to keep from Mary Ball in Birmingham, Alabama, Tuve Floden in Rockford, Illinois, and my father in Canton, Ohio. Rayline's daily record makes clear that girls expected gifts from fellows—flowers, candy, trinkets including inexpensive jewelry (Rayline wore a handcrafted ring from Sam but only a diamond would qualify as signifying engagement), and fellows were expected to pick up the tab for movies and food, but no one was put under serious obligation in the enjoyment of one another's company. This included a lot of friendly letter writing just to keep in touch, even among fellows and girls who didn't actually date. The diaries contain references to having received many, many more letters from many more different people than the chance selection I inherited, sometimes with second hand greetings from a correspondent's other correspondents.

Rayline's major complaint about Sam was that he was too possessive with his plan to have exclusive claim on her for four to five years while he attended medical school before they married. She was not happy with his intention to attend Marquette University in Milwaukee where he could keep an eye on her. As she remarked on May 5, 1919: "if he does come here to school I'm going to let him know right from the start that I'm going out with whom ever I please. And another thing, he won't have much time or money either in fact to take me out a great deal."

Part of Tuve's appeal was that while he wrote entertaining newsy, letters with humorous flirtation and was obviously interested enough to write, she didn't really know if he "gave a snap" for her—her frequent phrase meaning really interested. Tuve knew how to play the game too, mentioning other girls he was going out with. Rayline characterized Sam's letters as seriously romantic but dull and while she burned all of them after she finally broke up with him, the one example quoted in full in her diary, January 14, 1918, seems to justify her description. He returned all her letters to him for safekeeping when he thought he was about to be sent overseas: "My darling: -- I loan these precious letters to you until the end of the war at which time I shall claim them again along with the one who sent and wrote them. If I do not come back burn them and forget. I love you-your Sam." As it turned out, Sam's departure was delayed until August 13.

All the fellows were gallant to all the girls and the girls appreciated and responded to gallantry, even Jeanette, who was part of Rayline's boy-girl crowd, but whose "affliction," as Rayline remarks sadly from time to time, made it a foregone conclusion that she would never marry. Also illustrative of the kind of general gallantry is a little gold scarf pin I found among my mother's jewelry, a plain bar about 2 inches long and less than a quarter inch wide with "Rayline" engraved in gothic letters on the front and *"From The Three Trusty Guards"* on the back. Two of them are identified on June 30, 1918 when she and Sam took the 6:30 P.M. interurban trolley from Mukwonago to Milwaukee and went to her home on Layton Boulevard where Hans Jennings also appeared and they all went downtown. Rayline wrote, in reference to the fact that so many men were in the military, "I felt so conspicuous and selfish with two men when most girls haven't any. Well, I've sure roamed around a lot without anyone too, so I guess I was entitled to both." After dinner at Toy's and rushing to the depot so Sam could catch his train—destination unspecified except that he was returning to an army base, she adds, [Those] "two Trusty Guards sure are nice to me. It would have been nice to have the other." I wish I knew who the third one was. She must have received the pin before she began her diaries and before Sam became so proprietary about her or perhaps he just didn't consider Hans and the other "guard" serious competition.

Tuve returned to the United States early in 1919 while Sam was still overseas where he would remain until nearly the end of July. Tuve's letter postmarked Rockford, February 19, 1919 referred to his recent two day visit to Milwaukee to see both Rayline and his friend and former University of Wisconsin roommate, Bill Tierman, who was teaching at South Division High School.

> Dear Genevieve:
>
> It almost broke my heart to tear myself away from you after our short honeymoon—but we'll both have to be brave and wait until I can think of some excuse for visiting my Milwaukee wife. (It's hard to be a polygamist).
>
> After receiving directions from every member of your family, including your mother's brother, I easily found the Polish Church and later the South Division High School. Bill was just going to leave the building and had I prolonged my stay at 874 [Layton Blvd.] I should have missed him. We dissipated terribly before I departed, eating ice cream at the Arcade and then sitting around the Schlitz Palm garden seeing the sights and sipping some port.

After discussing his train ride to Beloit, part way by chance with Daddy Wones of the Phantom Lake YMCA whose offer of a camp leader position the following summer he turned down, he caught an interurban trolley home to Rockford. As the letter unfolds, it becomes clear why Rayline doesn't know where she stands with him. He has made good on his pre-war plan to leave teaching, has a new job, and has re-entered the Rockford dating scene:

> Saturday morning I completed arrangements with my new employers and they are going to pay me enough so that I can afford several 3c stamps, and even risk going out with young ladies who must have flowers. Saturday afternoon I made up for some of [the] sleep I should have had while I was touring Milwaukee in a street car at 2 A.M. And at night [back in Rockford] I was dining and indulging in a card party.

He goes on to describe various family and friends' dinner invitations "to entertain the returned hero," and having been asked to give an address to the "Girls Patriotic League" about his

Downtown Milwaukee, early 1920s.

experiences overseas that went well despite his clearly facetious claim to nervousness. Sunday evening he took his mother to church, adding "(Honest, cross my heart)" making clear that church going was as unusual for him as for Rayline. Monday he began his new job with a special lunch to celebrate the 36th anniversary of the company (that he never names), some employees' birthdays and his joining "'the bunch' as it is called." He described his work as "interesting for my job is to learn cotton, the manufacture of hosiery, the managing of the concern, bookkeeping, etc."

Then he returns to his social life with a curious reference that Rayline must have understood: "I got only one valentine this year and that was from the girl friend you helped me buy the flowers for. She is a very nice and thoughtful little girl. And she always takes such pains and uses such good taste in selecting appropriate cards. It's a gift, I suppose." His last bit of information is typically Tuve:

> One of my former pupils, a bashful Swedish girl as I remember her, called me up last night and asked me to go to a dance Saturday. So I am going to take my first fling at indoor sports next Sat. p.m. Her father must sell dancing pumps [slippers] and he is using this means to get me out where I can damage enough of them so that it will pay him, in the trade he gets to allow his daughter to run the risk of dancing with me.

He closes with, "Remember me to the family and Gladys. As ever just '2V,'" adding a new address in Rockford at the bottom of the page, suggesting he has moved from the family home but without saying whether to an apartment or rooming house.

Rayline's diary account of the visit, February 13 and 14 reveals that she is now uncertain about her feelings for him but more than hints at the reason. She was taken by the romantic image of the returning soldier. "Well, Tuve was here to-day- & now that I've seen him I'm not so wild about him." He was still the tall, handsome Tuve, taking her to the movies downtown, dinner at Toy's, then to another first run movie, and finally Tillema's where they probably went to dance. They talked for a while after he brought her home. But she was disappointed because he wasn't in uniform. As discussed in connection with Tuve's and Sam's war time experiences, Tuve wanted to put the war behind him while Sam took advantage of his stay in Europe, traveling whenever he could and collecting post-cards. Sam was as agreeable to wearing his uniform for Rayline to show him off at social affairs as was my father. Rayline does not seem to appreciate that Tuve experienced combat, was wounded, and lost a boyhood friend to a horrible death in the trenches while Sam got to Europe when the war was about over and Carl never went overseas.

The following day, however, she has second thoughts. "Now that I've seen Tuve again I guess Sam had better hurry back if he wants to find me his sweet-heart for I'm quickly losing my heart to Tuve." He picked her up at 9:30 A.M. and they went to the Normal School. "I have never have seen anyone as surprised as Mr. Wensthoff when he saw Tuve," she says in reference to her history teacher. While he was always proper in dealing with her, she knew the teacher found her attractive and she couldn't resist flirting just a little bit. When she told her school friends that she wasn't going to finish the semester, they were all sure she was engaged, but she suspects it is unlikely anything serious will develop with Tuve:

> Had lunch at the Badger Room. He bought me the most gorgeous corsage of French violets that I have ever seen. Poor kid had to pay $3.50 for them. Tuve is so different from the time at [the YMCA] camp. I would like to know what he thinks of me. He sure was darling to me to-day-I wonder what Mr. W. thinks. Well, forget all about Tuve, Rayline, for most likely you'll never here [sic] from him again.

But she did, and meanwhile continued comparing her feelings for him with Sam.

Tuve's next letter, March 4, 1919, follows up on the dance invitation:

> I had a rather 'punk' time at the dance with my former pupil. Imagine my surprise when I rang the doorbell at the address furnished, and the door was opened by the wrong girl, not the one I had pictured at all. She was just as nice as the other but it nearly knocked me over. The floor was rough and the orchestra couldn't play 'Home Sweet Home' so that we could recognize it.

Tuve reported that his speech to the Girls Patriotic League went so well that he was booked as the main attraction at the next Sunday night service at his church. "Imagine me in a pulpit talking to a bunch of dyed-in-the-wool Methodists." He refers to a letter from Rayline where she said his recent visit to Milwaukee was too short and explains his idea was that if he didn't stay around too long he'd be invited back, adding, "And then it's expensive to chase around with a young lady who insists on having flowers right in the middle of winter. (Honest, I'm only kidding.)" He details his rigorous Friday and Saturday social schedule—a dance, basketball game, and a Mardi Gras celebration. "I enjoyed every bit of it but had to sleep until 1:30 p.m. Sunday to even get started on catching up on my sleep." His letter reveals the nature of Rayline's letters: "I know how busy you are visiting 'Glad', writing to Mary Ball, visiting movies with Grandpa, and attending club meetings but I am forced to ask you to please spend a few leisure moments in keeping me informed as to your health and behavior." He closes grandly: Yours pedagogicly [sic] Tuve John Floden."

The final letter in the collection of 22 letters from Tuve, April 1, 1919, is post-marked Peoria and written on stationery of the city's Hotel Jefferson. Tuve explains his long silence is because he has been almost continuously on the road, evidently on sales trips, most of the time with his boss—to Minnesota and Chicago and back to Rockford; after his present trip alone to Peoria they will go west together. He doesn't have time to write when he is with his boss who likes to go to movies and shows after working hours, noting that when they were in Chicago they saw, "Business Before Pleasure"…"and I nearly laughed myself sick at those two Jews, Potash and Perlmutter." He engages in a few pleasantries recalling time spent at Phantom Lake and adds:

> You know girls are the same the world over. Our minister has some daughters, and I was being nice to one of them and took her home from church one evening and she told me her birthday was on the fifteenth of April and that she likes violets with a rose in the center. So you see it's getting to be a universal custom.

He ends the letter, "If you write when you get this, I'll just get a nice letter when I'm home between trips this time."

Rayline's reaction when she receives the letter, April 2, 1919, shows she is still intrigued with Tuve, but playing it cool, by the rules: "There is happiness in my young life again. Heard from Tuve. He has been galivanting [sic] over the countryside for the firm & very casually informs me that if I write to him immediately he would get a letter between trips. Now if I should write he'll think I'm chasing after him."

This is the last letter from Tuve that she saved and apparently took her time answering, if she ever got around to it at all. She soon had other concerns but, meanwhile, to further examine the matter of courting patterns, passing remarks in Rayline's diaries indicate that Glad operated much as she did with special interest for a while in "Smith," sometimes identified as "Lt. Smith," while also dating "Roy" and "Bill" and apparently others who remain nameless. As Rayline tussled with her feelings about Sam and Tuve, she repeatedly expressed a certain wistfulness about her friend Mary who entertained no doubts that she was in love with "Tuck'" to whom she was engaged. Tuck, short for his surname Tucker (his first name is never mentioned nor whether he was originally from Birmingham or Milwaukee) was more than ten years older than Mary and had some kind of job that kept him away for long periods, including an overseas assignment in Paris. Mary's letters, however, indicate that despite her certainty about Tuck, she was in no hurry to get married and had at least three other fellows regularly taking her to movies, dances, and dinner and, like Rayline, admittedly indulged in a little "vamping." She obviously also knew how to play the game. An opinion she shared with Rayline about a mutual friend who had sent a Christmas card to a fellow who had shown no interest in her whatsoever is reminiscent of Rayline's characterization of Margaret Breed: "Poor Babe, she certainly is a nut on some subjects. Mostly long pants." Mary's letters reinforce Rayline's diary entries about boy friends as illustrative of a larger, patterned context rather than simply personal flirtatiousness.

In her letter of March 21, 1920, Mary enclosed a clipping of a syndicated newspaper column by Helen Roland, "As A Woman Thinketh," posing the question, "When is a woman most interesting to men?" and supplying answers that pretty well covered what I was gleaning from the diaries, such as:

> When she isn't trying to be interesting.... When she is sufficiently experienced not to be easily shocked—and sufficiently innocent not to be easily kissed...When she is sufficiently spirituelle to appeal to his higher nature—and sufficiently human to appeal to the other ninety-eight per cent of him...When she likes him well enough to be glad when he calls—and not well enough to be miserable when he goes...When she has too much sagacity to pursue him—and just enough audacity to sit back and make him pursue her.

The column, obviously recent though undated and unidentified as to source, must have struck a resonant chord with both girls.

The issue of whether to complete her course of study at the Normal School was complicated by the fact that new opportunities for employment outside the home were now becoming commonplace, if not exactly taken for granted, for girls like Rayline, although getting married remained the inevitable goal. Her comments, quoted in an earlier chapter, about the cost of her schooling being a strain on family finances more than suggest that it was her idea to seek higher education after graduation from Downer Seminary in 1917 and, though soon disappointed with her decision, she felt she had to stick it out. Attending the Seminary, particularly since it was connected to a women's college, probably imparted expectations to seek higher education that she might not have entertained had she gone to a public high school. In her circle of Downer friends it was becoming customary but not obligatory for girls to go to college, perhaps to prepare for a career but more importantly to meet men with the best social and financial prospects as husbands. Going to college for an MRS. degree was probably already an old joke. Her friend Mary who was formally engaged did not go to college as far as I'm aware. I'm sure that Downer College, even if Rayline's parents could have afforded it, held no charms after Downer Seminary as simply more of the same and an all-girls school, at that. At least the Normal School was co-ed, but it wasn't much fun or glamorous like the university at Madison that her neighborhood friend Ada Kroening was attending and Glad, still at the Seminary during 1918, was planning to attend.

Rayline had put in one semester at the Normal School by the time she began her first diary in 1918. On January 2, when classes resumed after the Christmas break, she stayed home because of a snowstorm, but managed to get to Glad's house later for her initiation into Gamma Phi Kappa, a local sorority. On January 3 she wrote: "Went to school today and hate it more than ever," a sentiment to be repeated about as frequently as her indecision about Sam and Tuve. Part of the problem was that she cut so many classes, lab' sessions, and exams that she had to struggle constantly to make up her missed work in a full schedule that included English, History, Chemistry, Art and Design, and the "S & P of Food." I believe the last two were part of the new Home Economics program that she had chosen over the usual teacher preparation curriculum and that S. & P. stood for Selection and Preparation. There is obvious satisfaction, despite the complaining tone, in her entry of June 11: "Worked all morning on calorie balance sheets in the S.& P. of F. Some job! I was the only one in class who knew what Miss Johnson was talking about." She suffered mental agony over quizzes and exams in all her courses as "fierce," even "fiendish," but got good grades—at least those reported in the diaries were in the high 80s and 90s after she had expressed worry about flunking. She got similar grades on the class assignments in the miscellaneous papers at the bottom of the shopping bag holding the packets of letters.

Many of Rayline's absences in 1918 could be chalked up to bad weather in an exceptionally cold and snowy winter. However, since grade school her parents had allowed absences on flimsy grounds of weather and sniffles and, as noted in her "Auto-Biography," her parents loved to travel and took her out of school to go with them on extended trips. Thus, she was constantly under pressure and anxious to stay abreast of schoolwork; failure was unthinkable. She had no choice but to attend school regularly when she was a boarding student during her first two years at Downer Seminary and apparently enjoyed Downer enough to attend faithfully even as a commuter student during her last two years. But she slipped into skipping classes at the Normal School although it made keeping up with her studies more burdensome. Entries like those for January 24 and 25 show up at regular intervals: "Have my Eng. work all up to date..." and "Only four more history notes to get in and one quiz to make up," for the beguiled Mr. Wensthoff.

As the flu epidemic worsened, she commented on October 15,

139

"Went to school and I think it is mean that Normal has to be open when all other schools are closed. Everyone has to have his temp. taken every day." She went to school the next day but her parents expressed worry that she might contract the flu traveling on the crowded street cars which was all the excuse she needed to stay home for more than a week—and then face more make-up work! (Thanks to Rayline's resolve that I learn from her mistakes, I earned a lot of gold paper stars for semesters of perfect attendance during my grade school years and was so conditioned that I never cut classes, right through grad' school.)

Besides frequent expressions about hating school, another recurrent and related theme was that she would wind up an "Old Maid School Teacher." It is usually mentioned somewhat tongue in cheek, but so frequently and sometimes so seriously that it takes on the function of a code term, whether or not Rayline was aware of it, for young middle class women's changing social and economic options. Even Mary jokingly expresses fear of becoming an "Old Maid School Teacher" in one of her letters. Traditionally, teaching had been about the only occupation open to women like Rayline, but as a matter of custom, and even law in some places, married women were not hired as school teachers. Teachers were women who worked because they had to, and they had to work because they were not married. It would be bad enough, or maybe not bad at all, just being an old maid if family finances provided the means to live comfortably, but it still implied no man, at least no suitable man, found you attractive enough to propose. Almost by definition, a career as a school teacher, rather than just filling in a few years before marriage, was tantamount to spinsterhood.

While Rayline was going to a teacher training institution, she had no desire to be a teacher. She apparently saw majoring in Home Economics as an acceptable alternative, not only enhancing her role as homemaker once she was married, but possibly, in a pinch, as preparation for employment as an interior decorator, a new field that was opening up to women. Although it is mentioned only once and that was in Mary Ball's letter of March 3, 1920 regarding a Downer friend who was planning to take a course in interior decorating in Chicago, Rayline had a real interest in the field and natural talent. She attributed her related interest in architecture and impressive technical knowledge to having helped her father with his estimating and other office work in his contracting business and often going with him to inspect jobs he was working on.

On September 17, 1918, however, when she and Margaret Breed registered for the new school year she noted in her diary, "I'm the only one who is going to take second year Home Ec. And so they are not offering any course! Darn my luck. So out of desperation I've decided to take the Primary Course. Here's where I'll be an old maid school teacher sure."

On January 7, 1919 she comments about returning to school after the Christmas recess: "Oh how I hate that place & the thought of teaching." Margaret Breed had quit school at the end of the fall semester of 1918 and Rayline decided to quit during the second semester but waited until June of 1919 to clean out her locker and officially terminate her student status. Meanwhile, she began thinking about other options. She had stayed in touch with another friend who had left the Normal School early in 1917. On January 13, 1919 she wrote, "Esther Lindquist called up this eve & I'm thinking quite serious[ly] of going to Business College with her. I think I'd rather do that than go to Normal. But still that would mean no loafing Saturdays and vacations. Oh well, you can't have your cake and eat it too." As much as Rayline claimed to hate the thought of being a schoolteacher, she was fully aware of its advantages over office employment. At that time the workweek was 5-1/2 to 6 days long with only a week or two of vacation all year.

She never followed up on the idea of business college. "I would like to get a job," she wrote on January 23, 1919, "but I must admit either I'm too timid or I haven't any push in me to go out & find one." She contemplated writing a family friend to ask if there were any openings where she worked at the local Red Cross office, but evidently never got around to it. On March 23,

1919 her cousin Jeanette helped her check the "want adds" to find employment. Jeanette spent her entire working life in the office of a large manufacturing firm but I don't know if she attended a business college or learned on the job after graduating from high school. In light of Rayline's early comment about her attending school as a drain on family funds, I assumed, from the perspective of my generation when girls expected to work after completing their education, that she felt some pressure from her parents to bring in money. But it becomes clear that while they might have considered her advanced schooling an unnecessary expense during hard times, they never expected her to go to work to earn her own keep, let alone contribute to the family's finances.

Her diary entry for March 26 indicates she was simply bored for something to do and interested in the possibility of earning extra money for luxuries, but even that was beyond Lalla's comprehension. "Goodness, I'm getting tired of staying around home. Every job I see in the paper mother has something to say about [it]. Glad called up and she is getting such good looking new clothes & things with the money she earns." Glad had graduated from Downer Seminary in June of 1918 but waited a year before enrolling at the University at Madison. Her father, Reinhardt Boerner, was a well to do physician so I don't know why she got a job except to fill the time and indulge herself and, perhaps, like Rayline, she wanted a sense of her "own" money no matter how generous her parents might have been meting out "spending money." In any event, it appears that Glad didn't keep her job very long.

As new opportunities were opening up for women to earn their own money, Rayline's diaries reveal that even women in her mother's circumstances at the time had much more control over the family purse strings than is commonly assumed. A woman like Lalla expected that her husband would be the provider of financial support but, if she thought about it at all, she would have seen her use of it as entitlement rather than dependency. Part of her responsibility in running a household was the prudent management of money. During the period of financial difficulties when Rayline began her first diary, it is obvious that Lalla was fully informed about Daniel's total economic situation as a mutual concern. Certainly, she spent money without his oversight because she had been able to buy the Phantom Lake property as a surprise for him. Rayline looked forward to marriage in her diaries as being in charge of her own household (in contrast to disagreements about her mother's methods), not as exchanging dependence on a father for dependence on a husband.

When Margaret quit school, she was contemplating eloping with her steady beau Dave (Rayline never mentions his surname, but always disparages him as "a kid") and going on the stage with him, evidently as a dance team. Rayline considered this "nutty" because she thought Margaret was not sufficiently "dainty" for such a career. By early April of 1919 we learn that Margaret is working at the Racine Library and earning $30.00 a month. Apparently she was still living at home and dependent on her parents as this was hardly a living wage even in 1919. Eventually, she became a professional children's librarian in Raleigh, North Carolina where she met and married a local man and sent me wonderful books when I was a child.

Rayline mentions visiting with her cousin Antoinette and seeing her regularly at family gatherings and parties, but I had to check with Antoinette's son Robin to help verify my recollections of what I had heard about his mother's life at this time. She too had gone to the Normal School and would have been teaching grade school. Teacher certification for the primary grades only required two years and since she was two years older than Rayline, they did not attend Normal School together. Antoinette had three siblings and had to work if she wanted more than bare essentials before marriage.

Although Rayline complained about being bored after leaving school, her days from the spring of 1918 to the spring of 1919 were filled with shopping—usually with her mother, dating, attending club meetings that were held one or two evenings a month at members' homes to chat and play cards, helping her mother with house work and her father with office work, going to the movies, and continuing to agonize about Sam and Tuve.

Despite the financial uncertainties of the contracting business, my maternal grandparents appear to have been typical of the comfortable middle class in the first decades of the 1900s with leisure time and disposable income. Rayline's diaries indicate they spent significant amounts of both, particularly my grandfather, on what sociologists call voluntary associations, primarily Daniel's involvement with Freemasonry. Although such groups are still active, this was the heyday of national and international fraternal organizations offering inspirational and recreational activities, fellowship and (understood, if not crassly mentioned) a potential source of contacts to help men further their careers and improve their economic prospects. Masonry, the oldest, largest and, at least in the eyes of its members, the most prestigious, was the model for fraternal groups that proliferated in the late 19th and early 20th centuries such as Knights of Pythias, Benevolent and Protective Order of Elks, Fraternal Order of Eagles and others, including the Knights of Columbus, the Roman Catholic answer to Masonry, founded in 1881.

While not avowedly anti-Catholic, Masonry traditionally is considered no friend of Rome insofar as several Popes since the early 18th century have issued encyclicals denouncing it as atheistic and heretical. This seems to have been totally irrelevant to my grandfather but the antipathy to Catholicism figured in my father's Masonic affiliation, as will be discussed later. Daniel was a 32nd Degree Mason meaning that besides his basic membership of three degrees as a Master Mason he was active in many of Masonry's component groups, each with its own rituals, degrees, regalia, and purposes—the York Rite and Scottish Rite, and sub-groups of Knights Templar, Shriners, and so on. He and Lalla also belonged to the Order of the Eastern Star, a group associated with Masonry open to men and women, but do not appear to have been very active in it.

National women's organizations, developed in the 19th

Jennie Schuette (Mrs. Charles) Kuehn and Hattie Schuette (Mrs. Sherman) Spurr, *THE AUNTS*, ca. 1910.

century to promote social reforms such as temperance and women's rights such as suffrage, did not begin to attract the number of women that drew men to fraternal organizations and are not even mentioned in the diaries and letters. Women's small card clubs, however, were ubiquitous and mention of Lalla's club meetings show up about as often as references to Daniel's "Masonic doings." I know from some of the names of women who happened to be mentioned in the diaries—Mrs. Tegtmeyer, Mrs. Graper, Mrs. Nicolai, and Mrs. Fick—that one of these clubs was the *Kränzchen*, a generic German term for such groups, meaning a "little circle" or wreath comprising eight to ten members. I don't know if there were any Catholic members but I do know they belonged to different Protestant denominations and Mrs. Fick was Jewish. Lalla's other club, the Mission Band, also was still in existence when I was a child. It originated among women of Norwegian ancestry and, given its title, probably was formed by Lutheran ladies for more lofty purposes than playing cards. My grandmother might

Father Louis Peschong, ca. 1921.

have been invited to join by one of her sisters-in-law, Inga or Lou; certainly not by her mother-in-law who disapproved of card playing. Lutheranism, the official denomination of Norway, was not strict enough for her and she became a devout Methodist.

In Lalla's later years, her clubs met for lunch at restaurants where they could reserve space to play cards rather than meet at each other's homes and be bothered with preparing food. These clubs just ceased meeting as the members became incapacitated or died, and other clubs sprang up. Bridge gradually took precedence over the games of poker, hearts, 500, rummy, and bunco mentioned in Rayline's diaries. Rayline did not join her mother's clubs; she had her own club made up of Downer Seminary alumni. Although Gladys dropped out when she went to Madison, Mary, Margaret, Irma, Thyra, Helen, Grace, and others along with various non-Downer friends who joined over the years continued meeting until the women were well into their eighties. Rayline outlived them all.

She had been introduced to cards at a very early age when she was given a "stake" to join in poker games around the family table. She could keep her winnings but if she lost, she had to accept bad luck or bad judgment like the grown ups and be a good loser. Even Pa, known as a formidable player of all kinds of card games, insisted on this rule although he spoiled and indulged her otherwise.

Skat, a variation on the quintessential Milwaukee German game of Schafskopf or Sheepshead, was very popular during the period covered in Rayline's diaries. She mentions her father, his uncle by marriage Sherman Spurr (husband of Hattie, one of *THE AUNTS*) and his close friend, Father Louis Peschong, playing skat at our house, a custom that continued through my early childhood years. Father Peschong also was a frequent dinner guest at Layton Boulevard as well as a visitor at Phantom Lake. He, in turn, entertained Lalla, Daniel, and Rayline at his cottage on Wind Lake a few miles from Milwaukee where he and Daniel enjoyed fishing. My grandfather was apparently as comfortable in Catholic territory as Father Peschong was fraternizing with a prominent Mason and his family. Rayline's diaries indicate that the friendship was unusual and Rayline, herself, had picked up some taint of anti-Catholicism.

The two men met when Daniel landed a major building contract at St. Francis Seminary in Bay View on Milwaukee's far south side where Father Peschong was the chief administrator. They hit it off immediately in their approach to business and discovered they also shared common interests in fishing, the outdoors, skat, and entrepreneurial ventures. About 1908, Daniel and Father Peschong bought a large tract of standing timber and a sawmill near Minocqua, Wisconsin, but before they could become lumber barons a forest fire swept through and wiped out their investment.

Rayline noted in her diary of September 27, 1919 that it was Father Peschong's 61st birthday, so he was about 15 years older than Daniel. He evidently could relax and enjoy a sense of family life in the Danielson household in a way that was precluded among lay Catholics. On February 4, 1919 Rayline wrote in her diary, "Father Peschong was here for dinner this evening & he did the queerest thing. I was sitting on the davenport & he reached around me & kissed me, but in much the same way one would kiss a little child. I suppose some people would get all excited about such actions. It seems perfectly natural to have him around. I feel more at ease with him than I do with any minister that I have ever known." But he was so frequently in her parents' company that Rayline wondered if he was trying to convert them and on March 2, 1919 she thought it a bit excessive that they went with "Father Louis" to "some kind of a card party at a Catholic church."

He is sometimes referred to as "Father Louis" in the diaries to distinguish him from his brother, also a priest, "Father Johnny," whom I never met. According to what Rayline told me, Father Johnny was as stuffy and doctrinaire as Father Louis was "open minded." She also told me they came from Belgium. There are passing references to both Father Louis and Father Johnny visiting but the only other extended mention occurs on February 8, 1920: "Daddy & Father Peschong went to a Skat Tournament at the Auditorium to-day. Father Louis didn't wear his Roman collar either. He'd make a stunning looking man in a regular nifty suit." Daniel, of course, always wore nifty suits.

Father Louis retired from the seminary to take on the less demanding job of parish priest at St. Augustine's Church on the south side. I called the church for further information where Father Kiliszewski was most helpful. Father Peschong's official title as administrator of the seminary was Procurator, he moved to the St. Augustine post in 1920, and he had indeed come from Belgium— Belgium, Wisconsin, where he was born! His parents were from Luxembourg, the original Belgium's tiny neighbor, and émigrés from both countries had continued to live in close proximity to one another. Another cautionary case where oral tradition can be correct but you have to get it right.

Rayline frequently stayed overnight with her friend Glad after their club meetings. The Boerners lived on Fond du Lac Avenue in the then upscale, more northwesterly part of the predominantly German area immediately north of downtown. My father also was a north sider and although of more modest means had somehow become almost part of the Boerner family since the time he and Glad were quite young. Both were only children and Glad looked up to him as a kind of big brother. In his letters he refers to her as "Sis" and even as his sister. Although Rayline's first mention of Carl does not occur until August 19, 1918, the wording indicates Glad must have spoken about him on earlier, unrecorded occasions: "Glad's Carl came [home] to-day & she is all thrills, of course." Then nearly a year elapses before we hear about Carl again.

About the time Carl was discharged from the army at Camp (later Fort) Dodge in the early spring of 1919, he contacted Glad to find a girl for him to go out with during the month or so he expected to be in Milwaukee before leaving for a new job. According to his own admission, it was only on a sudden whim that he had specified "a black eyed girl" and Glad immediately thought of Rayline. Rayline, however, was hesitant for while she dated other fellows, her regulars of long standing, she still felt a certain obligation to Sam about taking on any new beaux he didn't know. Rayline once told me that Glad had assured her Carl would show her a good time but was not interested in serious commitments and she'd never hear from again after he left Milwaukee. She did such a good job of promoting Carl, however, that Rayline became a bit insecure, or perhaps challenged. On April 12, 1919 "Glad called up to say that Carl will be home next Sunday. Goodness I hope I get some new clothes by then so I can make a hit for he leaves for China the end of May." I was astounded. "China?" I asked myself. I knew Carl never went to China, and then realized that Rayline had jumped to an exotic conclusion, perhaps on the basis of Glad's touting Carl's talents. He actually was going to Canton, Ohio. Rayline never bothered to correct this initial entry in her diary.

He was about to take a position with The Berger Manufacturing

Co. that made sheet metal products. Headquartered in Ohio, Berger had or was developing branches in Boston, Toledo, Philadelphia, Chicago, St. Louis, Kansas City, Los Angeles, and Dallas. Carl was on his way to Canton in 1919 to meet with the Berger people and decide whether to stay there or go to one of their other plants.

April 14, Rayline spent the night with Glad and wrote, "I sure must get some clothes for Carl is coming home Sunday & Glad wants me to go out with him & Smith and her." The next day she wrote that if Carl liked her when they would finally meet "and Glad gets a bid for the Shriners May Ball [the big social event of the season], Mrs. Boerner is going to have Carl take me but I'm not going to think about [it] for if I plan I surely won't go." Carl's visit to Milwaukee was delayed and by this time Rayline is really eager to meet him, but on May 4 she wrote:

> I sure have the darndest luck in 17 states. Carl came home yesterday & he & Glad came out this afternoon to see me [and] of course I wasn't home. Glad made a date for Wednesday & of course I'm going to that fool dance with Hans [Jennings] & mother won't let me break the date. So now we're up a tree for I sure do want to meet Carl before the Ball Saturday. Oh yes, I forgot Carl is going to take me to the Shrine Ball. That is a little brightness in the darkness.

Amazingly, still tucked away at this page of the diary was the little calling card engraved with the name "Miss Gladys Marie Boerner" that had been left at Rayline's door. A penciled message on the back says, "I brought the ruff neck out but you weren't home. Coming out Wednesday night. Glad." Beneath that was a penciled Star of David with pseudo Hebrew writing and the words, "That means you're invited for the Shrine Dance, Carl." I wonder what Rayline made of the Jewish connection that she would discover played a special part in Carl's life.

On May 6, Rayline compliments herself for getting out of her date with Hans:

> Hans called up & I really out [ought] to hold a political post for the diplomatic way I got out of going to that dance. Then Glad called up & Carl has gotten tickets for 'Business Before Pleasure' & I'm so glad now that I cut that date with Hans for I'd heaps rather see 'B.B.P.' than go to that 'junkie' dance.

And, on May 7, she writes:

> 12: o'clock! have just gotten home from the theater & I've met the wonder Carl. He sure is a big peach, a prince of a lad & heaps of fun. Glad sure made a good 'Chap.' [chaperone] & I know I had a heaps better time with Carl & Glad than I would have had with Hans at that 'prize fighters' dance.

May 8, the story continues; Rayline anticipates Carl's attentions but is still concerned with all her options.

> Jane [AKA Jennie] Walters was here all day & Aunt Alice all after-noon working on my evening dress [making over a prom' dress]. It is real good looking but I don't like the skirt for some reason or other. I wonder what Carl thinks of me. I hope he sends me flowers to wear Saturday night.
>
> Hans called up and he was real good natured too—And he asked me to keep Sunday night open for him so he can't be peeved.
>
> Sam sent me some kind of booklet. Wonder if I'm ever going to hear from my friends Tuve and Ben.

By May 9th, I think I am already at least a glimmer in my father's eye as Rayline wrote:

> Carl called up at noon & asked me if I wanted to go to the Base Ball Game. And of course I went. He is fresh but so darn cute about it that I couldn't put him in his place. Then we went to Charlie Toy's for supper & then to the Butterfly & home. He stayed until twelve talking & I guess we are going to hit it off very good.
>
> Bill Miller [Mueller, one of Glad's beaux and Carl's friend], the cat [cad?], told Carl that I was engaged. Now where the deuce did he get that from?
>
> Carl sure is a funny duck & a lot of fun too.

And, finally, May 10:

> Well, to-night was the big night, the 'Shrine May Ball.' Carl and I danced a straight program. Of course I blamed it on to him, but I must admit I was not peeved with the idea. [It was customary at formal balls for girls to be given small printed programs for prospective partners to sign up for numbered dances, the names of many different fellows were evidence of a girl's popularity—Carl hogged her program]. He is a splendid dancer but used the 'strangle hold' on me. Glad was inclined to be peeved I guess because I wore Carl's 'fez' & to tell the truth I was the only 'female' on the floor with a fez on. Went to Charlie Toy's after & who should be there but Hans and the Mitchell bunch [unidentifiable].
>
> Can't say I'm wild about 'Smith' nor do I like the man that Helen [Klann] was with. Carl and I sure did have a good time to-gether but I'm going to have to put him in his place even tho I don't want to.

Rayline stayed overnight at Glad's house and the two girls talked until 4:00 Sunday morning, "hashing over" the ball. Rayline admits to her diary how smitten she is but doubts Carl is serious about her although he picked her up that afternoon and they went to the movies at the Butterfly and the Princess and then took a long walk along Lake Michigan.

Back home on Monday, May 12, Rayline admits, "I guess there is no doubt about it, but I am a born flirt & very fickel [sic] maiden. That darling Carl didn't call up to-day but I hope he does real, real soon." She got a letter that day from Sam with the news he expected to be home by mid-June and commented: "Well, I'm not going to worry about my affairs until the time comes. No need in crossing the bridge until I get there."

Nor did she see or hear from Carl on May 13 but filled the page discussing him. On the morning of May 14 she got a post card from him from Racine where he probably had gone to visit his Aunt Mary Ruemler and her family. Rayline recorded in her diary that the card "was headed, 'G.B.B.E.H.B.B.D.' meaning, 'Great big brown eyed heart breaking baby doll'." She received a second card on May 28 from Lake Mills where he had gone a few days earlier to visit friends and relatives. The cards eventually turned up in the bunch of miscellaneous papers discussed in Chapter One, but she began keeping his correspondence systematically in packets with the first letter he wrote, post-marked Madison, June 1, 1919.

Apart from the brief trip to Racine and the period of May 27-June 8 when he was at Lake Mills and also spent some time with friends at the university in Madison, Carl managed to see Rayline just about every day from their first date until his departure for Canton on July 5. They took in many movies, went on many long walks (on one of which the stone was lost from the ring Sam had given her and she wondered if it were an omen), and fell deeply in love in spite of Glad's characterization of Carl as fancy free and Rayline's commitment to Sam. Where Rayline had agonized between Sam and Tuve, her diaries are now filled with her attraction to Carl and what to do about Sam, and whether she would marry Carl or Sam or neither of them. On June 14 she took stock of the situation:

> It really is strange how much better I feel after telling Carl about Sam. I don't feel half so guilty & hypocritical. I don't know what it is I see in Carl. For he isn't especially good looking. He hasn't money or family. And the queer part is he is short & I've always 'fallen' for the 'Tall ones.' Also he isn't attentive & thoughtful the way Sam is and not the tiniest bit romantic or sentimental. And he does say and tell some of the most shocking stories.

Carl suggested she see how she felt when Sam returned and gave her until Christmas time to make her decision when he would be home again for a few days. He was quite agreeable to her continuing to go out casually with other fellows—movies, restaurants, dancing; he just didn't want to be "second fiddle" to Sam. And as Rayline had finally told Carl about Sam on this occasion, he told her about all his past "love affairs," but she doesn't provide any details.

Meanwhile, Carl won over and got to know Rayline's family. I don't think it was calculated although he was aware that he made friends easily. He was one of those people who fit in quickly, wherever they are. He was asked to stay to dinner, went with Rayline when she called on Jeanette, visited at Phantom Lake— even going to the Y Camp, attended a Shrine event with Daniel, and joined in family gatherings like helping with the entertainment at a kids' party THE AUNTS hosted where he wore his uniform as on other occasions to please Rayline. The war was still on people's minds; Rayline noted Red Arrow Day on June 6 was celebrated with parades to welcome home the 32nd Division. On June 18, Carl went with Rayline and her parents to Hartford for the day where Daniel wanted to check on a large gas holding tank he had under construction. They were enjoying a roadside picnic lunch, when they "saw a regular cyclone & that sure was interesting." I bet it was—a funnel shaped cloud! Carl was not so blasé when he adverted to the "tornado" in one of his letters.

They got home about 11:30 where they talked for an hour and Carl told her he had really fallen in love with her. She still was not sure how she felt about Sam or didn't feel free to express her true feelings to Carl that she had already confided repeatedly to her diary. She exceeded the allotted space in her diary for June 20 and continued her account on a Memoranda page at the back: [I] "wish I could give him a different answer but that wouldn't be fair to Sam & I may be only carried away with him. He is a prince to let me have until Christmas to decide. He says I should wear 'Nux' & when 'Nux' comes back to him he'll know he has lost, and until 'Nux' comes back he is going to be true to me, which I think is a very wonderful thing of him."

I had tried to dismiss "Nux" as one of those maddening but inevitable items in personal papers that would forever defy deciphering. A Web search only brought up nux vomica, a homeopathic medicine, with nux signifying a nut in Latin. My original theory that it might be an old brand of perfume didn't quite fit the contexts where the term was used. It wasn't until I began work on the next chapter discussing Carl's background that I made the connection: It was his fraternity pin, although I still don't know why it was called Nux.

On May 20 she wrote: [Carl] "asked me to wear 'Nux' for him to-morrow night. Mother & Glad will be about ready to wring my young head off. Well, I should worry, it will be lots of fun." The occasion was a club meeting when Rayline stayed overnight at Glad's house with the day's diary entry taken up mainly by the fact that Grace West was the first in the group to bob her hair and had broken her engagement. Rayline's final comments were, "I surely had to stand some teasing to-night about Carl. Well, it doesn't bother me much." It appears Glad didn't mind Carl giving Nux to Rayline but Lalla did, just as she had insisted Rayline return Miller Mureson's fraternity pin. On June 9 Rayline wrote, "Gave back

'Nux' even tho Carl didn't like it," but two days later she wrote, "He insisted I take 'Nux' back. I suppose Mother will have a dozen fits." I suspect she didn't wear it openly, at least not at home.

Rayline had missed her friend Mary and looked forward to seeing her as always but was particularly eager for her to meet Carl and to talk with her about him. Mary liked Carl immediately, but favored Sam in comparing them as competitors for Rayline's favor. Before the year was out, Mary had moved over to Carl's side but in the meantime Rayline had to deal with Sam. She was convinced she didn't love him anymore, if she ever did, but she was wryly aware of her own inconstancy. On June 24, incidentally her parents' wedding anniversary, she wrote: "Read a part of my last year's diary & I wasn't in love with Sam when he came up on his furlough but by the time he left I thought I really loved him. And now I doubt my feelings again. I see it would never do for me to marry a traveling man."

Initially, I think Lalla considered Carl just another one of Rayline's many beaux like Hans, Miller, Don, Morey and the rest who were simply entertaining company when her true love, Sam, was not there. If Carl seemed to monopolize her time, well, he would be going away soon. By June 26, however, Lalla got wise to the seriousness of their attraction for each other and "harped all day about Sam & Carl." Lalla truly subscribed to the importance of one's word being one's bond, and Rayline had let Sam labor under the misapprehension that she cared only for him.

One can't help but feel sorry for poor, unsuspecting Sam when he finally got to Milwaukee on July 30: "I met Sam at the depot & he can't begin to compare with Carl in looks in his uniform—I didn't want him to kiss me and I had an awful time keeping myself from drawing away. I know I'll never marry him & I don't see how I'm ever going to tell him." He brought a cameo and other gifts from France and prior to his arrival had sent a dozen roses to Rayline's home. What astounds me, however, is that instead of going off some place to be alone after their long separation, they went to the Alhambra movie theater and met Glad who "lied most marvelously about my not going out or falling in love while Sam was gone." I can't imagine what Glad was thinking and that Rayline wasn't upset but seemed amused. Perhaps Glad assumed Carl would revert to his old carefree, uncommitted ways in Canton and forget about Rayline, "Nux" notwithstanding.

Sam evidently stayed at the city YMCA where earlier in the spring Glad had noticed on the bulletin board he was signed up for a "tent," that is serve as a counselor, for the second period at the Phantom Lake Y camp. On August 1, Lalla, Jennie Walters, Rayline and Sam all drove out to Phantom Lake and were joined later in the day by Glad and Mary who came out on the interurban trolley.

Many of the pre-war staff had returned to the camp and Rayline's diaries indicate an effort to return to the kind of socializing that had gone on between the Y boys and the Floraydan Lodge girls, in this case, Glad and Mary. A new name appears on the counselor staff, just the last name, Graus, who takes quite a shine to Mary. On August 15 Sam arranged for a box of red roses to be sent by special delivery to Rayline at Phantom Lake to mark the second anniversary of their engagement. Rayline commented in her diary that "Two years ago to-night I promised Sam to be his for ever after, and I thot [thought] that that was what I wanted, now two years later I'm tired of my bargain." Perhaps prophetically, the roses had been improperly packed and were wilted, and Sam had become aware that Rayline had changed. The next evening the girls went over to the camp for a program and played the piano but when Gerb' playfully lifted Rayline up to the pulpit in the camp assembly room, "Sam got wild," and when the girls didn't save a place for him at their table at supper time, "Sam blew up sky high about it," blaming Gerb' and Graus.

Rayline and Sam left the group to talk, "and we had it out hot & heavy, & then we had the talk we have both been dreading but knew was coming since he got home." She concluded, "I feel wonderful that Sam & I have had this talk. We are going to be on lots better terms now." But she never mentions telling him about Carl.

Meanwhile, Mary's 'Tuck' came to Milwaukee on August 19 for a five day visit and Rayline was favorably impressed initially, but toward the end of his stay she had some reservations about a certain lack of devotion to Mary and his ladies' man attitude toward all the girls. She also noted that Graus was showing increasing interest in Mary. Rayline and Sam had a brief falling out on August 21 and though Rayline thought they had made up, Sam stopped calling or writing for nearly a week when she got a letter "as if there had never been a fuss." He let her know (to her great relief) that he had decided to go to medical school at Northwestern where Graus was enrolled rather than Marquette. On August 31, back at Phantom Lake, she reported having had "a fairly good talk" with Sam and "told him about Miller," adding, "I will have to work up courage to tell him about Carl next." I'm not sure if she ever really told him about Carl.

Her diary entry for Sunday, September 7 fills the whole page and continues on a Memoranda page:

Oh, I wish I weren't ever put on this earth! Sam has just left (2:00 A.M.). We started in to talk at 10:30 & even now we haven't arrived at any definite solution to our problems. He wanted us to not see or write each other for four years—surely a kid's plan. Well, we compromised on Xmas. Poor me—now I have Sam's & Carl's fate to decide at Xmas time. One thing Sam doesn't realize that Carl does [is] that attentions help a lot to sway judgement a favorable way. I dread this explaining the whys and wherefores to everyone [evidently a reference to her family, especially Lalla who had "harped on Sam and Carl."] The trouble with Sam is he takes everything too seriously & dramatically. I would be surprised if Carl wouldn't win out. Sam wanted me to return everything he had given me, but then I sure would have had some explaining on my hands. [She must have written to Carl about this because in one of his letters at this time he thought it was petty and opposed the idea.] I wanted to tell Sam about Carl but the mood he was in it would never have done. The only thing I hope is that he doesn't do anything rash or foolish because of his disappointment [that she broke off their engagement indefinitely].

But he did, although he built up to it gradually. Rayline received a bunch of roses on September 20, her birthday, without any sender's name but since they were ordered from Racine she knew they were from Sam. On Sept. 25 Mary wrote to Rayline and included a letter Sam wrote to her in Birmingham seeking sympathy in his problems with Rayline. Rayline must have destroyed Sam's letter but Mary's letter indicates she already knew from Rayline about the September 7 break-up and characterizes Sam's letter with her own twist on a case of sour grapes: "like a kid who wants cake but when he can't get it, eats crackers and pretends he wanted them anyway."

On September 29 Rayline is still weighing Sam and Carl: "Heard from Carl this morning & again this afternoon. He certainly is a dear & from the way he writes he is truly in love. I am beginning to believe that I am in love too. I can't remember of ever having this feeling toward Sam." Actually, she expresses her fondness for Carl over Sam in her diary early in their relationship and frequently thereafter, but she liked the status quo of having two men "wild" about her and a lot of other second string beaux besides. Rayline expected to get married—eventually, but at this point she wasn't sure who it would be since she still thought Christmas would be the day of reckoning.

She was thus still undecided when Carl managed to get back to Wisconsin for a weekend to take her to the University of Wisconsin homecoming game on November 1. Her account of the game spills over into the memoranda pages. Carl showed her all around the campus, and they had a wonderful time even though Wisconsin lost to Minnesota 19 to 7. Two items are worth special note. They visited Glad and had lunch at her dormitory, Barnard Hall, but Rayline wrote, "there is still a little rub. She hasn't been rushed by any sorority which surprised Carl and me greatly." This is not the last we will hear of Glad's difficulties at Madison. And then at the game: "One thing that nearly knocked me over was to see Tuve Floden. Even tho I didn't see him to speak to him, I'm satisfied now that that is over. I've a sneaking feeling that Carl is the one I'm going to love, honor and obey." Carl managed another weekend visit to Milwaukee on November 7 when they double dated with his cousin Eugene Kern and his girl friend.

By November 11, the break with Sam is complete as Rayline wrote in her diary, "I had the most horrible letter from Sam this morning. It was written in a fit of anger I know," but she resolves to return all his gifts despite Carl's view of the matter. There is a real sense of relief: "I can honestly say that I'm glad, yes, happy that it is all over with Sam & I haven't one pang of regret either."

Perhaps the clearest evidence that Rayline is through playing courting games and is seriously considering marriage is that shortly after the break-up with Sam when Carl was off in Canton, Irvin Hansen, one of the Y camp crowd whom she never dated suddenly showed up, eager to go out with her. She went on a few dates with him as she did with Hans Jennings when he put in one of his unexpected appearances, but to her own surprise she found she didn't mind staying home and waiting for Carl's daily letters and funny surprises—jokes, clippings, riddles, and small gifts.

6

Carl

Carl's background was as typical of Milwaukee as Rayline's and yet very different, and while both of Carl's parents were German speakers born in Europe they also had very different backgrounds. His mother, Rose Kern (her baptismal name was Theresa) came from the town of Heinrichsgrün in what was then part of the old Austro-Hungarian Empire. The area was known as Bohemia and encompassed largely German but also some Czech

Carl, about four years old, in Little Lord Fauntleroy suit. He remembered this trip to the photographer because of the Papagei, the prop parrot

speaking communities in the northern borderland of what became Czechoslovakia after World War I and the Czech Republic after World War II. It was called the Sudetenland by the Nazis after invading and occupying the region in 1938. The Czechs, perhaps understandably given the special atrocities committed on the town of Lidice in 1942, were among the most precipitate among the east Europeans in the forced expulsion of ethnic Germans from their countries after the war, although some exceptions were made for Czechs' German spouses and professional people needed in the cause of national reconstruction.

Rose's parents were Johann Nepomuk Kern and Anna Schindler Kern. Johann Kern was a manufacturer of saddles and harnesses—purveyor to the Habsburgs, according to family tradition. I am indebted to my second cousin, Gwen Samp, for this and other details about the Kern family. Gwen's grandfather, her mother's father, John Kern, was my grandmother Rose Kern Oestreich's brother. Gwen's personal knowledge of her mother's family is similar to my knowledge of my mother's family because, like me, she grew up in her maternal grandparents' home in Milwaukee.

While genealogical minutiae of names and dates quickly become tedious to unrelated readers, a few details about the Kerns are of general interest. The emigration of my mother's forebears (and perhaps many more people than we realize) differs from the stereotypic story of poor peasants leaving Europe to till the soil and improve their lot in life in America. Likewise the Kerns followed a different pattern. The senior Kerns were comfortably middleclass but they *sent* their adult or near adult children to America to urban destinations, with the means to ease the journey and make a good start. Oral tradition handed down to cousin Gwen has it that our great grandmother, Anna Kern (whose family might have been bakers), saw to it that even the boys knew how to cook in order to care for themselves if needed. The siblings anglicized their given names and seem to have adapted quickly and well to America, but maintained strong familial ties across the Atlantic. As to ethnic origins, they considered themselves Austrian. In his letters, Carl refers to his mother's sister, Anna Lehrer, as "my aunt in Austria," although by this time it was Czechoslovakia. The continuing closeness of the Kern ties between Europe and America is reflected in the fact that when Aunt Anna learned of Carl's engagement she sent my mother lovely gifts of lace collar and cuff sets and, when I was on the way, she sent yards of lace trim for baby garments she made herself. This so-called "pillow lace" at which she excelled is produced by casting bobbins of thread around straight pins stuck into a firm cushion or "pillow" that outline a pattern drawn on paper. Grandma Rosie also knew how to make pillow lace, but Aunt Anna was the family virtuoso who designed her own beautiful and complicated patterns.

Altogether there were twelve Kern siblings, born between 1858 and 1880; the tenth and twelfth died before reaching the age of two. Rose was the seventh child, born in 1870. Her older siblings, in descending order were Joseph Karl (called Karl), Franziska or Frances—"Fanny" (Lorenz), Emily (Kastenak), John, Joseph—"Joe", and Anton— "Tony"; her younger siblings were Anna (Lehrer), Robert, and Mary (Ruemler).

Karl remained in Heinrichsgrün possibly because he was the eldest son who would take over the family business. Fannie migrated first, followed by Emily, apparently in something of an au pair capacity to family friends or perhaps relatives in the Philadelphia area. My grandmother Rose left Heinrichsgrün at about the age of 12 accompanied by her older brothers John, Tony, and perhaps Joe, and also stayed briefly in Philadelphia, presumably with the same people as her sisters where, she once told my mother, she was treated "like one of the family." For unknown reasons, apart from the possible attraction of Milwaukee's large German speaking population, they all moved to Milwaukee where they married and raised their families, except Emily who had married and remained in Pennsylvania where my father visited her on his way to Newport News in 1918. Anna also emigrated to Milwaukee but had a boyfriend back in Heinrichsgrün and returned home to marry him while Mary, the youngest child, lived in Racine after her marriage.

The Kern siblings who came to Milwaukee settled in what my father said was once known as "the wooden shoe district," in this case meaning Germans, not Hollanders. Roughly a little over a square mile, its southern boundary, Juneau Avenue, is about a half mile north of Milwaukee's main business street, Wisconsin Avenue—known as Grand Avenue until 1922, and extended north to North Avenue. Originally, it was bounded by Third Street on the east and 13th street on the west, but by the time Carl was a child it was expanding farther west and north. Carl's home was on 12th Street between Brown and Lloyd Streets.

The Kern siblings' mother visited her children in Milwaukee and died during one such visit. She is buried in Calvary Cemetery, the oldest extant Catholic Cemetery in the city, founded on the then far western outskirts in 1857, less than a decade after Forest Home was established as a non-denominational cemetery by Episcopalians on Milwaukee's south side.

I know far less about my father's childhood and extended family than I do about my mother's background; and I know

On the left: Baby Carl, 1895, and his parents Rudolph and Rose Kern Oestreich

On the right: Carl, ca. 1900. These unusual photographs are printed on slightly convex metal discs, 6" in diameter, the earlier one is matte finish and the later one glossy. They are marked on the backs with small logos of Chicago companies: Photo Button Co. and Medalican Co., respectively.

even less about the Oestreichs, my father's father's family, than I do about the Kerns. I grew up among my mother's relatives in my maternal grandparents' home, but it required a trip of several miles to visit my paternal grandparents. By that time, they had moved to a home my grandfather built after he retired in a still rural area of the suburb of West Allis west of Milwaukee. Their property included several acres of land with a small barn where my grandfather kept a horse. My father never understood his father's fascination with farming, and joked that the only reason for the horse was, "To plow the field and make manure to raise the grain to feed the horse to plow the field and make manure to feed the horse to plow the field..."

A letter from Rayline had made reference to her visiting with Carl's parents when his father, to Carl's annoyance, brought up his interest in farming. Carl says in his letter of September 23, 1920, "I've told him hundreds of times to forget [farming]...You know, mother is no farmer and if it wasn't that bulls have such deep bass voices I couldn't tell them from a cow nohow."

During my later childhood, I sometimes spent several days at a time with "Grandma Rosie" but that was after "Grandpa Rudy" had died in 1933. For some reason I addressed them by both kinship terms and their names in contrast to calling my other grandparents just by their given names. I only saw my extended Kern kin, and not all of them at that, on special occasions. Grandpa Rudy had no relatives that I know of in Milwaukee at that time.

My father knew little about his father's background and early life partly because of his father's natural reserve and partly because his father apparently wanted to put his past behind him. Rudolph Oestreich came from a town in Prussia called Berlinchen, Little Berlin, long ago swallowed up by Berlin itself, where the family owned a grist mill. The only reason that he gave for leaving was that he did not get along with his stepmother, but other considerations such as his distaste for Prussian militarism and monarchy also must have influenced his decision, given his involvement in the Socialist Party in Milwaukee. I was under the impression that he cut all ties with his relatives in Prussia and was surprised to discover from my father's letters that apparently there was still some contact, at least through Carl's cousin Hans who had served in the German army and was attending the university at Jena. Hans cannot be identified in any way with the Kern family.

Rudolph was born in 1864 and came to the United States in the 1880s when he was in his early twenties. The city directories list his occupation as carpenter and painter and my father refers to him in one of his letters as a cabinetmaker. I still have a sturdy humpback wooden toy chest and a charming miniature chest of drawers that he made for my father when he was a child.

Carl surmised that his father had received a fairly good education in Prussia because he could help him with his high school algebra. In an uncharacteristic burst of anger, my grandfather once made a tantalizing remark that my father happened to overhear. His parents had been living in their West Allis home for at least a year but his mother still had not completed unpacking. Finally reacting to the clutter, Rudolph snapped at her, "Maybe the Kerns lived like this but not the von Oestreichs." "*Von* Oestreich!" my father exclaimed. His father grinned sheepishly but shrugged off further discussion. Had he dropped evidence of an actual connection to the aristocratic Junker class from his name or had his Prussian sense of orderliness prevailed over Rose's Bohemian approach to life and he merely used the term "von" metaphorically?

Young Rudolph evidently was drawn to Wisconsin because he had relatives, surnamed Draeger as well as Oestreich, who had settled around Lake Mills in Jefferson County, and he had at least one cousin in Milwaukee itself who was Rose Kern's first husband. She had a son who died in infancy and then her husband died not long after of a highly virulent form of tuberculosis referred to in those days as "galloping consumption."

The German community in Milwaukee was based on commonality of language rather than national, ethnic, or religious identity, and even the language was divided by a variety of dialects. When the first German speakers began arriving in Milwaukee in the late 1830s, what we know as Germany was a conglomerate of separate states. The city's intellectual and cultural life was greatly enriched by the influx of well educated "fortyeighters," fugitives from reprisals for their unsuccessful efforts in 1848 to rid Europe of monarchy, particularly in the German states. It was not until 1871 that Germany was unified through the masterminding of Otto von Bismark, Prime Minister of Prussia, and the former King of Prussia became Emperor Wilhelm I of Germany. Thus, in Milwaukee, as elsewhere in the United States, besides immigrants from the German states—Prussians, Bavarians, Saxons, Hanoverians and the like—there were the German speaking Austrians and the German speakers from Switzerland along with people from the German language enclaves in Hungary, Russia, and other parts of eastern Europe. They were further sub-divided, sometimes bitterly, into Roman Catholics and Protestants, particularly Lutherans (whose separate synods in Milwaukee as elsewhere in America reflect strong doctrinal differences among adherents of their faith), and Jews, also from a variety of German speaking regions, who seem to have gotten along better with the various sets of Christians than the Christians did among themselves.

I don't know how Rose Kern from the staunchly Roman Catholic Sudetenland met and married men from Lutheran Prussia, but she told me she met my grandfather at the cemetery where she was visiting her first husband's grave. This was certainly not at Calvary Cemetery. I don't know whether she broke with the Catholic Church at the time of her first marriage, but she was no longer Catholic when my father was born; he was baptized and later confirmed in a German Evangelical Lutheran church. German was his household language and it never occurred to me to ask him when and how he learned English. He had a natural talent for languages and mimicry and was a great raconteur. When I was a child, I remember him telling jokes (which I didn't understand but convulsed his relatives) with dialog between people speaking different German dialects leading to suggestive misunderstandings.

His Yiddish was good enough for him to pass as Jewish. In

fact, he once told me he dated a Jewish girl in the East, having made friends with her brother and his friends; her family discouraged the relationship when they realized Carl was not Jewish. It may have been when he was located at Newport News. He referred matter-of-factly to his old outfit, "the QMC," as "the Jewish Army" because the Quartermaster Corps was supposedly attractive to Jewish recruits with a tradition of expertise in mercantile matters. He was drawn to the wit and warmth of Jewish ethnicity, identifying with it, for example, in referring to his "Jewish intuition" when he saw through insincerity. In December of 1919, he and three friends went to a newly opened "Hungarian Restaurant" in Canton that he likened to a synagogue because, "The four of us were the only ones that were not Jewish—and I'm partly."

Although Carl and his father differed drastically in their political and economic philosophies, they agreed in their opposition to anti-Semitism. I really regret that I barely knew Grandpa Rudy and know so little about him personally because he was associated with one of the most interesting phases of Milwaukee's political history. In 1910 it was the first major American city to elect a Socialist mayor, Emil Seidel, and was in the only Congressional district that ever sent a Socialist to the House of Representatives, Victor Berger. Whereas my mother's side of the family were all Republicans and devoted to the tenets of capitalism and free enterprise, my paternal grandfather was a Socialist and active in the cause of organized labor. He worked for many years at the Milwaukee shop of the Chicago, Milwaukee, & St. Paul Railroad.

On January 31, 1920 Carl complained to Rayline that his father had passed through Canton recently on his way to Washington, D. C. and had not let him know. Two days later he passed on further information from his mother that his father had written to her every day he was in Washington. Carl was astounded as his father seldom wrote to him, explaining in jest when Carl once complained about it that there was no point in having a wife if she didn't handle the letter writing. What I found most interesting is that my grandfather went to Washington at all. It must have been in connection with the controversial re-election of the Socialist candidate, Victor Berger, to Congress in 1918, and suggests that my grandfather's involvement in Milwaukee Socialism went beyond mere party membership.

After serving one term in Congress Berger was defeated in his bid for re-election in 1912. He won again in 1918, but as the owner and editor of the Socialist paper *Milwaukee Leader* his 1917 editorials opposing America's entering into World War I led to his being indicted on federal charges of sedition. Berger and his Milwaukee associates were moderate, evolutionary Socialists dedicated to honest government and the gradual achievement of practical reforms through the ballot rather than doctrinaire revolutionary action, let alone Anarchism that the opponents of Socialism lumped with Socialism. In Milwaukee the Socialists had been part of a larger effort in consort with Progressive Republicans to rid the city of a notoriously corrupt regime, but the irrational hysteria generated by the Russian Revolution and the "Red Scare" that swept the country after World War I made them suspect on a national basis. Shortly after his election in 1918, Berger, along with several co-defendants, was convicted and sentenced to 20 years in Leavenworth Prison. Congress, deeming him a "felon," refused to let him be sworn into office. A special election was held to fill his seat in which he ran again (his case was on appeal and he was free on bail) and he again won. The case went all the way to the Supreme Court which voided Berger's conviction on January 31, 1921, and he went on to serve three terms in Congress. Given the dates, it appears that my grandfather was part of a delegation to Washington in support of Berger in the special election.

Apart from the personal issue, Carl's comments on his father's trip are a tip-off to a common practice at this time, now forgotten, whereby people kept in personal touch with each other before the widespread use of automobiles and the development of a national network of all-weather roads. Even telephone lines were still limited in their coverage, with long distance service prohibitively expensive to be used mainly in emergencies. It took me a while to recognize from a number of brief references in the diaries that people who were about to embark on a long train trip customarily wrote in advance to friends who happened to live en route to be at the depot when the train would stop there to take advantage of the opportunity for at least a brief visit. Sometimes local people even boarded the train to the next stop as Carl did when Rayline wrote to him that Margaret Breed, whom he had met by then, was coming through Canton on a trip to the East Coast. On February 2, 1921 he wrote, "Well, I gave Marg her little surprise. I hopped the train she was on, found her and went to Alliance with her, and took the street car [interurban trolley] home."

In view of their political differences, it is understandable if Carl's father did not let Carl know he would be passing through Canton in order to avoid arguments on the Berger issue. I suspect that my grandfather's political views were no more acceptable to the Kerns than his religion. It was only after I became re-acquainted with my cousin Gwen in the late 1990s (we had met at least once as children) that I learned her grandfather had also rejected the Catholic faith. She recalls he was badgered by his oldest sister Fanny to return to the fold. Although, according to what I heard from Carl, his mother socialized regularly with her siblings and their families in the old north side German neighborhood, I have a hazy recollection of my mother saying that Fanny and some of the other devoutly Catholic Kerns did not visit Rose at her home in West Allis until after my grandfather died.

On a number of occasions when Carl complained in his letters to Rayline about his father's politics or farm fixation, he would temper his criticisms that, thanks to his father, he had been saved from "the ring" [papal ring] or "the Micks," a term of opprobrium that originated against the Irish Catholics that Carl used in reference to his mother's family. Carl never ceased to be amazed by the Danielson family's friendship with Father Peschong. While Carl admitted "Father Louis" wasn't the usual run of priest he encountered through his Kern kin and genuinely liked the man once he met him, he could not resist regularly teasing Rayline in his letters to ask "Daddy Pesh" to say a mass or offer a prayer in support of some project of the moment.

Where the trip to Norway had been the outstanding memory of Rayline's childhood, Carl recalled his happy summers of swimming and fishing at Lake Mills where he was first sent alone on the train at the age of six to stay weeks at a time with Uncle John and Aunt Christine Bartels who had no children of their own. Aunt Christine, nee Draeger, probably was Carl's father's cousin but was called aunt according to the custom of children addressing adults, as discussed in the first chapter.

Carl had almost familial ties to Mr. and Mrs. Carl T. Mueller. "C.T." was a prominent pharmacist and by the time Carl was in high school or perhaps earlier he began working at the Mueller drug stores. Dr. and Mrs. Boerner were friends of the Muellers and also took a parental interest in Carl who always called Gladys's mother "Ma Boerner." Rayline had written about attending a card party at the Boerner's and Carl said of Mrs. Boerner, "Isn't she a great scout[?] I'm just as much Carl to her now as I was when she first saw me cleaning salve jars at C.T. Mueller's." Carl stood in a kind of big brother role to both Gladys and the Mueller's son Bill, also called Willy.

It is particularly frustrating not to have Rayline's letters at this juncture because Carl's truncated responses to whatever she wrote indicate that Gladys was really in love with Bill Mueller although, like Rayline before she met Carl, enjoyed dating a lot of fellows. In September of 1919 when Gladys had begun her freshman year at Madison, Carl wrote, "I'm hoping she gets over this 'Willy Mueller' stuff," but by the following February, when Gladys had dropped out of the university he wrote, "Tell Glad we'll rest lots easier when she and Willy run off. We know way down in her heart is Bill." In April we find the cryptic comment, "C.T. Mueller's remark about Bill seeing a friend on Mon. afternoon bothers me. Poor Glad." Then, an isolated post-script in Carl's letter of August 13, 1920 asks, "Sure about Bill's girl?" The meaning of a final reference to Gladys and Bill in mid-February of 1921 suggests a break-up: "if what you tell me about Bill is true then I'll believe anything anyone ever tells me from now on. I'm just a little bit fraid [sic] that sis is letting her imagination play pranks with her."

With the exception of his cousin Eugene, son of his uncle Joe, Carl was much closer to the Muellers and Boerners than to his Kern relatives. It was probably through the influence of these families that Carl decided to attend the university at Madison, his aptitude for mathematics leading him to engineering. My mother once commented that while his parents were hardly wealthy, they could have contributed something to their only child's education,

Carl as graduate of the University of Wisconsin, 1918.

but Carl worked his way through college, earning his meals washing dishes at the then new Barnard Hall dormitory and the Delta Gamma sorority house. On January 20, 1921, when my parents' letters began to concentrate on wedding plans, Carl wrote, "Promise me, bunches [honey bunch] you'll never make me—except in a pinch—help wash dishes. When I donned my cap & gown I decided that washing dishes had ceased to be a part of my life, and bunches dear you'll hardly blame me after those four years of service."

Writing to Rayline in September of 1919 regarding Gladys Boerner's anxiety about beginning her freshman year at Madison, Carl recalled his own experiences:

> about six years ago...I started for school with $80 and a helluva lot of nerve. And the first day there my fees [and] one week's room and board amounted to $56 and that didn't even start with the books. Nothing in the world could have dragged me home either. When I think about it now I smile, it seems so impossible. Glad hasn't a thing to worry about. Believe me tho, honey, I'd think twice if I had to do it again. Still?

Somehow, he managed to join two fraternities while at the university, Acacia and Theta Nu Epsilon. Acacia was founded in 1904 by Masons, partly in reaction to the frivolity and bad reputation attached to some of the Greek letter societies. Initially members had to be Master Masons but later required only a Masonic recommendation. Carl once mentioned that his father had completed the first three, Blue Lodge, degrees, but was not inclined to go further than this status of Master Mason. Carl's dedication to Masonry was independent of his father's affiliation and he became a Master Mason at Madison. He became a 32nd degree Mason while still in the army at Camp Dodge, Iowa.

He did not join Acacia until his senior year and because war had broken out, the chapter suspended initiations; he was finally initiated in 1938. Theta Nu Epsilon or TNE, that he seemed to have joined early in his college career, was often the kind of outfit Acacia had been founded to counteract. It was a spin-off of the Yale Skull and Bones but took on many identities of its own on different campuses where it was frequently interdicted by university authorities for rowdiness and operated sub-rosa. Its official gold pin featured a skull with an emerald right eye and a ruby left eye; the crossed bones of the original fraternity were replaced by crossed keys under the skull. I finally figured out that the word "Nux" meant Carl's TNE pin, but I don't know if this was its official name or some secret word he only shared with my mother when he gave it to her very early in their acquaintanceship, frankly admitting she was not the first girl to wear it.

If ever the word "daunting" had an appropriate application it was the task of dealing with my father's letters. First, there are so *many* of them to keep track of and while they are unmistakably love letters the affectionate parts are far from the total content and they are as much reflections on a range of now historical topics as are Rayline's diaries. Apart from the first letter Rayline saved that Carl wrote during a visit with old friends in Madison, they begin with his employment with The Berger Manufacturing Company in Canton, Ohio. I don't know how he got this job after his discharge from the army, but he entered civilian life during troubled times. The post-war years, particularly 1919-1920, were marked by national turmoil and unrest. As noted, the Russian revolution helped to set off a "Red Scare" resulting in persecution, prosecution, imprisonment and, in the case of foreigners, deportation of anyone suspected of leftist leanings, a reaction that eventually proved to be far out of proportion to the actual numbers and strength of any revolutionary and anarchist activists. The hysteria over national security was further aggravated and confused by major strikes during this period relating to the long-standing discontent of the American labor force with working conditions, particularly in regard to coal mining, steel production and, on the west coast, shipping. In the end, the strikers gained little and were forced to back down, but the effort heralded eventual success and profound social changes to come.

Carl makes light of the Red Scare, starting one letter to "My own little Bolsheviki," and betting with his father that the Bolsheviks would soon be turned out of power. He was not alone in this belief; in his letter of March 3, 1920, he mentioned that people were buying Russian rubles for virtually nothing in the expectation that the monarchy would be reinstated and the money would be redeemed at full value. The strikes, however, were something else. The fact that Carl was a white collar employee of a manufacturer of sheet metal products located in Ohio, a major center of the steel industry, put him in the heart of the action and unquestioningly on the side of management and the Republican party, as reflected in the letters he sent to Rayline between September 26 and December 17, 1919. The effect of social unrest continues to show up sporadically in his letters until they terminate in 1921.

Yes, dear [he replied to her inquiry] we have strikes here at Canton. The United Alloy is out, Timken Bearing Mills are out, and the Stark Rolling Mills are out. (Stark Mills belong to Berger—only a different name for the mill end of it.) So far six fellows have been nicked [? ink blurred]. Two I guess are dead.

Two days later:

The wops and hunkies are getting rough. They attacked an old fellow who has been with Berger's for about 30 years, and clubbed the old boy into the hereafter. I guess the ex-officers [military] working in the office end of the plant will be sworn in as deputies. Anyway, I've sent for my old shooting iron [his service revolver] and if I haven't lost all my accuracy let 'em come. I can't afford to let them mess up with the best little girl in the world waiting for me. I wish they would end the trouble. If that dear President of ours would only exert his efforts into other directions besides League of Nations something would undoubtedly happen, but that dash blank asterisk.

On October 1st, Carl reported: "Mother sent my uniform & gun, altho everything is quiet again and I hope that by next Tues. things will be settled." The next day he wrote, "Things are beginning to calm down. The boys at Youngstown are going back to work. Bethlehem and Gary are partially back & those last two are the biggest in the world. I knew if my old pop gun came I wouldn't get a chance to use it. Gee, and it works so good." A few days later he added that he expected Canton to fall in line with Youngstown because "winter's coming on" and, presumably, it would be hard to keep up picketing.

His next reference to the situation was written on October 20:

> Berger's are trying to open the mill tomorrow and maybe we will have fun and maybe we will not. It sure is a peculiar state of affairs. These steel boys were making 15 to 20 a day and still they were kicking. They ought to give 'em about 5 or 6 for 8 hours and then maybe we'd be on our way back to the good old days.

If winter was a discouragement to striking steel workers, it played into the hands of miners; the coal strikes became a growing source of anxiety across the country as cold weather drew on. On December 4th Carl began his letter on a jocular note, anticipating his Christmas visit in Milwaukee and referring to some kind of family dispute Rayline must have told him about. "Gee whiz old girl don't get on the wrong side of the folks just yet, wait till we get coal again. One plant after another is closing down here. Berger's got about three weeks supply and then it's sweet vacation time."

But, as he explained a few days later, "Berger's own their own coal mine so I guess we'll have coal all right." Since train locomotives were fueled with coal, however, the railroads cut back on service, resulting in bunching up of mail deliveries. "Darn those miners anyway," he groused. The far reaching effects of the coal strikes are noted in a letter dated December 12, 1919 that Carl received from his former teacher, Professor Van Hagen of the University of Wisconsin College of Mechanics and Engineering, and sent on for Rayline to read. "We are preparing to close the University on the 17th,-a week early. The action is due chiefly to the coal shortage. We have kept warm so far, but there is trouble finding enough coal to run all through the winter and quite a bit can be saved by closing."

It appears that shortages varied from place to place since Carl observed on December 13, "Isn't life funny? Now the coal strike is over and we can't get [steel] bars for rolling sheets. All orders are cancelled and the mill closes next week. Tuff very tuff on the rollers who had been striking."

Van Hagen's letter had been in reply to a letter from Carl who had told him, along with other news, of his new job with The Berger Company on "the sales engineering force." Van Hagen opined, "I should expect that would suit your peculiar talents very well."

Carl's subsequent letters to Rayline revealed that, once Berger was back in full production, his job covered a multitude of tasks, called for a multitude of talents, and entailed travel to different cities on company business. He was called upon to do original engineering designs, analyze and troubleshoot when problems arose, estimate jobs for Berger to bid on, and win over architects to specify Berger sheet metal products, including some standard items and some of their own patented specialties. In a pinch, he was called upon to do special drafting because his department head recognized Carl's artistic hand at "shading" and other details, but Carl didn't consider this real engineering. It was not immediately apparent to me when he called himself a "slipstick chauffer" that it was slang for an engineer, a slide-rule driver. Indicative of changing times even when horses were still commonplace is that in early October of 1919 Carl was given the task of designing "an aeroplane hangar."

Carl's letters frequently contain sketches and technical explanations of current projects. He discussed such things as the advantages and shortcomings of "metal lumber" for a building addition, why Berger's "Ribplex" was ideal in floor construction, and a "beam clip" system that Carl and a shop foreman perfected and the Chief Engineer tried to take credit for it. Carl often mentioned his new friend Howard Rupert, a Canton native and frequent partner in work assignments. On November 14, 1920 he wrote: "Listen to this old girl. Howard & I worked on a little job that was the meanest thing in the world to lay out. It was a fancy hip and valley roof with dormers and ventilators. The contractors wrote and said that in their 20 years experience they have never erected anything that fit together as pretty as that did and they congratulated the firm on its efficiency." No wonder he was smitten with a girl who could fully understand and relate to his professional challenges and triumphs, thanks to her familiarity with her father's contracting business specializing in the construction of large, steel framed buildings.

Perhaps Carl's most challenging job occurred in early January of 1921, just after his Christmas visit to Milwaukee: "And you ought to see what they thrust onto me. I have to redraw and recompute all our dope [product information] from pounds per square inch to kilos per meter and make all the reading in Spanish for our South American trade. Don't know a damn word of Spanish so I'll have to use an English-Spanish dictionary." He pulled it off to the company's satisfaction. Carl's competence attracted the attention of upper management and on a couple of occasions the head of the Boston office sounded him out about transferring there, but he was not interested as Boston was even farther from Milwaukee than Canton.

Although the strikes were coming to an end and the Berger Co. was back to normal, there was widespread unemployment across the country and a rise in crime. Carl mentions automobile theft and hearing shots one night in his usually quiet neighborhood, but it was all rather removed from his concerns until September 2, 1920 when he wrote:

> Finally, something exciting happened in this town. Last night while I was ambling along home two fellows stepped from nowhere and put a great big 45 against my tummy and told me to 'throw them up.' Well, they took my billfold, and luckily I deposited nearly all my money that noon, and my watch & chain. I talked them into returning my bill fold tho. They were just amateurs cause they were very excited and I kidded them about it. I'm glad in a way that it happened cause it is a good experience. Next time it will seem like old stuff. Too bad they got the watch tho cause mother gave it to me for commencement.

He enclosed a newspaper clipping telling of his reporting the holdup in which his name is misspelled Oestrech and that the robbers got $6.00. Despite his bravado in his initial account to Rayline, a week later he admitted, "You haven't any idea how powerfully persuasive a 45 is." I was familiar with this incident but always believed it happened in Madison right after Carl's graduation, perhaps because of the association with the watch. I'm sure I'm right about one thing, though, and that is my father telling how he could feel the gunman's hand shake as he held the 45 against his stomach. He must have said something if he got the billfold back, but I wonder whether he really kidded his attackers.

The hold-up story reveals a surprising detail in business practices this late in the 20th century. When Carl said that he had deposited nearly all his money, he meant it literally. In January of

1921, he reported, "Berger's pay with check now instead of money because of the many hold-ups." At about the same time, Berger's introduced another innovation in office procedures, Dictaphones, adapted from Edison's system of recording on cylinders. Although disk records had long replaced cylinders for music as they offered improved sound and longer playing time, they required cumbersome equipment and studio conditions. Cylinders remained the most portable and economical means of recording dictation and were used in offices up to the 1930s when they were replaced with cellophane-like belts and then wire and tape.

Carl's letters tell us a great deal about the day to day living of young professional men who began their careers immediately after World War I, were not yet married, and for reasons of employment were living away from their home towns. Many of his colleagues at the Berger Co. fit this category as did many of the men he socialized with at the Canton Masonic Club—some fell into both categories. Carl's living arrangements seem to have been typical. He rented a room in the private home of a Mr. and Mrs. Wess, 1222 12th St. N.E., which was within walking distance of his job, and took his meals elsewhere. His $10.00 a week rent included bed linens, towels and washing of his personal laundry and mending. He only made the bed and cleaned the room during a two-week stint when Mrs. Wess was seriously ill. The room had the essentials of bed, dresser, chair, and the like but, as will be discussed later, apparently no place to write. Carl installed his own record player, a Victrola.

The Berger Co. had an employees' restaurant where Carl usually ate breakfast but I can't be sure if lunch also was served there. Wherever he ate lunch, he was partial to a ham sandwich and a cup of coffee that cost a quarter. Dinner was usually at a boarding house but Carl provides no information on the number of men who ate there or the prices.

Carl, being Carl, was soon thoroughly at home in his rooming house and his letters contain regular reports on life with the Wesses who were probably only some ten years his senior but treated him more like a kid than a contemporary. He never mentioned their first names although they called him Carl as evidenced from quoted conversations. Mr. Wess was a German immigrant and we hear little about him except that he served in the German navy during the war. Mrs. Wess was new to the role of landlady so Carl made allowances for her bossiness and inquiring into and expressing opinions about his affairs. A strict Methodist, Mrs. Wess disapproved of dancing and never went to movies but the family did go to the opera when a company made a rare visit to Canton. Much to Carl's amusement, the opera was "Carmen" that he considered more "suggestive" in part than some burlesque acts or any of the movies Mrs. Wess wouldn't think of attending.

When he first arrived and asked her if the movies were open on Sundays in Canton because some cities had blue laws, she said smartly, "Yes, and so are the churches." In contrast to Rayline and her family and friends, Carl frequently went to church at Mrs. Wess's insistent invitations. I think he agreed partly for lack of things to do at the start (because he indicated he was not a regular church goer) and partly because he knew Mrs. Wess felt it set a good example for their son, Ralph, who was about five when Carl arrived in Canton. He drew the line, however, when Mrs. Wess suggested he teach Sunday school.

Carl was a Pied Piper and immediately became Ralph's idol, giving him a penny whenever a letter arrived from "our girlfriend," making him a sling shot and a bow and arrows (to Mrs. Wess's despair but giving Ralph status with the neighborhood kids) and going to elaborate lengths to perpetuate the myths of the Easter Bunny and Santa Claus. Ralph also picked up slang from Carl, once telling his mother "No can do," also to Mrs. Wess's despair.

Both Rayline and Carl's mother (*"Tante Rosie"* to Ralph) regularly sent Carl candy, cookies, and other goodies on which Ralph had an automatic claim. Ralph learned to recognize Rayline's letters and would take them up to Carl's dresser, delighting in Carl's surprise after he expressed disappointment not to have a letter waiting on the front hall mail table. When Carl learned Ralph had been adopted, he expressed pity for the "poor kid," although admitting the Wesses were excellent parents. The idea that being adopted was somehow a handicap or minor tragedy may have been fairly common at this time. At any rate, Rayline sometimes expressed a similar sense of pity in references to her childhood friend Ada Kroening who had been adopted and, like Ralph, was a well-loved child. Ralph was very upset when Carl planned to leave Canton. By this time he was in first grade and learning to write and Carl mentions writing to Ralph from Dallas in one of his letters to Rayline.

Just as Carl found a home away from home with the Wess family, rather than simply a rooming house, he immediately and enthusiastically availed himself of the Canton Masonic Club as if he had belonged to it all his life. His letters reveal ingenuously that his arrival on the scene must have been recognized early on as a real asset to the organization. Such fraternal institutions, among other functions, offered a ready-made social life for strangers to meet and make friends among like-minded men. Housed in the Masonic Temple at the corner of Market Ave. N. and Fourth St. N.W., along with other Masonic groups, its stationery proclaimed, "All Master Masons in Good Standing Eligible to Membership." In Carl's words, in early December of 1919, "If it wasn't for this Club I'd go wild. When there is nothing to do I stroll down here," to take advantage of its facilities or "chew the fat with some of the fellows." The club had billiards, pool, and card tables, a player piano, a record player, and access to space in the building for informal dances once or twice a month as well as formal, holiday dinner dances with an orchestra. It also sponsored picnics, dances at nearby resorts, and other outings. Carl's letters are reminiscent of the situation in Milwaukee and Phantom Lake where fellows and girls (sisters of the fellows or girl friends of fellows' girl friends) could enjoy each other's company without serious commitments until, as happened in a few instances while Carl was in Canton, a couple eventually paired off exclusively and planned to marry.

Carl was available when needed, with Rayline's agreement,

Sergeant Oestreich, Newport News, Virginia, 1918.

to escort girls to dances but he generally went "stag," dancing with different girls when not helping with changing records, serving food, keeping scores of card games that sometimes were held in connection with dances, and acting as "cloak room checker." After a few months, he finally got authorization from the club to buy three new records a month to stay current with popular music and retire overplayed ones. He liked "real jazz" as well as sentimental danceable tunes. His choices were nothing if not eclectic, to cite a small sample: "All The Quakers Are Shimmy Shakers," "Hindustan," "My Cairo Love," "My Baby's Arms," "Everybody Shimmy Now," "Yellow Dog Blues," "Your Eyes Have Told Me So," "Dardnella," "My Isle of Golden Dreams."

The big, formal dances brought out the older generation of Masons and Carl complained about their taste in music ("They consider 'Down in Bom Bombay' is still great stuff") and their monitoring of the dance floor to make sure partners did not dance too close together. Although he never smoked, Carl also helped organize and attended club "smokers"—male get-togethers to smoke and socialize.

When Carl traveled on company business, if time allowed, he visited the Masonic temples in other cities and wrote to Rayline about their buildings and the people he met. He also wrote that in making sales pitches for Berger products, he occasionally encountered fellow Acacians or TNE members that usually proved advantageous in getting a foot in the door and a fair hearing. Beyond these affiliations, he was instrumental in establishing a chapter in Canton of a new organization, American Officers of the Great War, sending Rayline a newspaper clipping on December 20, 1919 announcing plans for the chapter's first military dinner dance to be held in late January. Carl, his name misspelled Oestrick, was listed among the committee members planning the dance.

Since Rayline was unable to come to Canton, a friend arranged a blind date for Carl to attend the AOGW dance, and as soon as he'd taken the girl home when the dance ended at midnight on January 20, he popped back into the Courtland Hotel where the dance had been held, to get a note off to Rayline. The next day he sent a sketch and detailed description of a dress he admired that he felt would have looked better on Rayline than on the wearer, and enclosed a dance program along with his letter. The music, provided by "Wiesenberger's Society Orchestra," led off with the Star Spangled Banner followed by 20 dances designated by dance type rather than song titles, including familiar terms—One Step, Two Step, Fox Trot, and Waltz, and ones I'd never heard of—Paul Jones, Two Step (Ladies Tag) and One Step (Men's Tag). Thanks to the Web I found out these were "mixers" with complicated patterns for changing partners. Carl had mentioned Paul Jones as passé in his complaints about the older Masons' dance preferences but apparently it was still popular enough to rate inclusion on the AOGW program.

A week after the AOGW dance, he wrote about founding yet another organization: "Tonight bunches we're going to start what will be known as the Canton Engineers Club. This will be organized for technical purposes[,] that is we intend to have a reference library, discuss problems, etc." Nothing seems to have come of this idea; at least it is not mentioned in subsequent letters.

When I first discovered that most of the packets in the shopping bag were love letters, I was uncomfortable about revealing intimacies not meant for strangers' eyes or even mine, for that matter, but I need not have worried. It wasn't that my father was particularly circumspect, it was just that he and my mother had so many things to talk about besides being in love. Even the expressions of love are playful, slyly suggestive rather than blatantly sexual, and frequently funny like the contrived lovers' quarrels (so they could kiss and make up) when her letters started with "Dear Carl" rather than something more affectionate or when her alleged sarcasms brought threats of "spanky spanky" or kisses in multiples of millions as "punishment." A couple of times he returned pieces torn from her letters with his editing to make them more affectionate or positive. Rayline observed of the first letter from Canton, received July 8, 1919, when she was still engaged to Sam, "But one thing, he can't begin to compare with Sam when it comes to writing love letters." The single surviving note from Sam quoted earlier begins, "My Darling," and he talks about the day he can claim her. Later, as she was seriously comparing the two men, it was Carl's "attentions" in response to her interests and wishes, not Sam's possessiveness that won out. Besides their very frequency, the letters contain evidence of Carl's constant "attentions" in his references to the little gift or special memento—candy, books, a fancy powder puff, or trinkets he sent just about every pay day, when "the eagle sang."

Carl's sense of humor sometimes skirted the bounds of propriety and one of his surprise gifts probably was in response to, "Oh, you wouldn't dare!" On January 7, 1920 Rayline wrote in her diary: "I was so mad at Carl, I could skin him. He sent me a wonderful pair of silk bloomers, but I'm in a terrible mess with the family. I don't see why he ever did it!" But she relented: "I was angry with Carl last night for sending me those pink silk bloomers but today I can see the humor of it & I know he didn't mean anything." Underwear was an inherently funny subject—bloomers, drawers, BVDs, teddies, chemises.

The post card Rayline received from Carl early in their acquaintanceship headed "G.B.B.E.H.B.B.D." was an earnest of future correspondence. He loved to tease her with elaborately misleading initials to guess what he was getting for her birthday or Christmas. His first letters began, "Ray Dear," but once the matter of Sam was settled, he generally abandoned the nickname, Ray, and indulged in creative variations and permutations on the initials in that early postcard. "My Great Big Honey Bunch," shortened to "Bunches," and "Bundles" for "Bundle of Joy," "Bestest and Mostest Sweetheart," "Kiddo," "Kidlets," "Dear Bundle bunches and sweet cream puffs," to cite but a few examples. He also addressed her as his "Little Fat Rascal" and "Fatty" when she was put on a diet to gain weight to get back to her normal weight of about 100 pounds. He also called her "wifey" and "wiffy" and started one letter, "My dear little Jewish wife Raychel." Among the letters is a Jewish New Year's card sent in the fall of 1921. Asterisks of various sizes were kisses, and the words "I love you" would be buried in trick lettering. Once he sketched a small outdoor scene of trees and a lake with an island, titled, "Isle of View," with instructions to "Say it fast." When she had a mole removed from her neck he wondered if he would still know where to kiss her without his "landmark." Thankfully, the treacle is seasoned with humor, and there is a lot more than treacle.

The letters are a sample of life of the period, sometimes sounding as familiar as this morning's newspaper and sometimes with incomprehensible allusions and cryptic comments about long forgotten incidents and people. Carl frequently enclosed clippings with his letters: columns by humorist Ring Lardner, cartoons about courting, in-laws, and married life, and funny "fillers" from newspapers and magazines. One letter held a large four-leaf clover; Carl had a special knack for spotting "four-leafers" that he would triumphantly present to Rayline. Dozens of them were pressed between the pages of books at Phantom Lake. He also made little blueprints of her initials in attractive Gothic letters to serve as patterns in embroidering linens for her hope chest and because her friends admired them he obliged with patterns for their initials too.

He loved puns and the kind of joke that takes a moment to appreciate, e.g.: "Anthony calls on Cleopatra and the maid says she can't see him. She's in bed with tonsillitis. 'Damn those Greeks,' he says." A kind of formula punning joke was popular at the time—some of the better ones: "You tell 'em, Mayonnaise. I'm dressing." "You tell 'em, Wells Fargo. I can't express myself." And a pre-diesel era example: "You tell 'em, Locomotive. I've got a tender behind." Drawing on the funny papers, Carl sent Rayline a telegram on her 22nd birthday, September 20, 1920: "CONGRATULATIONS FROM DINTY MOORE CLANCY MONAHAN JIGGS MAGGIE AND CARL."

The letters also are a compendium of then current slang. "Give it the East and West," to look something (or someone) over carefully. "Hold your thumbs," for luck, like crossing one's fingers. "All of a sudden" or "sudden" meaning right away or soon; "when I finish this letter, I'm going home all of a sudden," or "if I can't get home by Easter it will be pretty darn sudden after it." "Fussing a girl," an expression Rayline used more frequently in her diaries than Carl did in his letters, meant to make a fuss over a girl with gifts, dinner, movies but without serious interest in her. Rayline suspected that Tuve was fussing other girls when he was away from her and then, early in her attraction to Carl, she wondered if he was just fussing her. "Hop Off," was to get married. "S.O.L." occurs frequently and if the letters don't stand for "S___ Out'a Luck," as they do today, given the contexts, the meaning is the same. I was surprised to find familiar slang phrases that were already in use prior to 1920 such as, to be "hep" to something and to "hang out" some place or with someone.

Particularly endearing and distinctive is Carl's use of German words and phrases for special emphasis and affection. After all it was his first language, but it's not easy to read because he wrote in the old script that even modern German speakers have trouble deciphering: *Siehst du?* Do you see, understand? *Nicht so schlimm*, not so bad; *Ach, Gewalt!* and *Ach Gott*, conveying surprised exasperation; *Schatz*, treasure, a traditional term of endearment. He closes a number of letters with *Jeztz muss ich gehen*, Now I must go. Occasionally, just for the sake of urbanity, he substituted *n'est-ce pas?* for *nicht wahr?* My favorite had to do with their agreement that both of them could go out with other people when they were apart, even after they were officially engaged, rather than just sit at home and miss parties and dancing. Carl had escorted the sister of one of his fellow Masons to a formal dance in Canton and described her as very good looking and a fine dancer, but *Niemand zu Hause*, nobody home.

It becomes increasingly obvious from my father's letters that while physical attraction had drawn him to Rayline at the start and continued to delight him, he really did admire her for her mind—there was definitely someone *"zu Hause."* Very little of this comes through in the diaries as Rayline probably saw no reason to repeat what she had written to Carl. His half of the correspondence, however, includes discussions and responses regarding books, including poetry—he was quite taken with Edgar Lee Masters' Spoon River Anthology and admired the Rubaiyat of Omar Khayyam, articles in the Literary Digest, stories in the Saturday Evening Post, movie plots and quality of acting—movies were as popular in Canton as Milwaukee, plays, vaudeville, and current events. Writing on December 6, 1919, for example, he adverted to war with Mexico being narrowly averted: "Well, what do you think of this man Carranza? I was all set in spending a winter in the south and watching bullfights, and now the darn fool apologized. 'S tuff!!'" Carl was semi-serious insofar as it appeared he might be called up to active duty as a member of the Army Reserve.

Two important national events merited recurrent reference: the 18th and 19th amendments to the Constitution regarding prohibition and women's suffrage. As Rayline had noted in a letter to George Gustafson, prohibition was already under serious discussion during the war. When it was officially enacted in 1920, many sober, law-abiding people flouted it, if only on a token level, as an expression of opinion that it was unwarranted. The Volstead Act that spelled out the conditions of Prohibition allowed people to make up to 200 gallons of wine or hard cider annually for non-commercial home use. Daniel's basement winery provided the family's usual table wine, but Rayline complained in her diary that the house "smelled like a brewery" because her parents were making beer, and that was illegal.

Carl talked of an outing with some of his Masonic club friends over the course of several letters when they picked bushels of wild elderberries that they converted into wine for their parties. This was barely within the letter of the law of "home use" insofar as they didn't sell it. And the Oestreichs certainly were not serious drinkers but Carl's mother felt almost obliged to try her hand at dandelion wine and I think she was in violation of the Volstead Act when she sent some to Carl by U.S. mail. Rayline managed to lay her hands on a small bottle of whiskey that she sent to Carl as "medicine" when he was laid up with a cold. A rare N-word joke in Carl's letters was really a prohibition joke whose sentiments about spilled whiskey crossed racial lines when the main character with a bottle of bootleg hard stuff in his pocket slips and falls down. As dampness begins to spread down his leg he prays that "it's only blood I feels."

When women gained the right to vote in 1920, Carl began his letter, "My dear little Suff'," for Suffragist. In a subsequent letter he teased her that she wouldn't be able to vote because no one would believe she was over 21. On October 18, Rayline and Jeanette "went up to the aunts for a republican political meeting." When she wrote in her diary about actually casting her first ballot for Harding and Coolidge on November 2, 1920, the experience was something of an anti-climax: "Up at 5:30 this morning so I could go to the polling booth with Dad to cast my first vote. It wasn't anything at all. I was the eighth one to vote." Yet the whole matter of being among the first women involved in the elective process was important to her. During much of my childhood Rayline worked at our local polling place on election days, the only "wages" she ever earned, but she didn't do it for the money. She would be away all day handing out ballots and all night when votes had to be tallied by hand. Carl would fetch her home in the morning, bleary eyed and exhausted but with a sense of civic pride.

Sports also were discussed in season. Thanks to Daniel taking her to games from an early age, Rayline was absolutely avid about baseball as Carl soon learned. She said Daniel used to joke that when he "started on his second million"—he'd *started* on his first—he wasn't going to buy a yacht or polo ponies but a baseball team and he would coach at first base and Rayline would coach at third.

An initially puzzling feature of my father's letters from Canton is that about half were written on stationery from the Hotel Courtland and most of the rest on Canton Masonic Club stationery, with a few on letterhead paper of other hotels or The Berger Manufacturing Co. where he was employed. It was not until Carl was getting ready to leave Canton for his new job with the Berger Co. in Dallas in the spring of 1921 that Rayline received three letters written on heavy quality stationery he brags about having bought. They are embossed with a gold Shriners' logo of a fez surmounting a "cheese knife [scimitar] and claws." I could understand his use of hotel stationery when his work took him on trips to other cities, but the Courtland in Canton seemed strange since he stayed in a rooming house. Rayline's only reaction was to note that the Courtland paper was smaller than the Berger or Masonic Club stationery and its logo on the envelope usually meant a short letter.

The stationery turned out to be a tip-off to another once widespread but now forgotten practice relating to a significant technological change. I might never have discerned it without the preservation of such a large volume of correspondence from one person in Carl's kind of social situation. I gradually learned from the letters that besides the writing materials and desks in hotel guest rooms, the furnishings of hotel lobbies regularly included writing tables equipped with stationery, pens, ink (and, I assume, the essential blotters though they are never mentioned) for general use, even by people who might not be staying at the hotel. I don't know when the custom began but I have figured out what helped to start and sustain it—it was good for business—and that what finally obviated it had to do with the ink, not the paper.

In the era before radios, let alone television, it paid off as inexpensive advertising with the potential to reach a wide audience. The stationery featured attractive line drawings of the hotel and any hotels under the same ownership in other cities, along with information on amenities such as "absolutely fireproof." Sometimes daily rates were given—at this time, usually $1.50 to $2.00 for a single room with private bath. Letter writers not only disseminated an inviting image of the hotel far and wide, they even paid the postage!

Certain other institutions besides hotels regularly provided writing materials for people like my father, single men living away from home who expected this convenience almost as a natural resource wherever they went. At the outset, I thought it was just one of Carl's idiosyncrasies to use hotel stationery, but the only unusual part was that he took shameful advantage of a good thing in writing so many letters to the same destination. Perhaps not wanting to wear out his welcome at the Courtland, he alternated using stationery from the Canton Masonic Club but complained on occasion that there was no paper or ink at the writing desk and the person with the key to the supply room had gone home, or there were "other contestants for the writing table."

Another example is the YMCA stationery Tuve Floden used when he wrote to Rayline from Fort Sheridan that included the phrase below the national letterhead, "Public Correspondence Table at:" to be filled in with the name of the local Y'. Although Tuve referred to it as "Charity paper," he had to borrow some rather feminine stationery from his sister when he wrote to Rayline from his home; one of his letters is on the stationery of the Rockford High School Athletic Alumni Association.

Carl's expectation of free writing materials anywhere he

went is illustrated in the second last packet of letters containing correspondence after he started his new job with the Berger Co. in Dallas, April 21-June 1, 1921, just before my parents were married. He found a rooming house almost as soon as he arrived and, as a matter of habit, headed for a nearby hotel, The Adolphus, to write to Rayline. By his third letter he is using Berger Co. stationery in which he complains, "You see it's more difficult to write here because I can't find a convenient place. Not like Canton at all. At the Adolphus you ask the clerk for paper and he looks at me with that 'You don't stay here stare'. 'Sbad!" Carl's letter of May 31 is written in pencil on lined tablet paper for which he apologizes, "I got this paper at the Y. They didn't even have ink. I've never been in a place where it was so difficult to get paper. Nothing at the [Masonic] temple."

The next letter, April 1, is on the stationery of the John W. Low Post of the American Legion, thanks to Carl's cousin Eugene Kern, a navy veteran, who visited him in Dallas. Carl wrote: "Have you noticed that every time I write I have different stationery? You see, Eugene joined the legion and they have pretty fair writing rooms in the basement of the Southland Hotel, so I guess I'll use their rooms a while. As you said tho [probably in reference to the letter written in pencil], anything will do as long as I write." But Dallas eventually proved to be more like Canton, and apparently the nation at large, than it seemed at first. Although Carl availed himself of the Legion stationery from time to time, a great many of the remaining letters are on Adolphus stationery. Also, probably thanks to his Catholic cousin, Carl sent two letters on old "Knights of Columbus" stationery, reminiscent of the YMCA stationery Tuve Floden used during the war. It was subheaded "War Activities" with the K. of C. logo on the right and a picture of a bi-plane on the left and a blank line to name the local "camp." Carl closed one letter saying, "Father Pesh. I bet appreciates this stationery," with an arrow pointing to the letterhead.

Without beating the subject to death, I must note that there seemed to be an implicit message that, like eating quiche, men simply didn't buy stationery, at least not for personal, unofficial letter writing. Rayline, on the other hand, wrote of buying writing paper and receiving it as gifts, and Carl commented on her using fancy blue or beige stationery. That women were expected to have paper is underscored when Tuve wrote from Fort Sheridan encouraging Rayline and her "lady friends to lay in stocks of stationery" to write to lonely soldier boys.

Of course, hotels and some motels still provide their guests with stationery, at least note pads and pens you are welcome to take. This is an obvious holdover of the old function of corporate image and advertising, but those pens are ballpoints. I doubt that many people made off with the pens in use in my father's day, and even my school days. They were long, pointed, stained with ink that even when dry might rub off on one's clothing or catch on threads, and were totally useless without a supply of ink in a cumbersome bottle to dip them in at regular intervals as one wrote. These pens, that came into use during the 18th century, have a replaceable metal nib set in a handle, usually made of wood, and were an improvement on the prototype quill pen that wore down and had to be regularly sharpened with "pen knives." Although the first really portable writing instrument, the so-called lead pencil, has been around since the Renaissance, it seems to have had an image problem from the start as inappropriate for personal correspondence that calls for ink.

Experiments to improve writing instruments were just getting underway during the time my parents were corresponding and culminated in the ball point pen, invented long after the period covered in the letters. The first more or less practical fountain pens appeared shortly before World War I when Rayline was attending Downer Seminary, with Parker pens produced in Janesville, Wisconsin being among the early leaders. I understand it took a century or so of experimentation with various devices to create pens that carried their own ink, were easy to fill, and didn't leak. But fountain pens were costly, easily damaged, not yet fully dependable, and you still had to have a supply of ink on hand to refill them. We know Rayline sometimes used a fountain pen, but many of her diary entries are unmistakably written with pen and ink as are most of Carl's letters. As late as 1941 when I graduated from high school, my school desks still had inkwells in the upper right hand corner.

The widespread availability of complimentary writing materials was finally rendered unnecessary by the revolutionary change in writing instruments that began when the ballpoint pen was introduced in 1945 right after World War II but, as I well remember, the first ones performed poorly and were outrageously expensive. The problem of having an ink supply readily at hand when fountain pens ran dry was finally solved in the 1950s with the development of handy little packs of disposable cartridges that slipped into the fountain pen barrel without the messiness of bottled ink. They were soon edged out of a major share of the market, however, because the ballpoint pen was perfected about the same time and, like plastic items generally, had become increasingly cheap to produce. Ironically, the abundance of good pens began at the same time people were writing far fewer personal letters because of technological improvements such as cheaper and better long distance telephone service and air and automobile travel. (We need go no further with this subject.)

Because Rayline had already broken up with Sam by the fall of 1919, Carl did not have to wait until Christmas to learn which of them she would choose, but they did not become formally engaged until Carl's Christmas visit of 1919. His letters, meanwhile, reflect his sense of becoming part of Rayline's family and circle of friends. He exchanged local Shrine papers with Daniel—Canton *Crescents* for Milwaukee's *Tripoli Tattlers*, and borrowed Daniel's books on estimating while passing on business information, including the latest developments in the steel industry relevant to the growing popular interest in the stock market that would figure so dramatically as the 1920s wore on. He wanted to know the exact relationship of the aunts and uncles Rayline mentioned in her letters and inquired about Rayline's friends he had met. He spoke frequently and fondly of Phantom Lake, on one occasion joking that he'd been trying to reconfigure Floraydan Lodge to fit the name Carl into it too. As a young man on his way up in the world, Carl was drawn to the model of Rayline's Republican, enterprising, comfortably Episcopalian, Masonic family and, like Lalla, would even become something of a Norwegian by marriage, kidding Rayline in his letters about learning to like "ludafisk" [*lutefisk*].

Although, unlike Sam, Carl was not about to put off getting married for four or five years until he was fully established, he was more concerned than Rayline that they start married life with more than bare necessities. Rayline fantasizes in her diaries about eloping, inspired perhaps by the example of their neighbor's daughter at that time, but she realizes she would regret such a decision. While Carl thought about the possibility of locating in Milwaukee, Rayline had no objections to moving to Canton. She was even in favor of living in Boston when that possibility arose. She was open to adventure. By the beginning of 1920 they began making serious plans for the future, but wedding arrangements, including the place and date, remained uncertain for well over a year due to emergencies and unforeseen exigencies, as documented in the diaries and letters from 1920 until the spring of 1921.

Carl clearly established where he stood in one particular of married life before they were even formally engaged, writing on November 28, 1919: "J.B. Montgomery got a little girl this morning. I guess we want a boy." The a was underlined four times and an afterthought message was squeezed in between the lines: "(mono) (one) (singular) (compré?)." A year later on September 21, he reported, "One of my friends down here got a little girl on the 20th and he isn't pleased with his effort tho cause he wanted a boy. We'll be neutral and have an it. (no we won't!)." About a week later, he commented, "we'll be a typical American Family— Dad, Mother, <u>one child</u>, a Ford, a pup." Although he referred at times to a future "Little Carly" or "Carly Jr." this was usually in connection with something Ralph Wess did or said. I don't know why Carl was so adamant on this score because he enjoyed kids and they adored him, but the idea was perfectly acceptable to Rayline who more than once tells herself in her diary how lucky she is to be an only child. When I was a child and paid more attention to adult conversations than the grown-ups around me knew, I was aware that we were in the midst of a "Depression," so when my father spoke critically of couples in their circle of friends having *"another baby,"* I thought it was concern about the cost of raising children in hard times. Reading the letters and diaries, I learned otherwise. They never wanted anyone but me! And that was just fine with me.

7

Rayline and Carl

On January 1, 1920 Rayline wrote,

> I wonder what the year holds for me. Received a dear letter from Carl this morning [mail still was delivered on New Years Day]. It seems queer I look forward to the day when we get married, the same as he does. But when Sam talked about it, it made me have a queer feeling—I guess the difference is that I love Carl.

This was Carl's first letter following a ten day Christmas visit in Milwaukee, and after reporting that he slept most of the way on his train trip back to Canton, he recalled, "Last year, dear, I was in Des Moines. I didn't think then that I could be vamped but you win."

Their engagement certainly is the dominating theme in the later packets of Carl's letters from Canton and Rayline's diary entries, but both sources continue to deal with current news in the world at large and advert matter-of-factly to now scarcely known customary practices and details of domestic life in the 1920s. The long delayed electrical wiring of the house on Layton Boulevard occurred during the end of February, 1920 and the new fixtures

Lalla and Rayline had selected to replace the old gas lights and chandeliers were installed. As mentioned earlier, Rayline became adept and enthusiastic about sewing when she could jettison the old foot treadle for electric power, but that wasn't the only major new appliance to affect household activities. No mention is made of acquiring an electric washing machine, but I know they did, and unless carefully tended the wringer shredded garments into rags. Laundry is another of those domestic activities that was undergoing major technological change by the 1920s but remained unmentioned in the diaries unless something went wrong, or threatened to. On one occasion, Rayline saw "the coal wagon" on Layton Boulevard and breathed a sigh of relief that it did not stop at her house because she had a load of wash hanging in the basement. Most houses were heated with coal until after World War II and it was customary to locate the coal bin under a basement window that could be opened to admit a portable chute from the sidewalk into the bin. Delivery men unloaded coal from the wagon (or truck by the 1930s) into big canvas containers with metal frameworks that were carried on a man's shoulder and emptied noisily and dustily down the chute. It was not a good time to have laundry drying in the basement. On the other hand, people kept the ashes from the furnace in metal scuttles to scatter on slippery steps and sidewalks, saving the cost and negative environmental effects of salt used today.

Rayline and Lalla probably began doing laundry regularly when they got the electric washing machine because Daniel had preferred they send it out to be done commercially. With his "delicate stomach," the smell of boiling soap water made him sick. Bed and table linens along with sturdy clothing were literally boiled on stoves in huge tubs to get them clean. The electric flatiron was another welcome household item, replacing the aptly named sadirons that also had to be heated on a stove. As one iron cooled with use, the other was heating and had to be run over a rag before touching it to a garment to clear it of any stray bit of soot. And Rayline could at last try out the electric chafing dish Carl had given her for Christmas!

Carl was able to get away for a long weekend over the Easter holiday, arriving on Saturday, April 3, 1920. Although everyone knew he and Rayline planned to marry, Carl had a talk with Daniel formally asking his approval before he presented Rayline with her engagement ring. He had designed the setting himself, but the ring was too small and they had to rush around to find a jeweler to enlarge it so she could wear it right away. I had hoped that the letters with sketches of the setting would clarify some aspects of the ring that always puzzled me, but they merely verified what I already knew, that he actually obtained two diamonds. Rather than set both in one ring, he had a similar but not identical ring made with the other and presented it to her a year later, on June 6, 1921 when he arrived in Milwaukee just before their wedding.

When Carl had returned to Canton after Christmas and told his "boss" he was engaged and sought advice on buying a ring, his boss, probably "Monty" Montgomery, head of the Berger Engineering department, talked to his wife and they agreed to sell Carl two flawless white diamonds totaling nearly a carat for the price of one on condition he take both. They had been earrings the wife could no longer wear because her earlobe had been torn in an automobile accident.

Before Carl went back to Canton again on the Monday evening after Easter, they visited his parents, the Boerners, and C.T. Mueller to show them the ring. Many years later, in the 1930s, on the pretense of taking the rings to have the settings tightened, Carl worked with a jeweler friend to combine the two solitaires with two baguette diamonds into a new setting for a large star sapphire, Rayline's September birthstone, as a Christmas gift. This kind of recycling and resetting of gems seems to have been a fairly common practice, particularly in regard to inherited jewelry.

As to the engagement ring, on April 15, 1920 Rayline wrote: "I certainly dropped a bomb at club meeting when I showed my ring. I thought the girls would go wild—I had been there over an hour & kept my ring turned in, until the opportune moment arrived." Glad, of course, was in on the game. She had dropped out of school after the Christmas recess and was back home in Milwaukee with plans to make up lost work in summer school and re-enroll in the fall. A combination of factors contributed to what Rayline said Glad called a "nervous break-down." She was desperately disappointed not to have been "rushed" by any sorority, let alone Delta Gamma she had her heart set on, and she was having trouble with her class work.

Rayline mentions repeatedly toward the end of 1919 and the beginning of 1920 that relations with Glad were strained. Part of the problem was Rayline's closeness to Mary that Glad said made her feel unwelcome in the threesome. She seemed to accept Rayline's assurances that both she and Mary enjoyed her company, but now that Rayline was engaged they were back on their old friendly basis because it took care of what turned out to be the root cause of Glad's coolness. I wondered at first, as did Rayline, whether Glad regretted having introduced Carl and wished she'd kept him for herself, but Carl assured Rayline early in 1919 that he had never kissed Glad, "even playfully, charitably, or otherwise," and that it was really a brotherly relationship. Carl indicated in other contexts that "Willy" Mueller really was Glad's sweetheart since childhood.

When Glad and Rayline finally talked frankly after the engagement, Glad admitted that she resented not being confided in as to how things were going with Carl, having brought them together, and that she and her mother had worried that Rayline was not serious about Carl of whom they were so fond and would throw him over.

I don't know if the matter of uncertainty in friendships with girls is attributable to some quirk on Rayline's part or characteristic of the times. Rayline also makes repeated references to Ada Kroening's unpredictable friendship. Ada lived across the street and she, Rayline, and Jeanette had gone to grade school together and had once been very close but whereas Rayline and Jeanette remained lifetime friends, Ada eventually drifted out of the picture. Cousin Antoinette also was in an on-again, off-again relationship with Rayline for a while. Rayline did not think much of Antoinette's beau, Herb', referred to only by his first name and with the same scorn she felt for Margaret Breed's Dave, but she was more favorably impressed when Antoinette found a "new crush," Robin Middlemas, whom everyone called Bob.

When Carl had returned to Canton after his Easter visit in 1920, Rayline went back over her diaries and wrote on April 16, "last night I figured out how many times I'd seen him since I knew him, it was only 44 times. 'Only 44 times' but I'm ready and willing to spend my life with him." Upon the announcement of her engagement, Rayline immediately found herself the recipient of many gifts, as was customary—money, household goods, and trousseau items from family and friends. As she put it, it was "like one continual Christmas," and this was before the round of organized luncheon showers. When she entertained her club or there were other female callers at the house, it was expected that as a bride-to-be she would show them the accumulating hoard in her hope chest. Her future mother-in-law whom she refers to rather formally as Mrs. Oestreich or Mrs. O. was constantly presenting things, many that she made herself—table cloths, pillow slips, napkins, lace collar and cuff sets, and items not exactly to Rayline's taste that she doesn't specify but accepts graciously for the thought behind them. Meanwhile, as Carl and Rayline were merrily writing to each other about getting married and debating twin vs. double beds, reading in bed, big wedding or little wedding, getting married at Phantom Lake or Layton Boulevard, and many other matters, all plans came to a halt.

On May 18, 1920, a Tuesday, about 4:00 AM Daniel suffered a near fatal "stomach hemorrhage." The doctor came immediately and said he should move as little as possible and could have no food or water for a week or ten days. Rayline wrote several days in a row: "People in and out all day & the telephone rings continually."

She got a note off to Carl and by May 22 he replied:

"Bunches, bunches what one little twist of the pen can do to make life seem all wrong. I had to read your letter twice to realize what you were telling me. Ray, honey, we can't let dad go yet cause I've never really learned to know him and besides we need a grandad. If you need me, wire. In the meantime call on mother for any help at all. She'll be only too glad to be of assistance.

She decided there was no need for Carl to come to Milwaukee, and she also had to write to Lalla's old friend Cora Nichols in Kentucky to cancel a planned visit to Wisconsin. Carl's mother came to the house with flowers and called regularly for progress reports, but there already was an abundance of helpful and concerned kinfolk. It occurred to me as I followed the course of my grandfather's illness that if this had happened today he would have been rushed off to a hospital, given a blood transfusion and perhaps immediate surgery, and isolated in intensive care. Maybe the hubbub of a multitude of visitors responding to his own show of bravado was effective therapy in its day because he made a remarkably rapid recovery.

On Saturday, four days after the hemorrhage, "Daddy took a turn for the better during the night. He seems so bright and cheerful. He simply must get well. He has the grit & will power, that is certain." Nearby family members took turns providing meals so Lalla and Rayline could care for Daniel. Even Lalla's cousin Nettie who lived on the north side came to help. Jennie Walters's 86-year-old mother walked the six blocks from her home to visit with Daniel. At the end of the week, May 25, he was being fed egg white, and Rayline wrote that the doctor said, "that the next four or five days were the critical days. Daddy daren't move suddenly or he'll tear the tissue over the ulcer and start another hemorrhage."

On June 1, Rayline saw it as a good sign that the doctor did not pay his usual daily visit. The next day he said Daniel could eat some sweetbread.

The term refers to the thymus or pancreas of an animal, usually a calf, once considered a delicacy and appropriate invalid food. American food preferences have changed markedly since the 1920s. Except for liver, so-called organ meats such as brain, kidney, tongue, tripe, and the like are no longer seen in ordinary butcher shops and supermarkets, let alone listed on restaurant menus. I was reminded by a friend my age that up to about 40 or 50 years ago, "Sweetbread Salad Sandwich on Graham Bread" was a luncheon specialty of one of Milwaukee's fancier eating places. Today, beyond a limited "ethnic" demand, organ meats end up in pet food.

Daniel sat up in bed nearly all afternoon on June 3, and began attending to business, with Rayline "typewriting" for him. In a few more days, he was dressed and coming downstairs. The family meanwhile began returning to a normal routine of shopping, club meetings, and lots of movies. On June 15 Daniel took his first automobile ride, and on the 18th, just a month after the hemorrhage, Rayline went with him to Phantom Lake on the interurban train. On June 24, their wedding anniversary, Lalla and Daniel went out for the evening, and by the end of the month Daniel was nearly as active as he had been before his illness although Rayline noted he was still somewhat weak.

Carl managed a two week visit from July 4 to July 19, 1920 when they spent much of the time at Phantom Lake and even walked over to the Y' Camp, but Rayline observed, "Strange to say I've lost all interest in the camp." Mary was back from Birmingham for the summer and Tuck had some kind of temporary job with the Allis Chalmers Company in Milwaukee so the couples double dated but Rayline, as always, is bothered at Tuck's lack of "attentiveness" to Mary. Also, despite Carl's mother's generosity and even saying she loved her as much as she did Carl, Rayline was not entirely comfortable with her future in-laws, making the revealing comment toward the end of Carl's visit that his "folks came out [to Phantom Lake] to-day and it didn't bother me a bit."

As summer turned to fall, Daniel suffered a set-back and had to return from a trip to Two Rivers, Wisconsin at the end of September because he felt ill. While he soon was up and about, his health was an ever present cause for anxiety. September also was marked by Antoinette and Bob's engagement, with plans to marry in November. Rayline confided in her diary on October 15 that she couldn't help feeling a bit hurt that Antoinette would be married first, and then Antoinette really upstaged her by "eloping." It took everyone by surprise when she didn't show up for a party Jeanette held on October 17 nor the next day at the school where she taught. Her only reason appears in Carl's letter of October 22 responding to something Rayline had written, that she had run off because "she had a little tiff with her mother." Above all, I wondered why they went to Fargo, North Dakota and some God-forsaken sounding place called Moosehead, Minnesota.

When I turned for help to Antoinette's son, Rob, he didn't know what the tiff was about but supplied the information that his father worked for the Heil Company, a large Milwaukee firm that manufactured heavy equipment and containers, and his father was in North Dakota or Minnesota, "one of those northern states, anyway," on a job assignment of some kind. Fragmentary clues in Rayline's diaries between October 17 and November 11 fell into place, with recourse to a road map. Antoinette must have boarded a train for Fargo where Bob was temporarily located, and they were married on October 19 in Moorhead, Minnesota (well, it *looks* like Moosehead in Rayline's handwriting!) directly across the Red River from Fargo. They were soon back in Milwaukee and news of the marriage appeared in the society column of the paper. On November 11, they sent out printed announcements to family and friends.

Rayline, as usual, began counting the weeks until Carl's next visit and wondering where they would be at this time in the coming year. His birthday was October 26 and she bought him a gold watch fob with a Masonic Double Eagle design that he reported showing off with pride to the fellows at the Masonic Club. They were now talking seriously about getting married in the early spring of 1921. Although Carl offered to try to find suitable work in or near Milwaukee, Rayline was all in favor of moving to Canton. Besides longing for the adventure of living in a different part of the country, Rayline was concerned, as she wrote in her diary, that if they didn't get away at the start of their marriage, Mrs. O. would try to run their lives with her well-meaning but constant and often off-target helpfulness. Carl, by contrast, had no problem identifying with the Danielsons. After his most recent visit he even expressed his delight in the sentiment on the little plaque in the dining room on Layton Boulevard that now hangs on my wall. It shows an old fashioned "Gibson Girl" holding up a wine glass and offering a toast that resonates even today:

Constancy

'Tis better-aye, lift up the glass!
Once more I'll pledge it thus-
To die a good old Has Been-
Than to live a Never Was.

Carl arrived for his Christmas visit on the morning of December 24, 1920 and it is exhausting just reading Rayline's diary. They immediately went to his parents' home for lunch where the Oestreichs gave Rayline a ten dollar gold piece in a fancy little purse, but the bracelet Carl had asked his mother to find for him was too large and had to be returned for adjustment. Then they went to Glad's and exchanged presents and finally had Christmas dinner at Layton Boulevard. As a matter of both Norwegian and German custom, we lighted the tree and opened presents on Christmas Eve, not Christmas Day. Northern tradition also called for stockings to be hung up on St. Nicolas Eve, December 5, and opened early the next morning; as a child I thought St. Nicolas was a kind of advance man for Santa Claus to see if you really were being good.

On Christmas Day, Rayline and Carl had a turkey dinner at noon with friends of the Oestreichs and then went on to *THE AUNTS* who had arranged with Rayline that Carl would play Santa Claus at their annual Christmas party for all the Schuette family kids. Lalla's brother Uncle Will and Aunt Alice had them over for dinner on December 26 followed by a trip downtown to see a movie and a chance to "cuddle" a bit when they got home. On December 27, Rayline helped Lalla around the house and finished the wonderful black velvet dress, and then Carl took her to see "The Greenwich Village Follies" at the Davidson Theater.

On the 28th, Rayline did most of the work preparing a rabbit dinner "for the whole family," making me wonder if Daniel had gone hunting. Glad's long awaited dance at the Calumet Club was December 29. The next day they went to Nettie's for lunch, called on *THE AUNTS*, took in a movie downtown and got home about 7:30, and "wonder of wonders" the whole family went to bed early, "leaving Carl and me in possession of the davenport." He went home about midnight but was back the next day to attend a Booster Club luncheon with Daniel, returning at 7:30 to celebrate New Year's Eve at the Shrine Ball at the Milwaukee Auditorium. Carl was "all dressed up in his dress suit" and Rayline again wore her black velvet dress. Late though it was, Rayline recorded the events of the last day of the year and closed with, "Good Bye Diary. You have been a faithful friend and kept all my secrets within your pages."

She slept late the next day and when Carl came over they called on Jeanette. He left for Canton early on January 2. On Valentine's Day, Rayline was thrilled to receive a corsage of French violets surrounding her first orchids, a novelty that had been popularized as a fashion statement by President Wilson's wife. The New Year saw a continuation of trousseau gifts when *THE AUNTS* presented Rayline with those sensible muslin teddies that she thought "weren't worth taking home," and apparently told Carl as much because he joked about them in a number of letters.

On February 26 *THE AUNTS* held a joint party for Rayline and Antoinette attended by 21 of the girls' friends who brought gifts for their hope chests. I have a hunch it was intended originally only for Rayline but even four months after the fact, a "bridal shower" probably helped to regularize Antoinette's marriage in their minds. Typically, *THE AUNTS* questioned whether Pa was wise in buying Rayline sterling silver rather than plate flatware to start out married life. Pa disregarded his bossy sisters-in-law and, as I later learned more of the incident referred to in Carl's letter of February 20, went all-out getting additional serving pieces as well as the dozen complete place settings he had promised.

Some time earlier, her Danielson grandfather had given Rayline $500 as soon as he heard she was getting married, in case he might not be around for the wedding. He was in poor health and by the time of the wedding was living with his daughter Lou Waite in Colorado Springs.

Carl's letters resumed as soon as he was back in Canton. He had pretty well decided against the Boston offer while Dallas became increasingly attractive. As the story unfolds in Carl's letters from February 19 to 26, we are reminded that presidential inaugurations once occurred in March rather than January but, then as now, people speculated on the new administration's choice of advisors. Carl could not resist milking all the puns possible out of the fact that on February 18 he happened to be sent to the president-elect's home town, even before he got down to the news he was so excited about that he sent the letter special delivery (ten cents extra plus regular two cents postage). He had cadged stationery from Jacobs and Woolley, the architectural firm he was sent to contact, and circled the words Marion, Ohio on the letterhead. Writing on Saturday, his letter began:

> Friday at eleven o'clock A.M., Ralph Brown came in [to the Canton office] with a telegram which meant Carly dear had to hustle down to Marion. You

see W.G. Harding wants some drawers for his cabinet. I brought some muslin ones and told him the Aunts sent [them]. Seriously tho, I've been working from 6 P.M. to 12 P.M. and all day today till now (4 o'clock) and so before I go home I had to write to Mrs. Oestreich [Rayline] you know.

And now dear listen to this. Mr. Galvin, our mgr. of the newly created Dallas Branch and a friend of G.H. Charles [head of the Canton office], has asked me and made a good proposition to come to Dallas with him. It is an opportunity to get in on the ground floor with a good man. I told him as far as I was concerned I was 9/10 sold on the idea because if I don't go with him, it will be somewhere else. Of course I asked him for time to consult Mrs., so here it is. Game? My own boss, a fine city, good climate, near Mernie, and a driving power in an outfit rather than something being driven. I'd love to go.

Sometimes I wish I wasn't ambitious but look who I've got to fight for now.

There is a curious omission in Carl's written promotions of Dallas although I am sure it was discussed: the prosperity enjoyed throughout Texas as a result of the oil strikes beginning in 1901. Perhaps it is because the major "boom" for which Texas is famous did not get underway until later in the 1920s when they had already returned to Milwaukee.

Rayline's diary, Sunday, February 20, notes: [This] "afternoon I received a special delivery letter from Carl & he has had a pretty good proposition to go to Dallas, Texas and wanted my opinion on it. I sat right down and wrote him an eight page letter telling him that if he thought it would be to his benefit to go to the moon, I would accompany him." In 1921 that was saying something!

In his next letter Carl wrote that "as a matter of form" the Dallas job had to be posted and while his friend Howard who was slightly his senior at Berger's was eligible he was not interested because Canton was his hometown. Carl's next two letters discuss being sent on Berger business for two days to Toledo where he found a bargain in silk sox for himself (six pairs for $3.50) and by chance was able to attend some kind of lavish business party, courtesy of their Toledo agent who, at one time, had also expressed interest in Carl joining his staff. Rayline sings Carl's praises in her diary and declares her love, but the news of his Toledo trip so soon after his return from Marion gives her pause, "I don't like the idea much to have him go off on trips, & I have to stay home alone."

Dallas was still under discussion when Carl wrote on February 23, "I've been considering the proposition for some time and here is the dope."

> My intentions always were to get into a branch house for the simple reason you're part of a driving force then. Boston suited me all right but the draw back there was that they already had a going organization and the home office couldn't see my going when they could use me. In Dallas we must start and it is imperative that someone knowing the building products must be selected and in [that] it was to the advantage of the home office to let me go. Just what money I'd get wasn't definitely stated, but my limit was the sky. Partly commission that means. Mr. Galvin has all the ear marks of a real fellow, and as you so aptly stated, 'We have to take a chance.'
>
> Of course, it isn't next door to Milwaukee, but I know some people in Dallas.... [It turned out that the people he described had left Dallas before they arrived.]
>
> I've been asking around about people who have been in Dallas and everyone speaks well of it. I used to think that after one or two years [in Canton] you and I

would go back to Milwaukee and find something there. This means fini Milwaukee. Guess the folks will have to come south later. Nest ce pas? [sic]

Tomorrow morning I shall speak to Mr. Montgomery & G. H. Charles and the outcome of that visit will mean much.

You tell the world we'll have an electric fan, hot & cold water—and Prof. Mead (U. of W. water power expert) used to rave about the Dallas water, and a Mammy later. Funny world is right.

No reason in the world why we can't be happy after 25 years. Of course you might get a spunky spell but when you're in the wrong—no pity, if I'm wrong, you ball [sic] me out, but right or wrong a good night kiss, and I shouldn't be at all surprised if I'd sneak over a good morning one too.

I surely shall slip up home before I go, only honey I guess we'd better wait till June. Couple months more won't hurt either of us. You might collect some more teddies, see?

Lord, dear, I know you'll love it. You know, you'll be Mrs. Oestreich there, and not little Rayline, and in Canton it would take a long time to live down that training course I took at the plant; I mean it would take a long time to gain prestige.

Rayline was impatient that Carl was taking so long to decide and even suggesting they delay their wedding date, but the situation at least helped bring her closer to her future mother-in-law, now referred to as "Carl's mother," who called her for news. Rayline was appalled to learn Carl had not written to her for two weeks in his dithering over Dallas. Finally on February 24 came the triumphant announcement, "I think most of your outfits will be cool clothes cause it has been definitely settled now and we're Dallas bound."

After discussing the need to take a chance on the future, having "the folks," including Pa, spend the winters with them, and that Mernie was only an overnight trip away from Dallas, he got down to the issue at hand. "Bunches dear, seriously, I've grown lots older it seems in just a week, and I'm banking on you for a lot of help—advice. You're going to be a 50-50 partner in the C.R.O. firm and that's fair enough. I'd just as soon run off with you when I leave in a month or so—only we can have but one wedding. Check me?"

Rayline's reaction to the news when she received his letter on February 26 was simple and to the point: "To-day certainly was a big day—a letter from my beau-lover & we are going to live in Dallas. Well, that is one thing definitely settled."

The fact is that despite his joking and the impression he cultivated of being easy going and carefree, Carl was a worrier and tended to expect the worst. Rayline, was a gambler, confident she would win, and if she didn't, well, there was always a next time. She would only admit to her diary to being a "wee bit" nervous about the future but that was to be expected, and even on the eve of her wedding, while noting it would be easier if she weren't going so far away, she sounds as if she thought it was something she should say mainly because of Daniel's health, not an expression of her own anxieties.

Carl also seems to have worried more than Rayline that she would be homesick. In an earlier letter he had said she could go back to Wisconsin in the summer because she did not like hot weather. Now he wrote, "You know, I got to figuring, and I doped it out that we'll have no coal bills. That will be your railroad money to go home two months each summer." I'm sure they discussed the salary Carl would receive, but while no figures are provided some monetary inducement must have come with his new title: "Bldg Materials Mgr., Dallas Branch, Berger Mfg. Co." He drew an arrow from the title to a marginal note "That ought to look good in the Tattler," for Rayline to alert Daniel that he should notify the Milwaukee Shriners' publication editor what his future son-in-law was up to.

Carl's letters through March mainly concern his work for Berger including several trips to nearby cities and his diminishing interest in Masonic Club activities now that he would be leaving. He doesn't even bother going "stag" to the dances but just helps with serving food and making himself useful. Anyway, as he says in one letter, who wants to dance with girls who all "flunk" compared to Rayline. By April he begins winding up his affairs in Canton and reports on several farewell parties, including a dinner with the Wess family, and schedules a short visit to Milwaukee en route to Dallas, arriving on April 15. They went to the Oestreichs for lunch and then took in a movie at the Butterfly before returning to Rayline's home, little suspecting, when Carl left, the surprise in store the next day.

Diary entry, April 16, 1921:

The worst snow storm and blizzard of the year and I made my poor lover-man come out in it all. But I must admit I didn't have to ask more than once. The [street]cars have stopped running & so he had to stay all night. And I am back on the cot again. How different it all will be in two months time.

Carl got out here [to her home] about four & we haven't done a bit of sensible talking or planning. Really, love is a wonderful thing. And I am so happy & have such perfect faith & confidence in my dear Belovedest.

Carl went home late the next morning but was back by 2:30 and they went to two movies and had dinner downtown where they ran into Lalla and Daniel. Most of the snow was gone but he insisted on carrying her over puddles and snowy spots. Somewhere along the line someone must have warned Rayline not to expect Carl to be so devoted after they married because at this point, as in earlier instances, she writes that she doesn't believe he will change after they are married. Then the diary sounds like contrived romantic fiction because on the 18th she starts out:

> Surprise seems to come fast and furious in my life. Who should call me up this morning but Miller Mureson! Well, it ended up by Carl, Miller & I going to the Majestic this afternoon, & a real good bill too. Then over to Telemas [sic] for something to eat & as we wanted to dance we went to the Charity Bazaar but just our luck none of the orchestras were playing at dinner time.... Miller & Carl got along just wonderful.

Carl left for Dallas early the next afternoon. Except for noting that "the next time Carl leaves I'll be going with him," Rayline was too busy to dwell on his departure because it was Lalla's birthday with 30 guests to entertain. On the 20th, she had time to reflect: "Miller really was awfully sweet Monday. He said to Carl he hoped he'd be good to me & that they all couldn't win out." Carl even was agreeable to Miller taking Rayline to dinner and movies now and then.

Carl wrote en route from Kansas City where he met with the local Berger representative and arrived in Dallas on April 21. He located a boarding house near his rooming house where he would eat breakfast and dinner and use his lunch time to check out other eating places and get to know the city. Of general interest is the indication that single women were beginning to join the work force away from their homes; Carl notes a number of women school teachers ate at his boarding house. He wrote positive descriptions of Dallas as a clean city and while warmer than Milwaukee it cooled down at night. He also observed that the women dressed predominantly in shades of gray and he looked forward to Rayline standing out in more colorful outfits. As usual, he checked out the Masonic situation and soon had made friends, particularly with the local Shriners who held their big annual parade only a few days after he arrived. Carl scouted the housing market and discovered Dallas had very few apartments, just "little selfish bungalows," and the apartments were small and costly compared to Milwaukee and Canton. His opinion of the quality of much of the rental housing: "2 boards + a window = apartment house."

He was enjoying exploring on his own when after a week, cousin Eugene Kern breezed in, broke and looking for a job. Fresh out of the Navy, he'd had a falling out with his family when he returned to Milwaukee and decided to seek out Carl who noted ruefully that it was not a good idea to tell relatives, "If you're ever in this neighborhood…" because they might take you up on your offer as a serious invitation. He also commented to Rayline that if only half of Eugene's Navy stories were true he could understand why he didn't get along with his strait-laced family. He put Eugene up at his rooming house and finally found work for him at Berger's if he promised to forget they were related. Eugene vindicated his visit when he learned about an auction as he scouted out odd jobs, and Carl was able to get Rayline a new and very stylish gold mesh evening bag for $27.00, about half the regular price.

Meanwhile Carl bought Rayline's wedding ring, and after the problems with sizing her engagement ring, he erred in the other direction and the ring was too large. When they tried to have it made smaller after the wedding it broke. Rayline did not want a "substitute" for the actual ring used in the ceremony and never wore a wedding band, just her two diamond rings, and later the star sapphire ring. It was a definite departure from custom since almost all married women wore wedding rings but the custom of both husband and wife wearing them seems to have become common much later, after my own marriage in 1951.

Carl and Eugene soon found out about the shoddier side of Dallas, as reported in his letter of May 22. The night before, "a young lady driving a Ford drew along the curb near us and spoke. I went up to the machine and she said, 'Do you want to spend some money on me?' I said, 'Hell, no!' So did Gene. You see it's high time you come down so that you can keep those kind of ladies from disturbing me."

Since the period, 1920-1921, was marked by the revival of the Ku Klux Klan and the rise of other white supremacists, resulting in unprecedented numbers of unprosecuted lynchings of African Americans, I wondered if these developments, mainly in the south, would be reflected in my father's correspondence. It seems, however, that while the ceremonies of large gatherings of costumed Klansmen were colorful copy for the newspapers, the isolated occurrences of local atrocities were not widely reported and the true horror of the period only became generally known later as history, not current events. There is a curious irony in the fact that at the start I was afraid I would happen upon intimacies in my parents' courtship documents that I would be reluctant to write about, but now that I've almost completed the story I find my only real embarrassment is that my father blandly accepted the official white southern line on race relations. When he and Eugene were accosted by the "young lady," they were walking home from watching a "Klu Klux Klan parade," evoking his comment, "This country sure needs a body of men like that, to help the law and act as vigilants." I take some comfort that he was so uninformed about the situation in the South that he misspelled Ku Klux Klan. Unlike Rayline, Carl was a good speller.

Carl remained enthusiastic about Dallas but his work at the start was not what he expected. The new plant was still under construction, with the office area and warehouse barely started. Mr. Galvin turned over to Carl the full responsibility for scheduling and overseeing the various stages of work to complete the two buildings—framing, wiring, pouring cement, sheathing, roofing, and more. Carl was gratified that despite some painful bumps and scrapes he got on the construction site, he could handle the kind of assignment he had not even been asked about when interviewing for the Dallas job. It was a far cry from administering a department, visiting architects, and pushing Berger products with the prospect of earning commissions. Much of his time was spent outdoors and, after a severe case of sunburn, by early May he already had a darker tan, at least on the back of his neck, than he had ever achieved in a whole summer in Wisconsin.

He complained at the end of May that, "J. B. Montgomery touted me so high that Galvin expects me to do everything. And to make it worse, he's not at all appreciative." Besides leaving Carl strictly alone to direct work on the buildings, he also left it up to him to placate neighbors who complained about the noise of construction and deal with the unions. Carl was no friend of organized labor after his experience with strikes from the perspective of management when he was in Canton, but he managed to negotiate around union demands on the office building although he had to hire union carpenters on the warehouse as it had been contracted separately before he arrived.

To Rayline's annoyance, Carl was not ready to set a wedding date because he did not want to leave Dallas before he could be absolutely sure the new buildings were completed or close enough to completion that he could leave with a free mind and look forward to starting his real job in earnest on their return. They finally settled on June 11, a Saturday. Carl planned to return to Milwaukee on June 6 and Eugene decided to accompany him north as he had heard from a friend in Canada and decided to explore employment there.

By the end of April, Rayline concluded that as much as she had always dreamed of a big formal wedding at Floraydan Lodge with lots of attendants, she was content that it would be a small affair on Layton Boulevard with Mary as her only bridesmaid. Bill Mueller would serve as Carl's "groomsman." Carl had also favored getting married at Phantom Lake and expressed willingness to do whatever pleased Rayline, but he confessed he didn't think he'd be comfortable with a fashionably elaborate and costly affair. What really prompted both of them to scale down drastically was Daniel's health. The doctor had recommended an ocean voyage but Daniel felt too tired to even think of getting away for a rest. Adding to his difficulties, alluded to in one of Carl's letters but not mentioned in the diary, was a problem Daniel was having with some kind of court proceeding that finally got settled in his favor before the wedding but took a further toll on his energies.

As Carl's letters are filled with the day-to-day developments of his job, Rayline's diary is filled with day-to-day preparations for the wedding: arranging for a caterer; picking out invitations and announcements; buying the wedding dress, veil, traveling clothes and other new dresses; buying trunks not only for clothes but to ship wedding presents to set up housekeeping; ordering flowers; and finishing items she made for herself such as "a Pullman robe" for the train trip to Dallas.

Friends held parties in her honor beginning with a light luncheon and elaborate party favors hosted by Margaret and Jeanette in Racine on May 7. A week later, the Gamma Phi Kappa sorority celebrated the engagements of four of their members with a dinner at the Astor Hotel in Milwaukee and a gift for each girl, while the next week Helen Klann hosted a Club party for several brides-to-be who received bouquets. On May 20, Aunt Elisabeth Danielson held what Rayline designates "a miscellaneous shower" with lunch at her home where everyone gave her "such lovely things," as well as a family dinner in Rayline's honor on June 7. Aunt Inga Nelson followed the same pattern of a lunch and shower with gifts on June 3 and a dinner June 8. By this time Carl had arrived and attended the dinner with Bill Mueller. The menus are listed in detail in the Memoranda section at the back of the diary. They all began with "Fruit Cocktail" and were strong on chicken in different forms, but Elisabeth served sweetbread at her luncheon while Inga offered "filet of beef" at lunch and turkey at her dinner party.

Mary arrived from Birmingham on May 25 and spent the night of June 4 with Rayline on Layton Boulevard when Rayline learned, "She has broken her engagement with Tuck," and added, "for which I am very happy. She found out he has been untrue to her at which I am not surprised." The next night Rayline spent at Mary's home and marveled that Mary was so calm and cheerful "as if nothing has happened." But Rayline was outraged by Tuck and wished she could "kick him in the shins & tell him what I think of him."

The following morning they went to the Downer campus and visited their "old teachers" to tell them the news of Rayline's

Rayline in bridal dress with floor length veil. Driving to the depot.

7-4. Bridal party in the yard at Layton Boulevard: ring bearer Dorothea Danielson and flower girl Florence Martin; best man Bill Mueller, Carl, Rayline, and maid of honor Mary Ball.

wedding and then met Carl at the depot. "Had lunch with Carl and his cousin at Toys. Made application for a [marriage] license, saw Bill Mueller, did some shopping." She adds, "Carl gave me my diamond & it is a beauty. The setting is so much more gorgeous than the other one." The entry for the day ends on a sad note, however: "Poor Mary must certainly have a big heartache now."

Mary and Margaret spent most of June 7 with Rayline and on the 8th "Carl came out about one & we went to town. Made reservations to Dallas as we are going to travel in real style in a drawing room." It was a busy day topped off by Aunt Inga's dinner. Rayline closes with the terse information, "Heard from Glad & she can't come in Sat." Glad was still in Madison and Rayline had noted earlier that she expressed uncertainty whether she could get away as school was still in session. I'm sure she could have cut classes, especially to attend a wedding she was responsible for, but it would have meant seeing "Willy" who after so many years was jilting her. Rayline and Carl continued their friendship with Mueller after they returned to Milwaukee which perhaps solves the mystery of Glad distancing herself, although they must have remained on cordial terms with her parents since Dr. Boerner delivered me.

Meanwhile gifts poured in and on June 9 Carl's parents had dinner with the Danielsons and got to see the trousseau and wedding presents. On the 10th, Rayline and Mary did last minute shopping and completed packing her bags for her trip. Later Carl and Rayline met with the minister.

The final entry in the diary, June 11, 1921, "Our Wedding Day!" must have been written en route to Chicago where they changed trains for a direct trip to Dallas:

> Now I'm married & don't feel one bit different than I did yesterday. Up bright and early. Had my hair marcelled also had my picture taken to please the family. My flowers were wonderful & everyone said I made such a nice bride. We were married in front of the fireplace which was banked with palms & pink peonies

& blue larkspur. My flowers were lilies of the valley & sweetheart roses & Mary carried pink peonies & blue larkspur.

Everyone seemed to have a lovely time. Florence was flower girl & Dorothy [Danielson] was ring bearer & Bill Miller [sic] Best man & Rev. Bigelow Minister [of St. John's Episcopal Church].

The folks showered us with rice & paraded us all over town in Bill's Car. That was all.

I have never understood why no studio photograph was taken of the bride and groom together when everything else about the preparations and the wedding itself was so conventional for its time. The only pictures of the whole wedding party are outdoor snapshots. Also not mentioned in the diary but documented in a family snapshot is the fact that Daniel's brother Charles drove the newly weds to the train station in his car with placards on the back proclaiming, "Oh Boy Just Married" and "Ain't We Got Fun."

Right after the wedding, Lalla, Daniel, and Lalla's friend Jennie Walters went on a camping trip at a favorite site along the Wolf River on the Menominee Indian Reservation in the hope that some fishing and the fresh air would help restore Daniel's health. Their commodious tent, referred to as the "bear den," was shaped like a salt box with a mosquito net extension across the front. They soon returned to Milwaukee as Daniel's health only worsened.

The final packet of 20 letters, dated July 23-August 15, 1921, concerns the period Rayline was away from Dallas to be with her father who had gone to the Mayo Clinic in Rochester, Minnesota to undergo surgery for his "ulcer." It may have been cancer, but in those days the word was avoided, almost as if it were a form of venereal disease. He was accompanied by Lalla and his physician friend, Dr. Foster McNary. As a child, I heard the family talk about Daniel having had a portion of his stomach and several feet of intestine removed, and the details that Dr. McNary was present during the entire operation, with Daniel gripping his hand. Daniel was conscious and in pain because only a limited local anesthetic was used to avoid the risk of reflexive retching often caused by the general anesthetics available at that time. The surgery was a new procedure and Dr. Will Mayo himself lectured to an audience of doctors as he worked. He was impressed by Daniel's fortitude, having overheard him whisper to Dr. McNary something to the effect that he hoped they learned something from his ordeal "to spare the next poor devil this pain."

Fortitude seems to have been a family trait. Some years earlier, Daniel's father had lost his left arm in a freak accident involving a crane, an innovation in building equipment he had recently bought. As he was showing the grasping mechanism to a friend on a Sunday, not knowing the machine operator had also come in to make some adjustments and unexpectedly started the machine, it pinched off his arm but left his coat sleeve intact. He rigged a sling with an old pair of overalls lying at the site and with the help of his friend, who had nearly fainted, and the crane operator, got to the emergency hospital without losing consciousness or crying out in pain. According to family stories, this mishap along with others led to an early piece of occupational safety legislation requiring the operator to have a clear view of the business end of such equipment from the cab where it was controlled. With his missing arm and impressive white goatee and mustache, great grandfather Danielson was amused that he often was mistaken for a Civil War veteran and addressed as "Colonel." A currently familiar stereotype apparently goes back a long way.

Coincidently, Ben Egan, the former YMCA camp doctor, had joined the Mayo staff and was a particular source of comfort for Rayline and Lalla after Dr. McNary returned to Milwaukee. It is a tribute to Dr. Mayo's skill that Daniel lived nearly 14 years longer and, as noted, died of a stroke unrelated to his "stomach trouble."

Carl's first eleven letters in the final packet are addressed in care of Rayline's mother at the Hotel Campbell where they stayed in Rochester, with the rest sent to Layton Boulevard where Rayline went in advance of her parents to prepare for their return and then stayed to help care for her father during his recovery. My parents had been married just a month when Rayline left and she did not return for nearly six more weeks. Naturally, the letters concentrate on Daniel's progress. Carl considered it a good omen that he made the trip to Rochester by train, and walked into the hospital rather than being brought in an ambulance. Like previous letters, this small collection contains revealing insights into the period and unexpected tidbits of historical information.

I know from Rayline's stories that Carl had found a furnished apartment for them just before leaving Dallas for the wedding but all he could tell her about it was that, "It has a breeze." I suddenly appreciated the deeper humor having read the letters he sent before they were married, extolling the Dallas climate as not very different from Wisconsin in the summer and, in answer to her friends who harped on the heat down south, that you could always count on the cooling air "from the Gulf" toward evening. By early June, Carl found the heat overwhelming and had grabbed the first place he found that offered some kind of cross-ventilation, paying little attention to its size, layout, or furnishings. When Rayline left for Rochester, Carl went back to his old boarding house for meals and had to endure joking that the marriage hadn't lasted very long. The used Scripps-Booth automobile they acquired soon after moving to Dallas began listing to the left and Carl wrote it probably was as lonely for her presence as he was to hold down the "starboard side."

Although Carl now had a proper office to do the job he was hired for, it still was not as he anticipated. He noted on July 7, "Galvin said that the mills were all shut down in the East and that things were dead." I don't know if this was a lingering effect of the strikes or simply a slowed demand for Berger products. While Galvin had made a favorable impression on Carl in Canton, he was proving a disappointment as a boss. Writing on July 30, Carl complained:

> Everything is up in the air at the office. This
> starting an organization is all wrong. Never, never

again. None of us has ever been schooled in invoicing, billing, cost accounting and the like and tho we all do our best, there are many slips. I worked thru till dinner and after I get this letter written I'm going to it once more. And then our first semi monthly inventory went in today to[o]. Oh lord what a job. Sometimes I get so disgusted I'd like to kick up the whole thing and leave—and no place to go.

We'll hope tho, old girl, and we'll make it all right. Mullis is on a one week trip. I've got to do a lot of promotion work from the office.

Mullis and Carl became good friends and while I can't recall his first name, his wife Ella and Rayline hit it off well too. Ella was Canadian but I don't know about her husband. By Christmas time, she and Rayline had developed a circle of friends among local women and were planning for the holidays. When they commented it would be a strange Christmas for them they were both thinking snow, but one of the Dallas women took mild offense and said, "Why! We have lovely Christmases with fireworks and everything!" To a couple of northerners, that was really strange!

Rayline's old Downer friends, Irma Sichling and Mary wrote to her while she was away and Carl forwarded their letters to her. Mary, as usual, was spending the summer in Milwaukee and had a new beau. She was having a marvelous time and wondering whatever she had found so attractive about Tuck. Irma, who was now a teacher, wrote from a resort near Eagle River, Wisconsin where she and several other teachers were spending part of their vacation. I suddenly realized from these letters and recalling Mary's earlier letters from Birmingham, that they no longer contained the gushy effusiveness that characterized girls' writing as teen-agers. I also learned a 1920s slang term from Mary's letter for what my generation called "the curse"—"a visit from grandma"—and that women's rest rooms already had dispensers of disposable sanitary napkins—the commercial version of an invention of World War I Army nurses that freed women from washing and re-using soft cloth rags kept for the purpose. Mary had not taken along any "mad money" (another quaint term) and had to ask her date for a quarter; they both pretended he didn't know what it was for.

Another enclosure, dated July 21, 1921, is a two page letter from The Kuhns-Batchelor-Snivley Co, an investment firm in Canton, Ohio addressed "TO OUR CUSTOMERS." It caught my eye since increasing numbers of ordinary people had begun investing in the stock market. After several paragraphs of tortured prose about the need to investigate potential investments with great care, and listing examples of dependable stock issues, it seems to come perilously close to an invitation to buy on margin, considered a major contribution to the devastating effects of the stock market crash of 1929 that brought on the Depression of the 1930s.

> Perhaps you want to invest in something of this kind but haven't the money. This is not an insuperable difficulty. Consult with us and perhaps some way can be found to enable you to take advantage of present market conditions.

Carl had evidently dealt with this firm because he had written in April of 1920 when he was still in Canton:

> I've got a new game for you but you must keep it quiet. You watch the stock quotations and if Pressed Steel Car gets better than 110-1/2 why you sing for joy and if it goes under that, then put more camphor balls in your God knows when box.

I doubt that my parents could afford to do any investing when they were first married beyond whatever Carl might have already bought, and Carl was too cautious to do anything risky or speculative, but the letter is interesting for another reason. Inventors were already experimenting with the duplication of business correspondence by means of a typed stencil on an inked drum but evidently such "mimeograph" machines were not yet common. The letter is obviously a carbon copy on standard weight paper so a typist could turn out a half dozen legible copies, at most, including the original, which meant typing (flawlessly) the same thing repeatedly even for a mailing of only 25 or 50 copies. Perhaps what by this time was mostly female office labor was still cheaper for some companies than the cost of labor saving equipment.

When Rayline returned to Dallas, she was no longer keeping a diary and, of course, there were no letters from Carl. In some ways, however, the Dallas interlude was like Lalla's and Rayline's 1906 summer in Norway—so out of the ordinary that it was recalled over and over, reinforcing family memory of it. The furnished apartment, breeze notwithstanding, was cramped and unattractive and they soon found an unfurnished place to their liking, the address of 2727 Colonial Ave. preserved on the envelope of one of Lalla's letters. They bought furniture to which Rayline added a few cherished family pieces sent from home.

Rayline, however, suffered intensely in the Texas heat, even with electric fans, and Carl was becoming increasingly dissatisfied with his job. When the telephone rang late one night and the connection was cut off before they could learn who was calling (a not uncommon occurrence at the time) Rayline became hysterical, certain that Daniel had suffered a relapse. Her reaction was very much out of character but she had kept her worries about her father and her unhappiness with Dallas to herself while Carl too had been putting on a brave front about his job. They decided on the spot to come home and take up Daniel's offer to join his business.

Once the decision was made, relief lightened the work of planning their departure and even had some humorous moments. It was more economical to sell rather than ship the furniture they had acquired and since Rayline was home during the day, she handled most of the sales, helped on two or three occasions by a new friend with dramatic talents who lived in the adjoining apartment. If a prospective buyer was wavering or too aggressive in trying to get her to lower the price, Rayline would stand next to the wall and surreptitiously tap an agreed upon code and the neighbor, purse in hand and dressed as if coming from outside (I understand that even in Dallas at that time, women wore hats) would go into raptures over the item in question, asking the price and pronouncing it a bargain. According to Rayline, it never failed. The first customer would point out that he or she "was here first" and would pay the asking price.

Then there was "Scrippsy." They had never taken out insurance because the machine wasn't worth it, but an insurance salesman kept pestering Carl who finally suggested they toss a coin. If the salesman lost, he would never come around again, but if he won, Carl would buy the limit covering every possible contingency. Carl lost and had paid one premium when "Scrippsy" needed some kind of repair and Carl took it to the garage. When he returned for it in the morning, all that was left was a twisted metal frame. The garage had gone up in flames during the night and the newlyweds enjoyed an unexpected windfall in the settlement that far exceeded what they expected to sell it for. It is worth noting that while automobile ownership was becoming common, even if "Scrippsy" had been new they probably would not have considered driving it back to Milwaukee given bad roads, fragile tires, limited speed, and distances between "filling stations." Long cross-country trips were still mainly for the adventurous with leisure time.

The number of Dallas stories always surprised me insofar as I knew my parents' stay there had not been long, but I was surprised to learn from Lalla's two letters at the bottom of that shopping bag that it was less than a year—roughly from mid-June of 1921 to early February of 1922, and Rayline was away for about a month and a half of that period. Lalla's letters on Daniel's business stationery dated January 28 and 31, discuss the safe arrival of Rayline's two trunks filled with items that not long before had been sent from Milwaukee to Dallas. She agrees with Rayline that it was better to sell rather than ship furniture and that she could buy new things in Milwaukee, implying Rayline and Carl would be setting up housekeeping after a stay with Lalla and Daniel to get their bearings and check out available housing. They never left.

As far as the letters go, the story ends here in 1922. But, then what? Of course, it is just the beginning of my parents' life together that started with the so-called Jazz Age and would include the Great Depression and another World War and its aftermath. So, having laid a necessary foundation at the outset, based on family oral tradition, for what was to come in the letters and diaries, I will complete the story without benefit of documented commentary but now largely as a participant observer. As with the letters and diaries, the subsequent story of my parents' lives both exemplify larger issues of technological and social changes, medical advances, and historical events, and illuminate details.

There does not seem to have been any formal decision for Rayline and Carl to stay with her parents. They just never got around to moving and by the time I was on the way in 1923 satisfactory arrangements about sharing expenses and responsibilities and respecting one another's individuality as a multi-generation household had simply evolved. It was not an unusual arrangement at the time except that we included a great grandparent instead of the more common case among my contemporaries of a grandparent sharing the family home. I was born at the house on Layton Boulevard because of my grandfather's legendary temper. Hospital births were pretty much the rule by then but infants, when not actually at the mother's breast during the usual five days or so of her "confinement," were strictly segregated in aseptic rows of cribs behind glass where you could look but not touch. Dr. Boerner knew that if Dan Danielson could not hold and kiss his first grandchild he would kick down the door.

Carl had been designated a partner in the Danielson Construction Company and while he held up his end in engineering and estimating, he simply was not cut out for taking the risks or

At Phantom Lake, ca. 1929: Daniel, Lalla, Pa, and Nancy. Carl took the snapshot.

engaging in the sharp practices on which Daniel thrived. Anyway, Daniel had begun cutting back on contracting to concentrate on setting up an assembly plant in the barn behind the house for producing Tie-To Inserts. Carl sought an additional source of income and found a new career. In 1923, he began teaching part-time at the Milwaukee Center administered through the University of Wisconsin Extension Division. Established in 1908 mainly in response to local business and industry calling for employees with special competencies, the Center, or Extension Division as it was usually called, was open from early morning to 10:00 P.M. and offered University of Wisconsin credit and non-credit courses. Carl and another faculty member organized a certificate program of non-credit courses in Building Design and Construction. His own course, "Estimating for Builders" was described in the University of Wisconsin faculty Memorial Resolution after his death as "one of the most consistently successful courses offered in the Evening School." Also in 1923, the Center was authorized to offer the first two undergraduate years in a number of fields that could be applied toward completing a baccalaureate degree at the Madison campus of the university. After occupying a succession of rented quarters, in 1927, the Center moved to its own facility on State Street, designed explicitly for academic programs.

Rayline said she sometimes wished for a home of her own but by 1928 other factors made it imperative that the family remain together. Lalla was confined to her bed for more than six months with a gall bladder condition and Rayline took over her care and management of the household. About the same time, Dr. McNary discovered I had a congenital deformity, torticollis or "wry neck," that was twisting my head to one side and pulling my spine out of alignment. Two years of nightly massage and wearing a removable brace during the day stabilized but did not improve the problem that was then corrected by surgery followed by six weeks in a cast covering most of my head and reaching below my waist. Typically, Rayline would not allow anyone to photograph me in either the brace or cast, so I would get on with my life and not engage in retrospective self-pity when the ordeal was over. I knew from the expression on the faces of people seeing me for the first time that I looked pretty awful encased in all that plaster of Paris. To my eternal gratitude, my parents stood up to a prevailing attitude that children should not have to endure such measures except as a last-resort in life-threatening situations. Rayline's cousin Jeanette, whose hunchback could have been corrected even at the beginning of the 20th century, was testimony to her parents' decision that a deformity was preferable to subjecting a child to the "torture" of prolonged confinement in a cast and, in their defense, the risks of dying of side effects of surgery at that time.

I soon learned to walk with the extra weight of plaster and apart from the fact that I bumped into things and couldn't go swimming I had a wonderful time. Visitors brought gifts and Carl decorated my cast with colored pencils. When he lettered the nickname, "Dangerous Nan McGrew," across the front (I had an arsenal of cap pistols) I went to admire it in a mirror and got my first lesson in optics. It read backwards! The operation took place in the summer of 1930, the same time the house at Phantom Lake was wired for electricity so no one had to worry I would blunder into a lighted kerosene lamp.

Although Carl's business association with Daniel was brief and he did not share his father-in-law's love of hunting and fishing, they participated together regularly in Masonic activities and Carl happily took over much of the maintenance of the Phantom Lake property, building rock gardens and a large goldfish pool, and scouting the countryside for fallen trees to cut up for use in the fireplaces. Despite Lalla's and my medical problems, the 1920s and even the early 1930s were good years. Though hardly inclined to cast aside convention and propriety in the supposedly totally abandoned spirit of the "Roaring Twenties," my parents and their circle of friends were not complete strangers to the culture of speak-easies, bathtub gin, and bootleggers during Prohibition. (Kids hear things!)

Carl after he received his commission
as a Captain with Nancy, 1930.

Carl and Rayline loved to dance and went to formal balls sponsored by the military and Masonic organizations Carl belonged to. Like just about every veteran, he was a member of the American Legion, but his major military association was the Sojourners, Masons who were or had been commissioned officers in the military services. He remained in the Active Reserve in the Quartermaster Corps and participated regularly in maneuvers held at Camp Douglas and other military installations around the state, rising to the rank of Captain in 1930. Although these activities were a welcome source of income when the Depression closed in, he really took part because they afforded him great personal satisfaction. We did not realize until World War II began how central his military affiliation was to his sense of identification and even manhood.

After his marriage, Carl renewed his youthful interest in stamp collecting, at that time the country's most popular hobby. With characteristic intensity of purpose, he helped found local philatelic organizations, corresponded with people around the world, and was in frequent demand as a speaker on the subject. For many years he was the volunteer curator of the large stamp collection at the Milwaukee Public Museum where he learned about the field of anthropology and introduced me to my life's work when I was six years old.

Just as the impact of the World War I influenza epidemic was relatively mild in Milwaukee, the city was exceptional in that the full force of the Depression did not strike there until about 1932-1933. Then, even "sheltered" children like me began to hear about school friends' fathers losing their jobs, "soup kitchens," the shame of possibly having to "go on the dole" (welfare), and the WPA (Works Progress Administration) along with other programs associated with "The New Deal." Although Carl was far from enthusiastic about "that man in the white house," when teaching opportunities diminished about 1933 he found employment as an administrator with the WPA, overseeing building programs around the state.

My family, like many others, got through the Depression by pooling their resources and strict economizing, but they were in more desperate straits than I knew. When the Depression began, Daniel was confident he would weather it as he had past "panics," but building construction came to a virtual standstill across the country just at the time his considerable investment in equipment and supplies to manufacture Tie-To Inserts should have begun to pay off. Then he had his stroke and Lalla took over. Drawing upon heretofore untapped business talents she got Tie-To specified in some federal construction projects and was able to pay off Daniel's debts and make the company profitable. The effects of World War II in getting women into the work force is a familiar story, but recalling childhood observations of women in my extended family and the neighborhood, I think more attention might be given to women's ingenuity and survival skills evoked by the Depression.

In the late fall of 1936, Pa fell and broke his hip at Phantom Lake and was taken by ambulance to a hospital in Milwaukee where, to everyone's surprise, he rallied and was sent home. Today, the hip might have been replaced or even set and pinned but in those days "no one" lived after a broken hip so he remained bed-ridden. The following spring he returned to Phantom Lake with Lalla in an ambulance. "Well, this should make the natives sit up and take notice," he said as they drove through Mukwonago. He died back in Milwaukee late in November at the age of 89. He had already turned his cottage over to Lalla a few years earlier and its rent paid the taxes and upkeep of the Phantom property during the Depression and beyond.

As I was finishing this story I came across another little trove, some of my mother's travel diaries that had somehow escaped the garage fire. The first contains the account of a trip to Florida in 1939, our longest venture to that date. It is illustrative of the way Americans in general were taking to the road and an indication of the easing of the Depression. Whether it was the direct of result of Franklin Roosevelt's programs or industrial gearing up for American participation in the war already raging in Europe remains a matter of debate, but the programs such as the Civilian Conservation Corps (CCC) were very noticeably responsible for enhancing the attractiveness of the landscape for the traveling public.

The diary is interesting and amusing both for its printed contents and what Rayline recorded in it. Leather bound and entitled, "Events and Places Visited," it offers useful advice and information about such things as National Parks and Monuments, distances between major cities and their populations as estimated for 1939, carrying money conveniently (travelers checks or letters of credit—credit cards came later) and small maps covering the entire world "To Trace Your Trip" that show no political boundaries or roads! Although it has brief sections on Bermuda, Cuba, the Panama Canal Zone, Hawaii and Canada and deals with some aspects of travel by train and ship—baggage, customs, and currency—reflecting an earlier, more affluent era, it is clearly an artifact of the increasing popularity of automobile travel in the continental United States. Several pages at the beginning that Rayline left blank were for "Autographs," presumably of new friends met along the way. Travel by air is not mentioned.

Carl, Rayline, Lalla, and I set out on December 22, "in the 'Blue Studie'" (Studebaker) at 6:00 A.M. on a day that was "clear & cold." It was a new car but the heater was inadequate so back seat passengers had to bundle up in blankets. As far as I remember, cars did not yet have radios, although ubiquitous by then in private homes. Carl and Rayline spelled each other driving as we headed first for Atlanta (to see *Gone With The Wind* country, the movie having just been released). Then, it was down the east coast to Florida and all the way to Key West, back to Miami, across the Tamiami Trail, up the west coast of Florida and on to Mobile and Birmingham, Alabama, Memphis, Tennessee, and Fulton, Kentucky for a brief visit with Lalla's old friend "Aunt" Cora and her husband, and finally home on January 6, 1940: "4324 miles without a mishap." We took in just about every historical and scenic site encountered en route, as listed by Rayline. She also kept meticulous accounts of nightly lodging for the four of us, usually at a "t.c." (tourist court), ordinarily $3.00 to $4.00 a night for two cabins or a two room cabin. We picked what looked like nice places from the roadside; well into the 1930s the presence of privies behind the little cabins signaled the lack of indoor plumbing. Sometimes we got good recommendations where we ate or bought gas. In Miami we were able to rent a whole house for $5.00. The most expensive place, $7.50, was a "Hotel Court" in Ocala, Florida (winter quarters of the old minor league Milwaukee Brewers) but that included a "Continental Breakfast," a real novelty. The Birmingham Athletic Club charged $4.75 for two rooms. Rayline sometimes commented on the quality of food if unusually good or bad though not the cost, but she recorded tolls for ferries and bridges, and various attractions' admission fees—in any case, seldom more than a quarter. And while she carefully clocked miles covered per day, she never cites the cost of gas, let alone concern herself with miles-per-gallon. She used the same diary for subsequent trips until it was filled in 1965. The term motel seems to have come into general use about 1950.

When the United States entered World War II in 1941, Carl was delighted to be called back to active service and would have entered with the rank of major. However, he had developed hypertension and despite his doctor's and his own best efforts he was unable to meet the army's physical requirements. Treatment of heart disease is certainly among the dramatic medical advances since World War II, but in 1942, Carl was simply notified his status was now "inactive—retired." The death of his mother that same year was an additional sorrow. With his army affiliation so important to him and the hope that this time he might even serve overseas, the rejection was crushing. Deeply disappointed but determined to contribute to the war effort, he applied for a job at the B.A. Froemming Shipyard in Milwaukee that built ocean-going tugs and other craft and soon was appointed Director of Training and Labor Relations (really meaning personnel relations). Absenteeism was a serious problem, despite national campaigns stressing patriotic duty on the home front, and Carl proved to have a natural knack for counseling and morale building. But he set a suspiciously suicidal pace, given his hypertension, often working 12 hour days, dealing with personnel problems and paper work during the regular shift, staying late for the beginning of the second shift, and arriving early to be available at the end of the night shift.

The shipyard closed soon after the war and in January of 1946 Carl became a full time faculty member of the Milwaukee Extension Division as an Assistant Professor of Civil Engineering and Superintendent of Building and Grounds. The latter job was farmed out as a part-time task among the faculty members on a yearly basis, a legacy of the Extension Division's ad hoc beginnings. With the enormous influx of students under the G.I. Bill, universities were hard-put to accommodate them and Carl's talents resulted in his being permanently in charge of the building program besides teaching one course a semester. Among other things, he arranged for the former POW barracks at the Milwaukee Airport to be moved to the Extension campus and converted into classrooms until a scheduled new building was constructed.

Meanwhile, news of post-war problems in Europe took on a personal dimension. Carl and his maternal relatives heard from Kern descendants living under terrible conditions in displaced persons camps in West Germany after their forced expulsion from the Czechoslovak Republic with only what they could carry. The American cousins sent help directly and through CARE, the then newly established private philanthropy Cooperative of American Relief Everywhere.

I had been off at Madison during the war and then earned my Master's degree at the University of Chicago. In the fall of 1947, Carl was promoted to the rank of Associate Professor and I began my first professional job as Instructor in Sociology and Anthropology at the Milwaukee Extension Division. I got the position before Carl and the rest of the family even knew I had applied for it, and started my teaching career in the barracks that still had their original Rauchen Verboten signs—No Smoking. In 1949 I left home again to enter Northwestern University to begin work on my Ph.D.

In 1951, I married Edward Lurie and was able to get my old

job back. Since Ed' still had course work to complete, we spent our first year of married life in Kenosha, Wisconsin, half-way between Milwaukee and Evanston, commuting north and south, respectively, on the old North Shore Interurban line. It was discontinued and demolished soon after we moved out of the area, an example of the effects of federal investment in interstate highways across the country taking precedence over maintaining public transportation by light rail and passenger trains.

Lalla died in the summer of 1953 after a mercifully brief bout with cancer. Carl had drawn up plans to remodel the house on Layton Boulevard but when work began that fall, he sank into a severe state of depression that required professional psychiatric help. He recovered and returned to his job at the Extension Division, to all appearances the same old Carl—always a soft touch, always ready with a joke appropriate to the occasion, always up to challenges in finding space to accommodate students and faculty. But how I wish there had been drug therapy available rather than electric shock, at that time the state-of-the art-treatment for depression. I cannot help but wonder if it was an underlying cause of the heart attack he suffered in the summer of 1955 at Phantom Lake; Rayline attributed it to receiving his discharge from the Army in April of that year.

Ed' and I were living in Boston and I rushed home and stayed with Rayline until Carl was able to leave the hospital. When Ed' and I came back to Milwaukee for Christmas, Carl complained he did not feel well and on December 27 he was stricken with a fatal heart attack at the age of sixty.

Rayline outlived Carl by some 40 years. In 1933 she had embarked upon what would be a lifetime of volunteer service with the Episcopal church becoming the youngest member ever to serve on the Board of Women Managers of St. John's Home for the Elderly in Milwaukee—a pioneer in accommodations and programs responding to Americans' increasing longevity. She held office and served in successor organizations to the Board and other diocesan, provincial, and national Episcopalian organizations. She also served for several years on the Budget Committee of the Milwaukee Community Fund, now the United Way, and volunteered at the Milwaukee County Historical Society.

A good manager with a head for investments, she lived comfortably on Layton Boulevard with rent from the downstairs apartments and income from the eventual sale of the Phantom Lake property and the Tie-To Insert Company, and filled more travel diaries on automobile trips with friends and relatives.

When I returned to Milwaukee in 1963 she finally got to do the international traveling she and Carl had dreamed of, beginning with the trip to Denmark and accompanying me to international anthropological meetings in Japan and India. She also went on tours to Europe and the Holy Land with friends, and took several Caribbean cruises. Unfortunately, her slides of these trips were lost in my garage fire.

When Rayline came to live with me in 1970, we became, in effect, the same age. She did not like celebrating birthdays, not out of vanity because she always looked younger than her years, but because "If people know how old you are, they treat you that way." We shopped together, traveled, played cards, entertained the extended family and mutual friends, recalled family history, adored our cats, paid for what neither of us liked to do—housework and yardwork—and also had lives and friends of our own. Frequently only one of us was home as I did fieldwork and Rayline went on trips. Our arrangements worked well but not because we agreed on everything. We had some major differences of opinion, but respected our differences. On election days, for example, while we often drove to the polling place together we simply cancelled out each other's votes.

As I approached retirement in the 1990s, Rayline hoped both of us would move to an apartment at St. John's and decided to take a small efficiency unit there for the time being. She was no longer driving and felt housebound and isolated when I was at work. There were activities she enjoyed at St. John's and old friends. She was in good health but many years earlier she had broken her right leg and though it healed and she walked unaided the bone began to deteriorate not long after she moved. Finally confined to a wheel chair, she was transferred to the nursing section of the home where she died in 1996.

A few years later, when I decided to sell my house and move into an apartment, I decided against St. John's, to the surprise of some of Rayline's friends—as I said, we didn't agree on everything. At that time St. John's didn't have a swimming pool or allow pets. Once settled, I eventually opened that shopping bag full of letters, my mother's special legacy almost demanding to be shared.